Human Rights and Economic Policy Reform

This book deals with the complex and challenging relationship between economic policy and human rights. In the context of the COVID-19 pandemic crisis, the need to address the conceptual and methodological (dis)connects between these two areas is more pressing than ever.

Inspired by the 2019 *United Nations Guiding Principles on Human Rights Impact Assessments (HRIA) for Economic Reform Policies*, this book brings together experts working on human rights and economic policy from a range of disciplinary perspectives, including economics, law, and development studies. The contributions reflect a huge body of professional experience in the academic, policy-making, advocacy and practitioner fields. They cover issues including the politics of evidence in the context of HRIA, economic inequality, child rights impact assessment of economic reforms, economic policy and women's human rights, tax regimes for multinational corporations and human rights, as well as the human rights impacts of the economic fall-out of the COVID-19 pandemic. The collection also includes the text of the *Guiding Principles* themselves. It constitutes a crucial volume for scholars, policymakers, advocates and others working on the burning topic of human rights and economic policy reform.

The chapters in this book were originally published as a special issue of *The International Journal of Human Rights.*

Aoife Nolan is Professor of International Human Rights Law and Co-Director of the Human Rights Law Centre at Nottingham University School of Law, UK. She is Vice-President of the Council of Europe's European Committee of Social Rights, which she joined in 2017. Her books include *Children's Socio-economic Rights, Democracy & the Courts* (Hart, 2011), *Applying an International Human Rights Framework to State Budget Allocations: Rights and Resources (*Routledge, 2014) and *Economic and Social Rights after the Global Financial Crisis* (CUP, 2014). She has acted as an expert advisor to a wide range of international and national organisations and bodies working on human rights and economic policy issues, including UN Special Procedures, UN treaty bodies, the Council of Europe, the World Bank, and multiple NHRIs and NGOs.

Juan Pablo Bohoslavsky is currently a consultant on finance and human rights issues for international organizations. He was between 2014 and 2020 the United Nations Independent Expert on Debt and Human Rights. He has worked at the United Nations Conference on Trade and Development (UNCTAD) and as a consultant for the Argentine state and the United Nations Economic Commission for Latin America and the Caribbean (ECLAC). His latest books are *Pinochet's Economic Accomplices: An Unequal Country by Force* (Lexington Boos, 2020), coedited with K. Fernández and S. Smart, and *Covid-19 y Derechos Humanos, La Pandemia de la Desigualdad* (Biblos, 2020). He holds a PhD in Law from Universidad de Salamanca.

Human Rights and Economic Policy Reform

Edited by
Aoife Nolan and Juan Pablo Bohoslavsky

Routledge
Taylor & Francis Group
LONDON AND NEW YORK

First published 2022
by Routledge
2 Park Square, Milton Park, Abingdon, Oxon, OX14 4RN

and by Routledge
605 Third Avenue, New York, NY 10158

Routledge is an imprint of the Taylor & Francis Group, an informa business

British Library Cataloguing-in-Publication Data
A catalogue record for this book is available from the British Library

ISBN13: 978-1-032-00613-0 (hbk)
ISBN13: 978-1-032-00614-7 (pbk)
ISBN13: 978-1-003-17491-2 (ebk)

DOI: 10.4324/9781003174912

Typeset in Minion Pro
by codeMantra

Publisher's Note
The publisher accepts responsibility for any inconsistencies that may have arisen during the conversion of this book from journal articles to book chapters, namely the inclusion of journal terminology.

Contents

Citation Information

The chapters in this book were originally published in *The International Journal of Human Rights*, volume 24, issue 9 (2020). When citing this material, please use the original page numbering for each article, as follows:

Chapter 1
Human rights and economic policy reforms
Aoife Nolan and Juan Pablo Bohoslavsky
The International Journal of Human Rights, volume 24, issue 9 (2020) pp. 1247–1267

Chapter 2
Human rights impact assessments and the politics of evidence in economic policymaking
Allison Corkery and Gilad Isaacs
The International Journal of Human Rights, volume 24, issue 9 (2020) pp. 1268–1289

Chapter 3
Human rights and democracy in economic policy reform: the European COVID-19 response under scrutiny
Matthias Goldmann
The International Journal of Human Rights, volume 24, issue 9 (2020) pp. 1290–1310

Chapter 4
Economic inequality and human rights impact assessments of economic reforms
Gillian MacNaughton
The International Journal of Human Rights, volume 24, issue 9 (2020) pp. 1311–1332

Chapter 5
Ex ante *children's rights impact assessment of economic policy*
Simon Hoffman
The International Journal of Human Rights, volume 24, issue 9 (2020) pp. 1333–1352

Chapter 6
Economic policy and women's human rights: a critical political economy perspective
Abby Kendrick
The International Journal of Human Rights, volume 24, issue 9 (2020) pp. 1353–1369

Chapter 7

Re-righting the international tax rules: operationalising human rights in the struggle to tax multinational companies
Olivier De Schutter, Nicholas J. Lusiani and Sergio Chaparro
The International Journal of Human Rights, volume 24, issue 9 (2020) pp. 1370–1399

Chapter 8

Guiding principles on human rights impacts assessments of economic policy reforms
Juan Pablo Bohoslavsky
The International Journal of Human Rights, volume 24, issue 9 (2020) pp. 1400–1428

Contributors

Juan Pablo Bohoslavsky, international consultant, Argentina.

Sergio Chaparro Center for Economic and Social Rights, Colombia.

Allison Corkery Center for Economic and Social Rights, USA.

Matthias Goldmann Max Planck Institute for Comparative Public Law and International Law, Goethe University Frankfurt, Germany.

Simon Hoffman Hillary Rodham Clinton School of Law, Swansea University, UK.

Gilad Isaacs School of Economics and Finance, University of the Witwatersrand/South Africa Institute for Economic Justice, South Africa.

Abby Kendrick Department of Politics and International Studies, University of Warwick, UK.

Nicholas J. Lusiani Oxfam, USA.

Gillian MacNaughton School for Global Inclusion and Social Development, University of Massachusetts Boston, USA.

Aoife Nolan School of Law, University of Nottingham, UK.

Olivier De Schutter UCLouvain, Belgium.

Human rights and economic policy reforms

Aoife Nolan and Juan Pablo Bohoslavsky

ABSTRACT

This article focuses on the vexed relationship between human rights and economic policy reform. It opens with an exploration of the reasons for the historic and contemporary nonalignment and disconnect between these areas. It then turns to an overview of the 2019 *Guiding Principles on Human Rights Impact Assessments for Economic Reform Policies*, developed under the mandate of UN Independent Expert on debt and human rights. Having introduced the different contributions to the Special Issue, the authors conclude by addressing the implications of the COVID-19 pandemic crisis for the relationship between human rights and economic policy reform. Will this crisis serve as an opportunity to accelerate mutual understanding or will human rights concerns remain subordinated to economic ones?

Introduction: a brief history of human rights and economic policy reforms

The vexed relationship between economic policy reform and human rights is a hot topic, with the global and financial crises that began in 2007–2008 rapidly accelerating academic, advocacy and policymaker attention to human rights and economic policy (dis)connects.[1] These disconnects have once again come into sharp focus as the economic fallout of the COVID-19 pandemic – 'plunging the world economy into a recession with historical levels of unemployment and deprivation'[2] – and its potential impacts on human rights have become ever-more obvious.

It is important to recognise successes and ongoing challenges in terms of work focused on the link between human rights and economic policy up to this point. On the one hand, there has been growing deployment of human rights as a discourse and a conceptual framework to critique economic policy-making inputs, outputs and processes in terms of their impact on human dignity, lived experience and life opportunities. On the other, there has been ever-greater recognition of the serious challenges with regard to leveraging human rights so as to engage meaningfully with economic policy-making – whether conceptually (in terms of standards), methodologically (in terms of tools) or in terms of practical impact.

Great strides have been taken on the conceptual front over the last decade through the development of understanding of the scope of human rights obligations from an economic policy-making perspective. This has included the elaboration and deployment of previously recognised but under-developed duties such as non-retrogression,[3] maximum available resources[4] and extra-territorial obligations[5] so as to address the effects of economic policy-making on human rights in the context of economic globalisation. At the same time, key human rights entities (including UN treaty bodies and UN special procedures)[6] and scholars[7] have engaged more directly with national and supranational bodies and systems that have a central role in economic policy-making. This includes bodies that had historically been regarded (and, in some instances at least, had sought to portray themselves) as 'outwith' the human rights schema. As a result, issues such as structural readjustment,[8] finance,[9] sovereign debt,[10] fiscal austerity,[11] tax justice[12] and aspects of international economic law,[13] can and are presented as topics of human rights concern to an ever-greater degree. In methodological terms, there has been an advance in terms of the tools deployed by those concerned with human rights to deconstruct economic policy – and, in turn, to reconstruct such.[14] Building on (and in some instances originating from) feminist and progressive economics, there has been significant progress in the development of alternative, more 'human rights consistent' economic models.[15]

However, despite these advances, human rights' impact on and traction in relation to economic policy-making remain weak. Tools and approaches developed by advocates and academics remain unembraced by key decision-makers on, and implementers of, economic policy. The foundational elements of mainstream economics that are not congruent with human rights remain largely unassailed.[16] Neoliberal economics' prioritisation of economic growth over human rights goals remains largely unmoderated. Human rights practitioners have the language and they are developing the tools but this has very definitely not resulted in wholescale reconfiguration of dominant economic policy-making paradigms or in a tempering of their negative human rights impacts.[17] While there are multiple reasons for this situation, it is in no small part attributable to the largely unassailed supremacy of economists in the fiscal and macroeconomic spheres, as well as the ongoing operation of human rights and economics actors in separate, watertight spheres. Both of these long-time factors continue to contribute significantly to the side-lining and undermining of human rights in the design and implementation of economic policy reform.

This is the backdrop against which the *Guiding Principles on Human Rights Impact Assessments for Economic Reform Policies* (*Guiding Principles/GP*), the motivating factor for this Special Issue, were created and will be operationalised. It is also the context in which the contributors to this Special Issue have developed their work on human rights and economic policy reform.

The *Guiding Principles on Human Rights Impact Assessments for Economic Reform Policies*

The *Guiding Principles* did not emerge from nowhere, whether methodologically or normatively. The methodological origins of human rights impact assessment (HRIA) lie in the introduction of environmental impact assessment in the 1960s.[18] From the 1980s on, there was a growing development and deployment of social impact assessment tools to identify the social consequences (for instance, in terms of poverty, inequity or health) of economic policies. Such impact assessment was particularly notable in the work of development-focused actors such as the World Bank Group, Asian Development Bank, African Development Bank and the UN Development Programme. The 2000s saw HRIAs evolve from being included as an element of social impact assessment to constituting autonomous policy tools,[19] with the focus on such work increasing exponentially in the last two decades.[20]

The rising profile and employment of HRIA – encouraged by a range of international and human rights actors,[21] including in the context of Guiding Principles developed by UN Special Procedures[22] – coincided initially with the growing traction of economic and social rights[23] and subsequently with growing concern about the impact of economic policy reform on human rights in the context of the financial and economic crises of the late 2000s. The last decade has seen a wide range of human rights actors, including UN Treaty bodies and Special Procedures, highlighting the duty to undertake HRIAs of economic reforms specifically.[24] However, prior to the *Guiding Principles on HRIAs of Economic Policy Reforms*, no consistent and comprehensive rights-based framework for conducting HRIA of economic reform programmes has emerged so far from the UN and its various human rights actors.

A brief history of the Guiding Principles

The *Guiding Principles* were developed under the auspices of the mandate of the Independent Expert on the effects of foreign debt and other related international financial obligations of States on the full enjoyment of all human rights, particularly economic, social and cultural rights (Independent Expert on debt and human rights/Independent Expert).[25] This is unsurprising given that one the principal areas of the UN Special Procedures mandate on 'debt and human rights' since its conception has been 'structural adjustment and its effects on human rights'. Initially, there were two mandates: that of the Independent Expert on 'structural adjustment programs', established in 1997,[26] and, a year later, the Special Rapporteur on 'the effects of external debt on the full enjoyment of economic, social and cultural rights'.[27] In 2000, these mandates were discontinued when the mandate of the Independent Expert 'on the effects of structural adjustment policies and foreign debt on the full enjoyment of all human rights, particularly economic, social and cultural rights' was established.[28] The 2005 broadening of the mandate from 'the effects of structural adjustment policies' to 'the effects of economic reform policies' to some degree set the scene for the broad scope of the *Guiding Principles*, albeit that the mandate was redefined and retitled in 2008.[29] Since 2008, mandate-holders have looked at a range of different economic policy issues from a human rights perspective, including in reports on the impact of economic reform policies on women's human rights, labour rights in the context of economic reforms and austerity measures, as well as the human rights impacts of tax evasion.[30] (Indeed, these reports contributed directly to the development of the *Guiding Principles*). An earlier set of Guiding Principles emanating from the mandate, on foreign debt and human rights, stressed the importance of HRIA in the context of lending activities.[31]

In 2015 and 2016, the Independent Expert paid official visits to Greece and the European Union institutions, respectively, in order to assess the impact of austerity policies on human rights.[32] During meetings with different stakeholders in the course of those missions, questions arose with regard to the legal framework to be applied in HRIAs and the methodology to follow if such exercises were to be conducted. Reflecting these important questions, the Independent Expert's report on his mission to the European Union highlighted the need to 'develop particular guidelines for conducting HRIA for macroeconomic reform programmes, building on the normative components of internationally recognised economic, social and cultural rights and on existing impact assessment guidelines and tools'.[33]

In its March 2017 session – the same one at which the Independent Expert's report on the European Union was presented and discussed – the Human Rights Council recognised that 'structural adjustment reform programmes and policy conditionalities limit public expenditure, impose fixed expenditure ceilings and give inadequate attention to the provision of social services, and that only a few countries manage to achieve sustainable higher growth under these programmes'.[34] The Council proceeded to request the Independent Expert to develop guiding principles for HRIAs for economic reform policies.[35]

The Human Rights Council considered and voted on the *Guiding Principles* on 5 April 2019.[36] The relevant resolution '[e]ncourages Governments, relevant United Nations bodies, specialized agencies, funds and programmes and other intergovernmental organizations to consider taking into account the guiding principles in the formulation and implementation of their economic reform policies and measures'. It also encourages national human rights institutions, non-governmental organizations and the private sector 'to give due consideration to the guiding principles in their work'.[37] The Office of the United Nations High Commissioner for Human Rights was requested to disseminate the *Guiding Principles*.[38]

Support for the resolution was not unanimous. Indeed, the voting patterns of Human Rights Council members with regard to it – effectively most high-income countries in favour, low- and middle-income countries against, and a few states abstaining[39] – reflects the historical geopolitical dynamics at the Council with regard to the debt and human rights Special Procedures mandate.[40] All Global North state members of the Commission on Human Rights voted against the mandate in 2000 and since then have continued to call for a vote and then vote against or abstain on resolutions renewing the mandate.[41]

The traditional, formal explanation for high-income country government resistance to the *Guiding Principles* (and the mandate more generally) has been that there are already international institutions with expertise on financial affairs dealing with these issues at the global level, specifically International Financial Institutions. However, the IMF has been explicit that human rights do not fall within its mandate, including in a letter submitted in the context of the drafting process of the *Guiding Principles*:

> Nevertheless, the mandate of the IMF is defined by the Articles of Agreement and its powers and responsibilities are limited to those entrusted to it by the membership. *This mandate focuses on macroeconomic and financial stability and does not, unlike the constituent documents of some other international organizations, encompass the promotion of human rights per se.* As an institution that is concerned with economic issues, the IMF is precluded from using its powers to support particular political systems or, directly engage in the promotion of human rights. (…) The IMF has not accepted the Declaration on Human Rights as the motivating principle of our operations. UN agencies have generally accepted our arguments as establishing the limits of our engagement and obligations on promoting human rights.[42]

During both the drafting process and the interactive dialogue at the Council in which the *Guiding Principles* were discussed, the Brazilian government asserted that the whole *Guiding Principles* project was biased as it assumed *ex ante* that all economic reforms (referring to austerity, fiscal consolidation and adjustment) have adverse effects on human rights. This is why the preamble of the final version of the *Guiding Principles* reads:

> Not all economic reform policy responding to economic crises is intrinsically against human rights, and economic reforms that are carefully formulated based on human rights can contribute to the betterment of human rights. In fact, responding to economic crises often requires actions by the Government that are dictated by the urgency to protect resources and assets that will, in the long term, serve to protect and fulfil human rights.

The inclusion of that statement did not however secure support for the *Guiding Principles* from all Human Rights Council members. Despite coolness on the part of some states, the *Guiding Principles* were nevertheless welcomed warmly by civil society and the profile of the *Guiding Principles* is steadily increasing.

Unsurprisingly, the work of the debt and human rights special procedure mandate has been a key driver of the *Guiding Principles*. Following the Council's endorsement of the *Guiding Principles*, the Independent Expert used the *Guiding Principles* in the context of official visits to Ukraine,[43] Sri Lanka,[44] Bolivia[45] and Mongolia[46] as a framework to assess contemplated and implemented economic reforms in those states. These reports were ultimately discussed with the relevant states during Human Rights Council sessions in 2019 and 2020.

The *Guiding Principles* have also received recognition from regional human rights institutions. For instance, the 'Business and Human Rights: Inter-American Standards', issued by the Inter-American Commission on Human Rights and the Special Rapporteur on Economic, Social, Cultural and Environmental Rights in 2019,[47] refer to the *Guiding Principles* as a relevant legal framework for the purposes of combating tax evasion.[48]

Ironically, despite the refusal of any European members of the Council to endorse the *Guiding Principles*, May 2020 saw the European Network of National Human Rights Institutions (ENNHRI) issue a statement on economic policies and human rights in the context of the Covid-19 crisis. ENNHRI explicitly cited the *Guiding Principles* when recommending human rights impact assessment of recovery measures in order to help protect people against discrimination and a widening of existing inequalities.[49]

The what, how and who of the Guiding Principles

Just as the *Guiding Principles* did not reinvent the wheel by centring on HRIA as a methodology, nor did they seek to outline 'new' human rights duties. Rather, they strove 'to identify and systematize existing human rights obligations, and also provide commentary on their implications' in the context of economic policy reforms.[50] This is in line with the approach of other soft law guiding principles in terms of particularising existing human rights obligations with regard to a specific thematic issue or group.[51] The *Guiding Principles* are explicitly based on 'all core international human rights instruments', the 'authoritative interpretation' of such by the treaty bodies, and the contributions of special procedure mandate holders.[52] The text of the *Guiding Principles* also makes clear that they are to be considered and applied 'in coordination and conjunction' with other

Guiding Principles, in particular those referring to business and human rights,[53] foreign debt and human rights,[54] HRIAs of trade and investment agreements,[55] and extreme poverty and human rights.[56]

While very much driven by concerns about the effects of the financial and economic crises of the late 2000s, the scope of the *Guiding Principles* extends to 'whenever economic reform policies may foreseeably result in impairment of human rights'.[57] Consistent with the notion of human rights as a proactive framework for policy-making, the *Guiding Principles* have both a preventive function (in the context of the design and implementation of short-, medium – and long-term economic reform policies), as well as a reactive function with regard to acute crises. This constitutes a crucial recognition that the negative impacts of economic policy are not limited to crisis contexts but extend to longer term processes such as fiscal consolidation or labour market reforms. Thus, while the *Guiding Principles* are applicable in the context of measures taken to address the immediate economic fallout of the COVID-19 pandemic public health crisis (for instance, short to medium-term state-funded work furlough schemes[58]), they will also be of direct relevance to more long-term economic policy responses – including those enduring beyond the duration of the pandemic itself (for instance, proposals to amend tax systems to ensure adequate future funding for social care).[59]

The *Guiding Principles*' section on 'Obligations of States' makes clear that states are obliged to manage their fiscal affairs and adopt economic policies to ensure that they 'respect, protect and fulfil all human rights', with their 'economic choices' complying with their international human rights law duties. This is required both when they act alone or as members of international financial institutions.[60] States and other creditors have the burden of proof of demonstrating that their proposed economic reform measures will realise, and not undermine, states' human rights obligations.[61] In turn, this implies a duty to carry out HRIA to evaluate and address any foreseeable effects of their economic policies on human rights.[62] Consultation on and the making public of the results of these HRIAs are stated to be important components of complying with this obligation.[63] The *GP* also respond to the risk of 'passing the buck' for human rights responsibility in the context of decentralisation, devolution or localisation of economic policy decision-making: they make clear that while although all levels of government have human rights obligations in the economic policy context, central government has ultimate responsibility for human rights compliance.[64]

Consistent with concerns about the impact of financial globalisation and the potential extraterritorial impacts of domestic economic policy measures, the *Guiding Principles* devote significant attention to the obligation of international assistance cooperation in order to facilitate the full realisation of all rights.[65] This not only entails a duty on states to respect and protect the enjoyment of the human rights of people outside their borders, it also involves contributing to the creation of an international environment that enables the fulfilment of human rights. In HRIA practice terms, this requires conducting assessments of the extraterritorial impacts of laws, policies and practices.[66]

The *Guiding Principles* also iterate that 'states, international or regional financial institutions and other non-State and State actors' – including, importantly, corporations – should not exert 'undue external influence' on other states so as to prevent them from using their policy space to design and implement economic policies, in accordance with their human rights obligations.[67] Undue external influence is defined as direct or indirect intervention in a state's economic affairs through the use of economic and/or political measures in an effort to influence states to adopt certain economic policies or to secure from them advantages of any kind that undermines their ability to give effect to their human rights obligations.[68] Examples of such measures would be conditionalities linked to financial assistance programmes or implicit conditionalities informally urged by international or regional institutions.[69] Giving effect to this requirement necessitates states to enact foreign investment laws in such a way as to include an obligation on investors to undertake HRIA through neutral entities in a transparent and inclusive manner.[70] Reflecting the fact that there is a particular risk of 'external undue influence' where states are facing financial or other crises, the *Guiding Principles* stress the importance of the systematic use of 'transparent and participatory HRIAs' in the design of economic reform programmes attached to international loans.[71]

The *Guiding Principles* focus directly on the obligations of public creditors and donors, including IFIs and bilateral lenders, to ensure that the terms of their transactions and their proposals for reform policies and conditionalities for financial support do not undermine the borrower/recipient states' ability to satisfy their human rights obligations.[72] HRIAs should be a mandatory element in the design of all economic reform and adjustment programmes, including in the context of debt management and financial assistance activities.[73] *Ex ante* HRIA – conducted sufficiently early to predate the conclusion of agreements – is particularly important in this context. Furthermore, release clauses with regard to specific conditions should be put in place where actual or potential adverse human rights impacts are identified.[74] The *Guiding Principles* also address private creditors, who are exhorted to assess the human rights impacts of their own actions as well as those of the activities financed by them, unless they have ascertained that debtor states or international and regional financial institutions have carried out effective assessments.[75]

In delineating 'applicable human rights standards', the *Guiding Principles* make clear that, when considering possible economic measures, states must be guided by existing international human rights law, including civil and political rights.[76] In line with the fact that non-discrimination and equal enjoyment of rights are key elements of international human rights law, states are required to ensure that economic reform policies and measures are not discriminatory. This requires the assessment of the discriminatory impacts of economic reform policies – whether direct, indirect, multiple or intersectional in nature.[77] HRIA for the purposes of the *Guiding Principles* must therefore include equality impact assessment such as to identify the potential and cumulative impacts of specific measures, to enable them to be addressed, and for alternatives to be considered. The *Guiding Principles* thus indirectly recognise and incorporate equality impact assessment.[78] Consistent with the general direction of travel of international human rights law with regard to equality,[79] as well as a growing understanding of the structural discrimination faced by women in the prevailing economic paradigm,[80] the *Guiding Principles* emphasise that economic reforms should promote substantive and transformative gender equality.[81] Methodologically, HRIAs should always include a comprehensive gender analysis.[82]

Notably, while the primary focus of the *Guiding Principles* is on human rights, concern with the environment is a central theme, consistent with the recognised interdependence of human rights and a healthy environment. Reference is made to the need to ensure that economic policy reforms do not hamper states' ability to meet their 'environmental obligations'.[83] Thus, all proposed economic reform measures should be informed by and align with individual and collective state measures to facilitate national and global environmental protection, recognising the interdependence between human rights and a healthy environment.[84] States should also consider how proposed economic reforms may impact directly or otherwise reduce a state's ability to address national ecological conditions and significant global ecological thresholds that affect the realisation of human rights.[85] Methodologically, the *Guiding Principles* make clear that a HRIA 'if carried out properly, can incorporate regulatory, *environmental* and social impact assessments and should contain a human rights-based budget analysis'.[86]

Unsurprisingly given the resource-dependent and oriented nature of economic reforms, the *Guiding Principles* focus in some depth on the obligations of progressive realisation and use of maximum available resources set out in Article 2(1) of the International Covenant on Economic, Social and Cultural Rights.[87] Fiscal, tax, debt, trade, aid, monetary and environmental policies should be designed and implemented so that they are 'deliberately directed' towards the realisation of human rights.[88] With regard to the latter duty, states are required to demonstrate that every effort has been made to mobilise all available resources (including though resource generation), even in times of economic crisis.[89] Reflective of a concern to secure human rights protection during crises and other situations of resource constraint, one Principle is entirely devoted to the issue of retrogression. This delineates the conditions which economic measures that result in backwards steps in terms of economic, social and cultural rights must satisfy in order not to fall foul of the international human rights law prohibition on impermissible retrogression.[90]

Turning to the section 'Policy Articulation', the *Guiding Principles* provide an important articulation of how fiscal policy, monetary policy and debt policy should be designed and deployed to ensure human rights realisation.[91] Policy coordination and coherence is central to ensuring this.[92] Financial sector regulation is identified as necessary to detect, prevent, manage and fairly allocate the human rights risks created by financial instability and illicit financial flows.[93] Unsurprisingly, given the focus of the Special Procedure mandate under whose auspices the *Guiding Principles* developed, particular attention is focused on the issue of debt. The *Guiding Principles* state that findings of HRIAs should be used to inform debt strategies, debt relief programmes and restructuring negotiations.[94] The *Guiding Principles* make the point that independent HRIAs carried out within regular debt management work and sustainability assessments can support early identification of where constraints on fiscal space due to debt servicing are leading to an undermining of states' human rights duties.[95] The *Guiding Principles* assert that debt should not be understood as 'sustainable' if the social and human rights dimensions of sustainability are ignored.[96]

Part IV of the *Guiding Principles* is devoted to 'Human Rights Impact Assessments'. Principle 17 sets out the basis and purposes of a HRIA, defining an *ex ante* human rights impact assessment as 'a structured process to review alternative policy options and analyse the impacts of proposed measures on human rights'.[97] The *Guiding Principles* make clear that HRIA of economic policy reform should not just identify human rights-related problems raised by specific economic reform policies (whether alone or together with other economic measures being or due to be implemented). It should also establish a list of preventive and mitigating measures to ensure conformity of the economic reform policies under consideration with the state's human rights obligations.[98] In terms of methodology, HRIA should involve the use of a variety of quantitative and qualitative tools and methods, including participatory ones, and carefully compare the human rights impact of different scenarios including budget cuts, tax increases, and measures against tax evasion and avoidance.[99] Rather than being a 'once-off' exercise, HRIAs should be carried out regularly – i.e. both *ex ante* and *ex post*.[100] Thus HRIA in this context is not just about the potential impacts of proposed economic policy reforms but also involves assessment of the actual impacts of policy change and implementation,[101] thereby enabling any negative human rights impacts to be addressed. HRIA as conceptualised in terms of the *Guiding Principles* is not solely a critical tool focused on human rights problems; rather, it can and should be deployed to contribute to the identification of means by which human rights realisation can be advanced through economic policy reform.[102]

HRIAs also have an accountability function. The *Guiding Principles* state that a HRIA can serve to ensure that accountability procedures exist and mechanisms are in place so as to secure the right to an effective remedy with regard to actions and omissions in the design and/or implementation of economic reform policies that may undermine human rights. It does so 'by requiring clearly articulated and justified policy choices that have been developed through inclusive participation of the potentially affected population'.[103]

While arguing for HRIA to form part of the 'policy continuum',[104] the *Guiding Principles* are not blind to the challenges posed to policymakers by crisis situations in which decisions about economic reform measures have to be made under extreme time pressures. The fact that a 'perfect' HRIA exercise cannot be carried out does not result in the elimination of state obligations in this regard: rather, in such situations, the government is obliged to complete and publish a HRIA 'to the extent possible under the circumstances before taking any policy decisions or actions'.[105] In addition, the government should publicly explain why it is unable to do a full *ex ante* impact assessment, undertake a fully compliant *ex post* HRIA, and take steps to remedy all adverse human rights impacts identified in either impact assessment as promptly as possible.[106]

The *Guiding Principles* emphasise the importance that participation, access to information and transparency be embedded in HRIA. This should be the case in terms of the inputs, process, outputs, and publicising of outputs of such exercises.[107]

The final Principle, Principle 22, addresses the tricky question of who should carry out HRIA. On the one hand, state actors will frequently be best positioned for the purposes of accessing and collating the data and other evidence needed for a 'robust' and 'credible' HRIA.[108] On the other, government or state actor conduct of HRIA of a proposed measure raises questions about whether such an exercise is in fact 'independent'.[109] This is particularly so where a state's independence (de jure or de facto) from any creditor or creditor-aligned institution responsible for designing adjustment programmes is open to question. Reflecting an appreciation of this issue, as well as the differing capacities and aims of different actors who might carry out HRIA, the *Guiding Principles* are 'flexible enough to be adjusted to the particular needs of government departments, advisory bodies, parliamentary committees, national human rights institutions, courts, international financial institutions, private creditors, international institutions or civil society organizations'.[110] However, any entity carrying out HRIA must be assessed against predetermined criteria. These should include, as a minimum, independence from the executive branch and any creditor/creditor-aligned institution, adequate funding, appropriate expertise, diversity of membership (including gender parity), engagement of affected communities, as well as credibility and legitimacy in the eyes of different stakeholders.[111] Consistent with the need to ensure participation of those affected by purported or implemented economic reform policies to the greatest degree possible, states should take steps to support the ability of affected communities and civil society generally to provide parallel information to assessment processes and, as far as possible, to conduct human rights impact assessments directly.[112] HRIA, as contemplated by the *Guiding Principles*, therefore has a crucial empowerment aspect.

Introducing the Special Issue contributions

This Special Issue brings together experts working on human rights and economic policy from a range of disciplinary perspectives, including economics, law, and development studies. The contributions reflect a huge body of professional experience in the academic, policy-making, advocacy and practitioner fields. All of the authors have a strong awareness of the importance of inter- and multi-disciplinary engagement. This is evident from the articles themselves, which address a wide range of different (legal, normative, economic, policy) frameworks and methodologies. The Special Issue's scope benefits enormously from this, with contributions ranging from political economy (Kendrick) to black letter international human rights law analysis (MacNaughton) to political science (Goldmann) to child rights (Hoffman) to law and economics (De Schutter, Lusiani, and Chaparro).

The *Guiding Principles* are the driving force behind the Special Issue and contributors engage with them in a range of different ways. Corkery and Isaacs use them as a springboard to explore the challenge posed by 'the politics of evidence' in the context of HRIA. Hoffmann highlights how they complement long-standing work in the area of child rights impact assessment. MacNaughton reviews the *Guiding Principles* from the perspective of economic inequality. Goldmann approaches them as a framework for strengthening democratic decision-making. Kendrick considers how gendered ideas might affect their potential as a framework for ideational power-oriented impact assessment. De Schutter, Lusiani and Chaparro address how the *Guiding Principles*, as part of international human rights law, can contribute to build a more solid conception of global tax justice.

Unsurprisingly, however, the Special Issue authors go well beyond the *Guiding Principles* to address key issues arising in relation to economic policy reform, human rights and human rights impact assessment.

In the opening article, Corkery and Isaacs argue that the way that evidentiary challenges are addressed in the field of HRIA pays limited attention to the political dynamics at play in shaping the methodologies through which evidence is created, selected and interpreted. In doing so, they engage with the long-standing challenge faced by those seeking to bring human rights to bear in an economic policy context: namely, the predominance of economics in human rights/economics interactions. The authors make clear that inherited limitations from both the fields of economics and HRIA pose serious challenges to the ability of the Guiding Principles – and other HRIA tools – to advance evidence-based policy-making meaningfully. Having identified the problems posed to HRIA by technical bias in neo-classical economics in particular, the authors set out a number of strategies to assist HRIA advocates to better navigate the politics of evidence, as well as take advantage of the space for contesting economic orthodoxies opened up by the imperative to audit economic reforms according to human rights standards.

The second piece, by Goldmann, addresses the relationship between human rights, economic policy and democracy, analysing a series of negative feedback loops between democracy and human rights in the context of economic policy reform. He details how economic reform policies driven by international and supranational financial institutions may compromise democratic self-determination and hamper the democratic participation of marginalised groups – an undermining of democratic institutions that has a knock-on effect on human rights. Arguing that such rights require a framework for legitimate redistributive decisions, the author asserts that any impairment of democratic institutions as a consequence of economic policy reforms will in the long run pose a risk to their realisation. Turning to the *Guiding Principles*, Goldmann outlines their potential role in strengthening human rights and democracy, particularly through their encouragement of states to subject economic policy reforms to democratic control. The author then demonstrates how the *Guiding Principles* can and should shape the European Union's response to COVID-19. In doing so, he hones in on the issues of transparency, participation and policy coherence – all of which are addressed in the *Guiding Principles* – and the role that these do and could play with regard to the EU's pandemic-related economic reform policies.

MacNaughton's piece centres on what she terms the 'current crisis of extreme economic inequality'. Having outlined the existing state of play, as well as the potential impacts of COVID-19, she places the blame for this on the long-standing impacts of neoliberal economic policy reforms. The article provides a detailed analysis of vertical (income and wealth) and horizontal (status-based) inequalities, including the relationship of both to international rights law as well as Sustainable Development Goal 10 on reducing inequality in and among countries.[113] Reviewing the *Guiding Principles* from the perspective of economic inequality, the author finds them wanting. In response, she argues for the inclusion of a specific principle on economic inequality to ensure that governments consider the impact of policy economic reforms on income and wealth inequality as critical causes of human rights violations. The piece as a whole makes clear the (COVID-19-reinforced) urgency of broader engagement with vertical inequality in the context of both international human rights law – including HRIA practice – and the framework for SDG 10.

Hoffman's piece focuses on an important group-specific sub-set of HRIA: child rights impact assessment (CRIA). He outlines the history and normative underpinnings of CRIA, highlighting the central role played by the UN Committee on the Rights of the Child in promoting such practice through its presentation of CRIA as a crucial element of state efforts to give effect to their obligations under the UN Convention on the Rights of the Child. This contributes to an understanding of the key role of UN treaty bodies in encouraging (and thereby indirectly advancing) HRIA. Having outlined the elements of CRIA and how they should be applied to economic policy, Hoffman reviews *ex ante* CRIA in practice in a range of national contexts, flagging that CRIA remains underutilised as a policy tool to assess how state budgeting contributes to the realisation of children's rights. In doing so, he provides valuable insights into methodological good practice and challenges for CRIA, including in relation to resource allocation. The significant overlap in aims and procedural steps of CRIA and HRIA renders the article's findings directly relevant to HRIA practice more broadly.

Kendrick's article brings us back to the issue of the political dynamics that may affect HRIA practice. She argues that, when considering the effects of economic policy reform on women's human rights, it is crucial to consider the political economy mechanisms through which these effects operate. In doing so, she provides greater nuance to our understanding of the causal channels through which economic policy reforms impact women's human rights than has been offered previously. The article directly challenges the treatment of the distribution of policy costs and benefits as outcomes of a given state of the world on the basis that economic policy reforms both shape and are shaped by those costs and benefits. Using a political economy model of economic policy-making, Kendrick shows how the choice of economic policy and its impacts on women's human rights are endogenous to various gendered political-economic forces, which have interest, institutional and ideational-based dynamics. She argues further that while the gender-related standards set out in the Guiding Principles on Foreign Debt and Human Rights are an ambitious step forward in addressing possible negative impacts on women's human rights, their relative salience in the shaping of economic policy will be mediated by those same political-economic forces.

The operationalisation of rights in the struggle to tax multinational companies is the focus of De Schutter, Lusiani and Chaparro's contribution. Having outlined what a national human rights-aligned tax policy would look like, the authors dissect how the existing international tax regime impedes individual states' ability to bring their national tax policies in line with human rights. The article thus reflects a key preoccupation of several pieces in the Special Issue: the direct and indirect impacts of economic globalisation on governments' ability to deploy their economic policy space in a human rights-aligned way. The authors discuss how international human rights law, including the *Guiding Principles*, can provide a stronger normative foundation to curb harmful tax competition and help resolve disputes over the right to tax multinational companies. The authors also highlight the paucity of practical tools to embed human rights norms into the process and substance of reforming international tax policies. They set out a framework of questions that policy makers and advocates can use to assess current efforts to rewrite the international tax rules so as to create an enabling environment for implementing human rights-based tax policies at domestic level – efforts that the economic impact of the COVID-19 pandemic have rendered more pressing than ever.

Fittingly, the Special Issue concludes with the text of the *Guiding Principles* themselves, together with a short overview of the process leading to their introduction.

Conclusion and challenges ahead

This Special Issue has addressed key themes in the debates on economic policy and human rights – both within the academy and beyond. It is clear, however, that while human rights and economic policy reform are as close to being on speaking terms as they ever have been, they and their proponents still often speak in parallel – and this is generally at the expense of human rights protection.

When plans for this Special Issue were drawn up and initial drafts of articles were prepared, COVID-19 had not yet reared its head. The challenges thrown up by this most recent global crisis engage directly with, and exacerbate, many of the issues raised by the authors – be it economic inequality (MacNaughton), tax rules and policy (De Schutter,

Lusiani and Chaparro) the role of international and supranational institutions (Goldman), gender inequality (Kendrick), children's 'invisibility' (Hoffman), and the methodological complexities of producing and understanding information on the links between economic reforms and human rights (Corkery and Isaacs).

Depressingly, the global response to COVID-19 thus far suggests that the spheres of human rights and economic policy reform remain separate and unequal. In April 2020 the IMF's 'Fiscal Monitor Report' was already warning that 'once the COVID-19 crisis is over, prudent fiscal policies call for appropriately paced, inclusive, and credible adjustments to put debt ratios on a firm downward trajectory' and that 'at the current juncture, making clear that support measures to address the COVID-19 crisis are temporary could help manage expectations (...)'.[114] The IMF's message that '[o]nce the COVID-19 crisis is over, high-debt countries should, in general, pursue fiscal consolidation supported by growth-friendly measures'[115] bodes poorly for human rights enjoyment given past experiences of similar post-crisis measures.

But are we – as Saiz stated with regard to the financial and economic crisis of the late 2000s – in a situation where 'despite the obvious human rights dimensions of the crisis, human rights have barely figured in the diagnoses or prescriptions proposed by the international community'?[116] This time around, the answer is (a tentative) 'no'. Despite the ongoing reluctance of IFIs to engage with human rights in terms of their work and its impacts, there have been significant statements on the part of international and regional actors on the need to ensure that responses to COVID-19 are consistent with human rights.[117]

However, where recovery discussions have focused on economic policy specifically, policymaker engagement with human rights appears to dissipate.[118] One telling example is the UN Policy Brief on policy responses to COVID-19. This document, which sets out the framework for the United Nations' urgent socio-economic support to countries and societies in the face of COVID-19, makes frequent and explicit reference to human rights. However, the section on 'guiding the necessary surge in fiscal and financial stimulus to make macroeconomic policies work for the most vulnerable and strengthening multilateral and regional responses' makes no mention of human rights.[119] This is notwithstanding references to the need to ensure support for vulnerable groups, as well as emphasis on the necessity of supporting SDG achievement and ensuring 'social and environmental sustainability within the framework of the 2030 Agenda and the SDGs'.[120] In the same section, the improvement of the evidence base for policy-making (including gender analysis) as well as the 'conduct of comprehensive impact assessments at the household level, and to undertake context-specific socio-economic impact analyses of the crisis'[121] are identified as areas of priority action. There is, however, no reference to HRIA.

That is despite the clear acknowledgement of the implications of COVID-19 and states responses thereto for human rights elsewhere in the document. This is reflected in, amongst others things, an annexe outlining indicators for monitoring the human rights implications of COVID-19, as well as a statement in the 'How We Will Deliver the Response' section that,

> the human rights implications of the pandemic call on the [UN Development System] to be proactive in ensuring that its efforts, as well as the local, national and international efforts it

> supports, address human rights concerns and advance human rights in the 'recover better' phase, as framed by the Secretary-General. To this end, with support and guidance from OHCHR, the UNDS will continue to assess the human rights impact of the COVID-19 pandemic and the extent to which responses respect human rights by using the 10 human rights indicators.[122]

This is a far cry, however, from asserting that such impact assessment should form part of the efforts of national government and other actors with central roles to play in the economic policy context.[123] Nor do any of the indicators set out relate to economic policy.

This is one significant, albeit necessarily limited, example that highlights the ongoing gap between human rights and economic policy-making. If human rights are not regarded as central to post-COVID-19 economic policy responses by all UN actors, then one suspects there is little hope for them featuring on the agendas of other institutions with significantly less institutional commitment to human rights. That said, this illustration also underlines the growing profile and recognition of scope for HRIA, something that can be leveraged by those seeking to advance HRIA of economic policy through the deployment of the *Guiding Principles*.

More positively, July 2020 saw the production of a 'Checklist for a Human Rights-Based Approach to Socio-Economic Country Responses to COVID-19' by the OHCHR, the UN Development Progamme and the UN Sustainable Development Group.[124] The Checklist includes a section on 'macroeconomic response and multilateral collaboration',[125] which is strongly in line with *Guiding Principles*. (These are expressly referred to as a resource in the document). Amongst other things, the Checklist asks whether stimulus packages have 'been developed and assessed with a human rights lens' and whether country analyses and strategies in relation to debt distress and sustainability incorporate HRIAs. It also includes questions focused on 'maximum available resources' and 'retrogression', as well as whether measures are in place 'to ensure IFIs and donors refrain from attaching conditions to their financing that could undermine the state's ability to respect, protect, and fulfil its human rights obligations in the allocation of resources and the design of policies'. Admittedly, the document proposes a rather simplistic yes/no assessment approach that needs to be further developed if it is to be line with more sophisticated and comprehensive HRIAs methodology envisaged in the *Guiding Principles*. However, it does demonstrate the increasing importance that the international community – or some parts of it at least – is attaching to HRIAs in the economic realm.

The COVID-19 crisis poses a real threat to human rights enjoyment. It also provides an opportunity to push ahead with the crucial task – for policymakers, for advocates, for scholars – of bringing human rights to bear on economic policy reform. The contributions to this Special Issue make clear that this opportunity is being and will continue to be seized with both hands. The *Guiding Principles* will have a key role to play.

Notes

1. It should be noted that this article takes 'reform' to mean change or amendment – it does not understand 'reform' necessarily to imply 'improvement'. This is consistent with the way in which that term is understood in the context of the UN *Guiding Principles on Human Rights Impact Assessments for Economic Reform Policies*.

2. United Nations, 'Policy Brief: A UN framework for the immediate socio-economic response to COVID-19', April 2020, 17, https://www.un.org/sites/un2.un.org/files/un_framework_report_on_covid-19.pdf (accessed August 8, 2020).
3. See, e.g. CESCR, 'Letter to States Parties on Austerity Measures', dated May 16, 2012, Reference CESCR/48th/SP/MAB/SW; A. Nolan, N. Luisiani and C. Courtis, 'Two Steps Forward, No Steps Back? Evolving Criteria on the Prohibition of Retrogression in Economic, Social and Cultural Rights', in *Economic and Social Rights after the Global Financial Crisis*, ed. A. Nolan (Cambridge: Cambridge University Press, 2014), 121; B. Warwick, 'Socio-Economic Rights During Economic Crises: A Changed Approach to Non-Retrogression', *International and Comparative Law Quarterly* 65, no. 1 (2016): 249; B. Warwick, 'Unwinding Retrogression: Conflicting Concepts and Patchy Practice', *Human Rights Law Review* 19, no. 3 (2019): 467–90.
4. See, e.g. A. Corkery and I. Saiz, 'Progressive Realisation according to Maximum Available Resources: The accountability challenge', in *Research Handbook on Economic, Social and Cultural Rights as Human Rights*, ed. J. Dugard et al. (Elgar, 2020 forthcoming); R. Balakrishnan et al., 'Maximum Available Resources and Human Rights' (Rutgers Center for Women's Global Leadership Report, June 2011); Abby Kendrick, 'Measuring Compliance: Social Rights and the Maximum Available Resources Dilemma', *Human Rights Quarterly* 39, no. 3 (2017): 657; R. Uprimny et al., 'Bridging the Gap: The Evolving Doctrine on ESCR and "Maximum Available Resources"', in *The Future of Social and Economic Rights*, ed. K. Young (Cambridge: Cambridge University Press, 2019), 624.
5. See, e.g. Committee on Economic, Social and Cultural Rights, 'General Comment No. 24 (2017) on State Obligations Under the International Covenant on Economic, Social and Cultural Rights in the Context of Business Activities', UN Doc. E/C.12/GC/24 paras 25–37; O. De Schutter et al., 'Commentary to the Maastricht Principles on Extraterritorial Obligations of States in the Area of Economic, Social and Cultural Rights', *Human Rights Quarterly* 34 (2012): 1084; M. Langford et al. (eds), *Global Justice, State Duties: the Extraterritorial Scope of Economic, Social and Cultural Rights in International Law* (Cambridge: Cambridge University Press, 2013).
6. See, e.g. Committee on Economic, Social and Cultural Rights, 'Public Debt, Austerity Measures and the International Covenant on Economic, Social and Cultural Rights', UN Doc. E/C.12/2016/1, 22 July 2016; UN Committee on the Rights of the Child, 'General Comment No.19 on Public Budgeting for the Realisation of Human Rights', (2016), UN Doc. CRC/C/GC/19; Special Rapporteur on Extreme Poverty and Human Rights, 'The Role of the IMF in Relation to Social Protection', UN Doc. A/HRC/38/33 (8 May 2018); Special Rapporteur on Extreme Poverty and Human Rights, 'The World Bank and Human Rights', UN Doc. A/70/274 (4 August 2015).
7. See, e.g. Matthias Goldmann, 'Financial institutions and social rights: from the Washington Consensus to the Lagarde Concord?', in *Research Handbook on International Law and Social Rights*, ed. Christina Binder, et al. (Elgar, 2020), 440; M. Dowell-Jones, 'Financial Institutions and Human Rights', *Human Rights Law Review* 13, no. 3 (2013): 423.
8. Committee on Economic, Social and Cultural Rights, 'General Comment No. 2 (1990) on International Technical Assistance Measures', para. 9.
9. See, e.g. D. Kinley, *Necessary Evil: How to Fix Finance by Saving Human Rights* (Oxford: Oxford University Press, 2018); M. Wachnefeld et al., 'Human Rights and Sustainable Finance', IHRB Inquiry Working Paper 16/1 (London: IHRB, 2016), https://greenfinanceplatform.org/sites/default/files/downloads/resource/Human%20Rights%20and%20Sustainable%20Finance%20-%20Exploring%20the%20Relationship.pdf (accessed August 5, 2020).
10. See, e.g. Committee on Economic, Social and Cultural Rights, 'Public Debt, Austerity Measures and the International Covenant on Economic, Social and Cultural Rights', UN Doc. E/C.12/2016/1, 22 July 2016; I. Bantekas and C. Lumina, eds., *Sovereign Debt and Human Rights* (Oxford: Oxford University Press, 2018); J. Bohoslavsky and K. Raffer, eds., *Sovereign Debt Crises: What Have We learned?* (Cambridge: Cambridge University Press, 2017).

11. See, e.g. M. Sepúlveda, 'Alternatives to Austerity: A Human Rights Framework for Recovery', in *Economic and Social Rights after the Global Financial Crisis*, ed. A. Nolan (Cambridge: Cambridge University Press, 2014), 23.
12. See, e.g. the Latin American civil society initiative on 'Principles and Guidelines on Human Rights in Fiscal Policy', 2020, at https://derechosypoliticafiscal.org/en/the-project (accessed September 8, 2020); the work advanced by the Independent Commission for the Reform of International Corporate Taxation (ICRICT), 2020, https://www.icrict.com (accessed September 8, 2020); ed. P. Alston and N. Reisch, *Tax, Inequality, and Human Rights* (Oxford: Oxford University Press, 2019).
13. See, e.g. the work of the IEL Collective, https://warwick.ac.uk/fac/soc/law/research/centres/globe/ielcollective/about/ (accessed September 8, 2020).
14. See, e.g. the work of the Center for Economic and Social Rights has developed on its OPERA framework. See CESR, 'The OPERA Framework. Assessing Compliance with the Obligation to Fulfil Economic, Social and Cultural Rights', 2017, https://www.cesr.org/sites/default/files/the.opera_.framework.pdf (accessed September 8, 2020). Analyses using the OPERA framework have been conducted in Brazil, South Africa and Spain, in partnership with national civil society organisations.
15. See, e.g. R. Balakrishnan, J. Heintz, and D. Elson, *Rethinking Economic Policy for Social Justice* (London: Routledge, 2016); S. Efange and J. Woodroffe, *The Audacity to Disrupt: An Introduction to Feminist Macro-level Economics* (London: GADN/FEMNET, 2020), https://static1.squarespace.com/static/536c4ee8e4b0b60bc6ca7c74/t/5f2940b2adaadd409fa60345/1596539086311/AFMA±resource±pack±-±The±audacity±to±disrupt±2020.pdf (accessed August 5, 2020).
16. For an in-depth claim that suggests that mainstream economics has foundational elements that are not congruent with human rights approaches, see S. Reddy, 'Economics and Human Rights: A Non-Conversation', in *Human Rights and the Capabilities Approach. An Interdisciplinary Dialogue*, ed. D. Elson, S. Fukuda-Parr, and P. Vizard (London: Routledge, 2012). See also, D. Elson, R. Balakrishnan, and J. Heintz, 'Public Finance, Maximum Available Resources and Human Rights', in *Human Rights and Public Finance*, ed. A. Nolan et al. (Oxford: Hart, 2013).
17. For a discussion of some of the reasons for this, see, e.g. A. Nolan, 'Not Fit for Purpose: Human Rights in Times of Financial and Economic Crisis', *European Human Rights Law Review* 4 (2015): 360.
18. International Association for Impact Assessment, 'What is Impact Assessment?', 2, https://www.iaia.org/uploads/pdf/What_is_IA_web.pdf (accessed August 4, 2020).
19. G. De Beco, 'Human Rights Impact Assessments', *Netherland Quarterly of Human Rights* 27, no. 2 (2009): 139, 141.
20. For an overview of the origins of HRIA, including its evolution from and relationship to other forms of impact assessment, see J. Harrison, 'Human Rights Measurement: Reflections on the Current Practice and Future Potential of Human Rights Impact Assessment', *Journal of Human Rights Practice* 3, no. 2 (2011): 162.
21. For an overview of key statements of UN treaty bodies and Special Procedures with regard to HRIA, see G. MacNaughton, 'Human Rights Impact Assessment: A Method for Healthy Policymaking', *Health and Human Rights* 17, no. 1 (2015), https://sites.sph.harvard.edu/hhrjournal/2015/04/human-rights-impact-assessment-a-method-for-healthy-policymaking/ (accessed August 5, 2020).
22. See Special Rapporteur on the Right to Food, 'Guiding Principles on Human Rights Impact Assessments of Trade and Investment Agreements' (December 19, 2011), UN Doc. A/HRC/19/59/Add.5; Special Rapporteur on extreme poverty and human Rights, 'Guiding Principles on Extreme Poverty and Human Rights' (July 18, 2012), UN Doc. A/HRC/21/39, paras 61 and 101. See also John Ruggie, UN Special Representative of the Secretary-General on the Issue of Human Rights and Transnational Corporations and Other Business Enterprises, Human Rights Impact Assessment – Resolving Key Methodological Questions (February 5, 2007), UN Doc. No. A/HRC/4/74. This report

fed into the Guiding Principles on Business and Human Rights. (See, Report of the Special Representative of the Secretary-General on the Issue of Human Rights and Transnational Corporations and Other Business Enterprises, 'Business and Human Rights – Further Steps Toward the Operationalization of the "Protect, Respect and Remedy" Framework' (April 9, 2010), A/HRC/14/27).

23. For more, see MacNaughton's contribution to this Special Issue.
24. See, e.g. UN Committee on the Rights of the Child, 'General Comment No.19 on Public Budgeting for the Realisation of Human Rights' (2016), UN Doc. CRC/C/GC/19, para. 47; Committee on Economic, Social and Cultural Rights, 'Public debt, austerity measures and the International Covenant on Economic, Social and Cultural Rights' (July 22, 2016), para. 11.
25. For more on this process, see the 'Introduction' to the *Guiding Principles* in this Special Issue.
26. Commission on Human Rights, 'Effects of Structural Adjustment Policies on the Full Enjoyment of Human Rights', UN Doc. E/CN.4/DEC/1997/103, (April 3, 1997) and 'Effects of Structural Adjustment Policies on the Full Enjoyment of Human Rights', UN Doc. E/CN.4/1999/50 (February 24, 1999).
27. Commission on Human Rights, Res E/CN.4/RES/1998/24 (April 17, 1998).
28. Commission on Human Rights, 'Effects of Structural Adjustment Policies and Foreign Debt on the Full Enjoyment of All Human Rights, Particularly Economic, Social and Cultural Rights', Resolution 2000/82 Adopted by the Commission on Human Rights, UN Doc. E/CN.4/RES/2000/82 (April 27, 2000).
29. Human Rights Council, 'Mandate of the Independent Expert on the Effects of Foreign Debt and Other Related International Financial Obligations of States on the Full Enjoyment of all Human Rights, Particularly Economic, Social and Cultural Rights', Resolution adopted by the Human Rights Council, UN Doc. A/HRC/RES/7/4 (March 27, 2008).
30. UN Doc. A/73/179, July 18, 2018; A/HRC/34/57, December 27, 2016; UN Doc. A/HRC/31/61, January 15, 2016.
31. Independent Expert on Debt and Human Rights, 'Guiding Principles on Foreign Debt and Human Rights' (April 10, 2011), UN Doc. A/HRC/20/23, para. 40.
32. UN Doc. A/HRC/31/60/Add.2, 21 April 2016; UN Doc. A/HRC/34/57/Add.1, 28 December 2016.
33. UN Doc. A/HRC/34/57/Add.1, 28 December 2016, para. 82(b).
34. Human Rights Council, 'Mandate of the Independent Expert on the Effects of Foreign Debt and Other Related International Financial Obligations of States on the Full Enjoyment of All Human Rights, Particularly Economic, Social and Cultural Rights', Resolution adopted by the Human Rights Council on 23 Mach 2017, UN Doc. A/HRC/RES/34/3 (April 6, 2017).
35. Ibid., para. 13.
36. Human Rights Council, 'The Effects of Foreign Debt and Other Related International Financial Obligations of States on the Full Enjoyment of All Human Rights, Particularly Economic, Social and Cultural Rights', Resolution adopted by the Human Rights Council on 21 March 2019, UN Doc. A/HRC/RES/40/8 (April 5, 2019).
37. Ibid., para. 3.
38. Ibid., para. 4.
39. In favour: Angola, Bahrain, Bangladesh, Burkina Faso, Cameroon, Chile, China, Cuba, Democratic Republic of the Congo, Egypt, Eritrea, Fiji, India, Iraq, Nepal, Nigeria, Pakistan, Philippines, Qatar, Rwanda, Saudi Arabia, Senegal, Somalia, South Africa, Togo, Tunisia, Uruguay. Against: Australia, Austria, Brazil, Bulgaria, Croatia, the Czech Republic, Denmark, Hungary, Italy, Japan, Slovakia, Spain, Ukraine, United Kingdom of Great Britain and Northern Ireland. Abstaining: Afghanistan, Argentina, Bahamas, Iceland, Mexico, and Peru.
40. Resolutions adopted in relation to the mandate and how States have voted them can be found at https://www.ohchr.org/EN/Issues/Development/IEDebt/Pages/Resolutions.aspx (accessed September 8, 2020).
41. R. Freedman and F. Crépeau, 'Supporting or Resisting? The Relationship between Global North States and Special Procedures' in *The United Nations Special Procedures System*, ed. A. Nolan et al. (Leiden: Nijhoff, 2017), 411, 420.

42. Dated July 27, 2017 (Emphasis in the original), https://www.ohchr.org/Documents/Issues/IEDebt/impactassessments/IMF.pdf (accessed September 8, 2020).
43. UN Doc. A/HRC/40/57/Add.1, December 31, 2018.
44. UN Doc. A/HRC/40/57/Add.2, January 17, 2019.
45. UN Doc. A/HRC/43/45/Add.1, March 2, 2020.
46. UN Doc. A/HRC/43/45/Add.2, January 3, 2020.
47. OEA/Ser.L/V/II CIDH/REDESCA/INF.1/19, November 1, 2019, http://www.oas.org/es/cidh/informes/pdfs/EmpresasDDHH.pdf (accessed August 10, 2020).
48. Ibid. para. 258.
49. ENNHRI, 'The EU Must Put Economic and Social Rights at the Heart of Its Economic Response to COVID-19', May 6, 2020, http://ennhri.org/statement-covid-19-esr/ (accessed August 9, 2020). The Greek National Commission for Human Rights, which was involved in the drafting process of the *Guiding Principles*, welcomed and recognised the importance of the *Guiding Principles* in 2019, available at See at http://www.nchr.gr/images/English_Site/CRISIS/GNCHR%20for%20IEs%20Guidelines%20on%20HRIA%20.pdf (accessed September 8, 2020).
50. *Guiding Principles*, para. 8.
51. For a detailed discussion of the legal status and purposes of Guiding Principles, see M. Sepúlveda, 'Human Rights Guiding Principles: A Forward-Looking Retrospective' in *Realising the Abidjan Principles on the Right to Education: Human Rights, Public Education, and the Role of Private Actors in Education*, ed. F. Adamson et al. (London: Edward Elgar, forthcoming 2021).
52. *Guiding Principles*, para. 8.
53. See note 22 above.
54. See note 22 above.
55. See note 22 above.
56. See note 22 above; *Guiding Principles*, para. 9.
57. *Guiding Principles*, Principle 1.
58. For a discussion of such schemes in the European context as well as the argument that emergency measures will be required in the longer term, see Financial Times, 'How to Adapt Furlough Schemes for Phase 2', https://www.ft.com/content/cdf73dc8-a298-4f08-ab89-76c10068e7ef (accessed August 8, 2020).
59. See, e.g. D. Campbell, 'Over-40s in UK to Pay More Tax Under Plans to Fix Social Care Crisis', *The Guardian*, July 26, 2020, https://www.theguardian.com/society/2020/jul/26/uk-ministers-looking-at-plans-to-raise-taxes-for-over-40s-to-pay-for-social-care (accessed August 8, 2020); For an overview of economic policy responses to COVID-19 across the world, see IMF, 'Policy Responses to COVID19', https://www.imf.org/en/Topics/imf-and-covid19/Policy-Responses-to-COVID-19 (accessed August 8, 2020).
60. *Guiding Principles*, Principle 2.
61. *Guiding Principles*, Principle 3.
62. *Guiding Principles*, Principle 3.
63. *Guiding Principles*, Principle 3.
64. *Guiding Principles*, Principle 4.
65. *Guiding Principles*, Principle 13. For more on the source of this obligation, see note 5 above.
66. *Guiding Principles*, Principle 13.
67. *Guiding Principles*, Principle 14, para. 14(1).
68. *Guiding Principles*, Principle 14.
69. On the responsibility of IFIs in this context, see Juan Pablo Bohoslavsky, 'Complicity of International Financial Institutions in Violation of Human Rights in the Context of Economic Reforms', *Columbia Human Rights Law Review*, 2020, 52 (forthcoming).
70. *Guiding Principles*, Principle 14, para. 14(4).
71. *Guiding Principles*, Principle 14.
72. *Guiding Principles*, Principle 15.
73. *Guiding Principles*, Principle 15, para. 15(1).

74. *Guiding Principles*, Principle 15, para. 15(1).
75. *Guiding Principles*, Principle 7.
76. *Guiding Principles*, Principles 5 and 6.
77. *Guiding Principles*, Principle 7.
78. For a discussion of the relationship between HRIA and equality impact assessment, see J. Harrison and M. Stephenson, 'Human Rights Impact Assessment: Review of Practice and Guidance for Future Assessments. Report for the Scottish Human Rights Commission' (SHRC, 2010), 23, https://fian-ch.org/content/uploads/HRIA-Review-of-Practice-and-Guidance-for-Future-Assessments.pdf (accessed August 8, 2020).
79. See, e.g. UN CEDAW, 'General Recommendation No. 28 on the Core Obligations of States Parties under Article 2 of the Convention on the Elimination of All Forms of Discrimination against Women', October 19, 2010, UN Doc. CEDAW/C/2010/47/GC.2, paras 16, 20 and 24; CESCR, 'General Comment No. 20 on Non-discrimination in economic, social and cultural rights (art. 2, para. 2, of the International Covenant on Economic, Social and Cultural Rights)' (July 2, 2009), UN Doc. C/E.12/GC/20, paras 8 and 9.
80. See, e.g. Independent Expert on Debt and Human Rights, 'Impact of Economic Reforms and Austerity Measures on Women's Human Rights' (July 18, 2018), UN Doc. A/73/179, paras 15–23.
81. *Guiding Principles*, Principle 8.
82. *Guiding Principles*, Principle 8.
83. *Guiding Principles*, Principle 14.
84. *Guiding Principles*, Principle 11(f).
85. *Guiding Principles*, Principle 11, para. 11(11).
86. *Guiding Principles*, Principle 17, para. 17(8). Emphasis added.
87. *Guiding Principles*, Principle 8.
88. *Guiding Principles*, Principle 8.
89. *Guiding Principles*, Principle 8.
90. Ibid. See, e.g. Committee on Economic, Social and Cultural Rights, 'General Comment 3: The Nature of the States Parties Obligations (Art 2, par. 1)' (December 14, 1990), para. 9 and note 3 above.
91. *Guiding Principles*, Principle 11(b), (c) and (e).
92. *Guiding Principles*, Principle 11.
93. *Guiding Principles*, Principle 11(d).
94. *Guiding Principles*, Principle 12.
95. *Guiding Principles*, Principle 11, para. 12(6).
96. *Guiding Principles*, Principle 12, paras 12(2)–(4).
97. *Guiding Principles*, Principle 17, para. 17(1).
98. *Guiding Principles*, Principle 17.
99. *Guiding Principles*, Principle 17, para. 17(4).
100. *Guiding Principles*, Principle 18.
101. *Guiding Principles*, Principle 18.
102. *Guiding Principles*, Principle 18, para. 18(5).
103. *Guiding Principles*, Principle 21, para. 21(1).
104. *Guiding Principles*, Principle 18, para. 18(1).
105. *Guiding Principles*, Principle 18, para. 18(2).
106. *Guiding Principles*, Principle 18, para. 18(2).
107. *Guiding Principles*, Principles 19 and 20.
108. *Guiding Principles*, Principle 22.
109. *Guiding Principles*, Principle 22.
110. *Guiding Principles*, Principle 22, para. 22(1).
111. *Guiding Principles*, Principle 22, para. 22(2).
112. *Guiding Principles*, Principle 22, para. 22(5).
113. United Nations General Assembly, 'Transforming Our World: The 2030 Agenda for Sustainable Development', UN Doc. A/RES/70/1 (September 25, 2015), 20.

114. IMF, 'Fiscal Monitor Report, WDC' (April 2020), https://www.imf.org/en/Publications/FM/Issues/2020/04/06/fiscal-monitor-april-2020 (accessed September 8, 2020), 24.
115. Ibid., 24
116. I. Saiz, 'Rights in Recession? Challenges for Economic and Social Rights Enforcement in Times of Crisis', *Journal of Human Rights Practice* 1 (2009): 277, 280.
117. See, e.g. UN Secretary General, 'COVID-19 and Human Rights: We Are all in This Together', April 2020, https://www.un.org/sites/un2.un.org/files/un_policy_brief_on_human_rights_and_covid_23_april_2020.pdf (accessed September 8, 2020); UN Secretary General, 'Shared Responsibility, Global Solidarity: Responding to the Socio-Economic Impacts of COVID-19', March 2020, https://unsdg.un.org/resources/shared-responsibility-global-solidarity-responding-socio-economic-impacts-covid-19 (accessed September 8, 2020); Inter American Human Rights Commission, 'Pandemia y Derechos Humanos en las Américas', Res. 01/2020, April 10, 2020, https://www.oas.org/es/cidh/decisiones/pdf/Resolucion-1-20-es.pdf (accessed September 8, 2020); Inter American Human Rights Commission, 'Derechos Humanos de las personas con COVID-19', Res. 04/2020, July 27, 2020, http://www.oas.org/es/cidh/decisiones/pdf/Resolucion-4-20-es.pdf (accessed September 8, 2020).
118. This is far less so when it comes to international civil society's work in this area. For an example of a leading civil society initiative in this area, see CESR's work on resourcing a just recovery from COVID-19, https://www.cesr.org/covid-19-recovering-rights-series-0 (accessed August 10, 2020). For an example of national human rights institution responses on this point, see ENNHRI's statement at note 49 above.
119. United Nations, 'Policy Brief: A UN Framework for the Immediate Socio-Economic Response to COVID-19', April 2020, https://www.un.org/sites/un2.un.org/files/un_framework_report_on_covid-19.pdf (accessed August 8, 2020). Similarly, the United Nations, 'Debt and Covid-19: A Global Response in Solidarity', April 17, 2020, https://www.un.org/sites/un2.un.org/files/un_policy_brief_on_debt_relief_and_covid_april_2020.pdf (accessed September 8, 2020) makes no reference to human rights despite their obvious relevance in the context of public debt vulnerabilities.
120. See, e.g. United Nations, 'Policy Brief: A UN Framework for the Immediate Socio-Economic Response to COVID-19', April 2020, https://www.un.org/sites/un2.un.org/files/un_framework_report_on_covid-19.pdf (accessed August 8, 2020), 23 (vulnerable groups) and 24 (SDGs achievement).
121. Ibid., 27.
122. Ibid., 33.
123. The section outlining the key indicators states that 'the following list of 10 thematic indicators has been developed to support national and international efforts towards a human rights-based policy response to the crisis, as well as an early warning tool' but the body of the report does not state that these indicators should be used as the basis of human rights impact assessment as such.
124. OHCHR, UNDP and UNSDG, 'Checklist for a Human Rights-Based Approach to Socio-Economic Country Responses to COVID-19', July 2020, https://www.ohchr.org/Documents/Events/COVID-19/Checklist_HR-Based_Approach_Socio-Economic_Country_Responses_COVID-19.pdf (accessed September 8, 2020).
125. Ibid., 17.

Acknowledgements

The views and conclusions reflected in this article are solely those of the authors and are in no way intended to reflect the views of any of the institutions to which the authors are affiliated. The authors would like to thank the following reviewers for their invaluable contribution to this Special Issue: Ilias Bantekas, Diane Elson, Conor Gearty, Beth Goldblatt, James Harrison, Ignacio Saiz and Margot Salomon.

Disclosure statement

No potential conflict of interest was reported by the author(s).

ORCID

Juan Pablo Bohoslavsky http://orcid.org/0000-0002-7059-281X

Human rights impact assessments and the politics of evidence in economic policymaking

Allison Corkery and Gilad Isaacs

ABSTRACT
The *Guiding Principles on Human Rights Impact Assessments of Economic Reforms* envision a policymaking process based on sound empirical evidence, so that the proportionality and legitimacy of reforms can be 'properly' assessed. Implicit in this vision is that methodological tools from economics should be drawn on, and adapted, to project or assess human rights impact. This article argues that biases inherent to these tools must be fully understood and addressed in order to meaningfully assess the human rights impacts of economic policy choices. First, it reviews relevant literature on human rights impact assessment, to give context to some of the methodological issues raised in the *Guiding Principles*. It then interrogates the claim that impact assessments can advance evidence-based policymaking, unpacking this idea with reference to a frame for advancing a more 'politically informed' approach to understanding evidentiary bias. Second, it explores bias in neoclassical economics. It does this by unpacking dominant styles of reasoning and policy devices, concluding that meaningful assessment of rights realisation does not easily fit within this cognitive infrastructure. Finally, it outlines a number of strategies that would help advocates of human rights impact assessments to better navigate the politics of evidence and contest economic orthodoxies.

It must, of course, be admitted straightaway that moral rights or freedom are not, in fact, concepts for which modern economics has much time. In fact, in economic analysis rights are seen typically as purely legal entities with instrumental use rather than any intrinsic value. – Amartya Sen[1]

Introduction

The *Guiding Principles on Human Rights Impact Assessments of Economic Reforms* reflect an ideal type of economic policymaking. They paint an aspirational picture of a process that can 'democratise' the economic policy arena by providing a 'clear and specific framework and process' for generating 'empirical evidence'. This, in turn, can generate public debate on how the 'proportionality and legitimacy' of economic reforms should be 'properly' assessed.[2] Implicit and explicit in the *Guiding Principles* is a call that human rights impact assessments incorporate 'well developed approaches' from the field of economics.[3] These approaches will be particularly relevant for *ex ante* assessments to predict the future consequences of a proposed policy and 'thereby provide the opportunity to improve it – or abandon it – before it is adopted and implemented'.[4]

Our central argument is that the ability of the *Guiding Principles* to be successfully deployed towards achieving these objectives is constrained by inherited limitations – from both the field of human rights impact assessments and from the field of economics. These limitations are likely to be exacerbated when the two fields are brought together, given the dominance of economics across a range of public policy areas – including those addressed by the *Guiding Principles*. As Richard Boele and Christine Crispin highlight, if an established discipline dominates a new area of practice, like human rights impact assessments, then 'it is more likely that their established methodologies and norms will have the greatest influence' on the direction such assessments take.[5]

The way that evidentiary challenges are addressed in the emerging field of human rights impact assessments pays limited attention to the political dynamics at play in shaping the methodologies through which evidence is created, selected and interpreted. The *Guiding Principles* do stress the importance of utilising 'a wide range of economic theory and evidence, expressed in language accessible to the public' and employing 'a diverse range of both quantitively and qualitative data'.[6] These injunctions are fully supported. Nevertheless, as described further below, 'mainstream' approaches to economic analysis narrow the range of theory, evidence and data considered 'scientifically' suitable – at times subtly so. Without a more politically informed perspective on evidence, there is a risk that impact assessments carried out in line with the *Guiding Principles* will be limited in their capacity to 'alter or subvert' powerful interests, as Jeremy Perelman cautions; such assessments may 'operate as process-oriented breaks on a largely unchanged, if chastened approach',[7] in this case, to economic reform.

As governments around the world scramble to respond to the economic fallout of COVID-19, contesting powerful interests could not be more urgent. There is considerable uncertainty about what the economic landscape will look like when we emerge from the pandemic. On the one hand, this presents an important opening for challenging economic orthodoxies. As the world faces the worst recession since the Great Depression, governments are debating large scale stimulus packages to provide unprecedented support to households and businesses. On the other, a short-term surge in spending – while vital – could lead to an even greater concentration of wealth. How packages are designed – and the values and priorities that underpin them – will determine how rights fair in post COVID-19 economies.

Part one of the article begins by reviewing relevant literature on human rights impact assessment, to give context to some of the methodological issues raised in the *Guiding Principles*. It then interrogates the claim that impact assessments can advance evidence-based policymaking, unpacking this idea with reference to a frame for advancing a more 'politically informed' approach to understanding evidentiary bias, which differentiates between *issue bias* and *technical bias*. Part two explores technical bias in neoclassical economics. It does this by unpacking dominant *styles of reasoning* and *policy devices*, concluding that meaningful assessment of rights realisation does not easily fit within this cognitive infrastructure. Part three outlines a number of strategies that would help advocates of human rights impact assessments to better navigate the politics of evidence, as well as take advantage of the space for contesting economic orthodoxies opened up by the imperative to audit economic reforms according to human rights standards.

The *Guiding Principles*, human rights impact assessments and the politics of evidence-based policymaking

The *Guiding Principles* extend the emerging field of human rights impact assessments to address economic reforms. This is an important step in terms of insisting that governments consider the implications of economic policy decisions for the rights of ordinary people. The *Guiding Principles* do this in an effort to shift the political dynamics around fiscal consolidation measures. Juan Pablo Bohoslavsky, who led the development of the *Guiding Principles* in his capacity as the United Nations Independent Expert on the effects of foreign debt on human rights, explains in an interview:[8]

> Austerity policies are often justified by an overly simplified or misleading diagnosis ... Policy decisions are frequently taken without sufficient consideration of less harmful policy options and reliable analysis of foreseeable outcomes ... Those who typically shoulder a disproportionate part of the cost of adjustments are the most disadvantaged groups who have marginal voice and political power, which makes their situation and the impact on their rights invisible.

This section focuses on how the *Guiding Principles* are constrained in achieving these objectives by inherited limitations in terms of how human rights impact assessments understand evidence-based policymaking.

Nora Götzmann provides a helpful grouping of literature on human rights impact assessments. This includes scholarly literature that identifies and elaborates the 'essential or original elements' of human rights impact assessment that distinguish it from other types of impact assessment; a broader body of literature on human rights-based approaches, against which these elements can be mapped; normative guidance from United Nations bodies, which, we would argue, is the category where the *Guiding Principles* fits; practical 'how to' guidance that outlines the stages or steps of human rights impact assessment; and actual examples of human rights impact assessments, as well as the scholarly literature reflecting on them.[9] To those categories we could add a sixth: literature that elaborates on the purpose of human rights impact assessment and seeks to 'make the case' in terms of what it can achieve and how it can benefit policymaking.[10]

A brief review of the literature covered in these categories reveals a strong focus on setting out the 'ideal type' of assessment. As Paul Cairney points out, setting out an ideal type can serve an analytical, as well as an aspirational, purpose. It 'helps us compare an artificial situation with the real world', in order to 'better explain reality'.[11] This, in turn, also allows us to assess how the ideal type is likely to be affected when applied in the world as it is. However, and notably from the perspective of this article, this last element has not featured in existing literature on human rights impact assessment.

While there is recognition of the gap between the ideal type of impact assessment and the reality of their application in practice, the reason for that gap remains largely unexplored. Implied in much of the literature, is that what is needed to move closer to the ideal is a better understanding of, and increased capacity to address, the methodological challenges of human rights impact assessments. In arguing this, the authors remove human rights impact assessments from a political context and pose their weaknesses as simply methodological and not political. Simon Walker advocates for 'greater professionalization' of human rights impact assessments, for example.[12] The World Bank concludes that more work is needed to 'enhance the quality' of human rights impact assessments. James Harrison makes this argument more explicitly, warning that the nomenclature of human rights impact assessment 'will lose its status as representing a robust evidence-based process' without 'shared normative understandings' of what that process 'should' involve.[13]

This suggests an overconfidence in the ideal type. It results in limited interrogation of the gap between the ideal and real world, as well as the implications of this for the effectiveness of human rights impact assessments. Two underexplored areas in the literature are worth noting, in particular. First, methodological challenges are only partially addressed. Second, the links between methodological challenges and political challenges are not made. There appears to be limited recognition that methodology is itself political, which forecloses interrogation of the political dynamics at play in shaping methodology. This is critical, because it is these dynamics that so often challenge the ideal.

In terms of methodological challenges, the difficulty of identifying appropriate quantitative and qualitative indicators is commonly highlighted. Scholars and practitioners 'unanimously agree' on the importance of using indicators in human rights impact assessment.[14] Reasons for this include that they 'heighten the objectivity and thus credibility of any assessment'.[15] They can also serve to 'make casual connections' between the policy assessed and the enjoyment of human rights.[16]

Selecting indicators for human rights impact assessment is a complex task that requires careful thought. However, there is little detail in either the *Guiding Principles* or the broader literature about how this should be done in practice. The *Guiding Principles* stress that that indicators used should provide information 'disaggregated by gender, disability, age group, region, ethnicity, income segment and any other grounds considered relevant, based on a contextual, country-level identification of groups at risk of marginalization'. They also suggest that the indicators included in the Sustainable Development Goals (SDGs) 'could serve as a source of useful *complementary* information to those working in a human rights impact assessment context' (emphasis added).[17] The literature stresses that indicators should be 'verifiable', 'specific', and 'relevant'.[18] What these qualifiers mean, particularly the last, is contestable.

A further methodological challenge is that of collecting and analysing data on selected indicators. The *Guiding Principles* note that assessment standards 'need to be adaptable to potentially different levels of data availability and overall capacity' and calls on governments to build strong information systems during 'good times' so that they are equipped for human rights impact assessments when necessary.[19] While cooperation between national statistical offices and human rights actors appears to be growing in in the context of measuring progress on the SDGs, there is still a long way to go to agree on concepts, definitions and methodologies.[20]

Unsurprisingly, then, many of the human rights impact assessments examined in the literature have focused almost exclusively on the use of qualitative indicators. Some have even reconceptualised indicators as 'key questions' regarding human rights conditions, developing checklists of varying scope and focus.[21] However, the ability of such approaches to provide information persuasive to economic policymakers is limited. Systematising thinking on what quantitative indicators will be relevant is therefore critical.[22]

Harrison places these methodological challenges within 'broader worries' about exercises in human rights measurement.[23]

> For instance, do we have sufficiently sophisticated methodologies for meaningful evaluation to be possible? Will the measurement of human rights privilege simple answers to straightforward questions over more complex and long-term problems and solutions? Will human rights maintain their transformational potential when utilized in technical measurement exercises?

He concludes that much of these concerns refer primarily to inwardly-focused evaluation (i.e. assessments of projects specifically aimed at promoting human rights). For the most part, he fails to consider its implications for outwardly-focused assessments (i.e. assessments of policies and practice in other fields). This reflects a general weakness across the categories of literature identified above in terms of how the wider policymaking context in which a human rights impact assessment is being designed and implemented affects its methodology.

Second, the links between methodological challenges and political challenges are generally not elaborated in the literature reviewed. Political 'pre-conditioning' is a 'perennial problem' affecting practice of impact assessment because it restricts the scope of policies and their impacts to be reviewed, notes the Center for Economic and Social Rights.[24] This problem has significant methodological implications, as well. However, these implications get little attention, beyond cautioning against the most extreme cases where the process is purposely 'manipulated' to result in particular findings.[25]

Two examples reveal how politics is embedded in methodologies for defining indicators and collecting data – beyond the kind of extreme cases of purposeful manipulation flagged above. The first is introduction of an 'improved' methodology for counting hunger, introduced by the United Nations Food and Agriculture Organization at the end of 2012. As Jason Hickel explains, the effect of the change was that calorie thresholds 'were adjusted downwards significantly'. This, he argues, allowed for a 'good news narrative' about progress on the Millennium Development Goals.[26] The second example is the politically-motivated failure to collect data on particular individuals and groups, which Alex Cobham terms the 'uncounted'. [27] This takes two main forms. Those at the bottom of income and wealth distributions are absent from statistics that underpin political representation and also inform policy prioritisation, and those at the top of distributions are further empowered by being able to hide income and wealth from taxation and regulation. This means that 'the uncounted at the bottom are excluded' and 'the uncounted at the top are escaping'. Cobham's conclusions make explicit what remains implicit in the *Guiding Principles*: improving data collection is not just a matter of dealing with technical difficulties facing government information systems. Rather, a 'radical and deeply political challenge to the power structures that lie behind the uncounted' is essential.[28]

Another area where politics and methodology intersect is in how the findings of an assessment influence policy decisions. The *Guiding Principles* stress, multiple times, that human rights impact assessment contributes to evidence-based policymaking.[29] As Bond and Pope highlight, the theory underpinning impact assessments reflects an 'information provision model', which assumes 'better information leads to better decisions'.

However, this is a poor representation of how decision-making actually works, they argue.[30] Even an 'optimized' methodology 'will fall short of hard science and significant further effort is likely to be required to persuade decision-makers to change policy'.[31] Nevertheless, there is little systemic inquiry into how human rights impact assessment processes interact with policymaking processes.

These two gaps in the human rights impact assessment literature – an insufficient grappling with methodological challenges and the absence of a recognition of the political nature of methodologies employed in human rights impact assessments – have corollaries in the broader literature on evidence-based policy making. The assumption underpinning calls for 'evidence-based' policymaking is that there is a gap between research and policy and that this gap can be bridged by addressing barriers to 'knowledge transfer' between researchers and policymakers. This has 'given rise to a veritable cottage industry of work' dedicated to knowledge transfer, in order to increase the use of evidence in policymaking, argues Justin Parkhurst.[32] This focus on scientific evidence (i.e. evidence arising from research) suggest a fairly narrow view of what should inform policymaking and a fairly simplistic understanding of how evidence is 'used'.[33]

To advance the debate among supporters and critics of evidence-based policymaking, Parkhurst advocates for a more 'politically informed' perspective on the use of evidence in policymaking. This perspective stresses that policies typically involve multiple competing social values and concerns and there can be different evidence bases relevant to each one.[34] Recognising this, two potential types of evidentiary bias can be identified. The first is 'issue bias', which he argues 'reflects the ways in which the invocation of particular forms of evidence can obscure the political nature of decisions'. It arises through practice or norms that routinely privilege certain types of evidence in a way that marginalises particular social concerns; this can be understood 'as an exercise in political power'. The second is 'technical bias', which he defines as the 'problematic use of evidence from the perspective of scientific best practice'.[35] Both types of biases can occur in the creation, selection and interpretation of evidence. Parkhurst also distinguishes between the 'overt' and 'subtle' politicisation of evidence. The former refers to deliberate strategies taken in pursuit of political interests, whereas subtle politicisation refers to cognitive mental processes or simplifying heuristics linked to existing values or beliefs.

These distinctions offer a useful lens for examining the potential of the *Guiding Principles* to advance evidence-based policymaking. To an extent, the *Guiding Principle*'s *raison d'être* is overcoming overt issue bias in that they demand consideration of evidence on social concerns that have been traditionally marginalised in economic policy decisions. The applicable human rights standards set out in Part III of the *Guiding Principles* make a compelling case for widening the set of concerns take into account – from narrow understandings of growth, debt sustainability, or financial stability, to concerns for the human rights impact of different policy choices. Principle 18 states this explicitly:[36]

> Throughout the policy cycle, economic reform programmes should be evaluated in accordance with whether they have ensured a fair and equitable distribution of social adjustment burdens, and not only whether they have reduced budget deficits and restored debt sustainability or economic growth.

The *Guiding Principles* also address the issue of technical bias, but to a much lesser degree. Principle 20, for example, calls for 'a diverse range of both quantitative and qualitative data' to be used in such an evaluation. But unless impact assessments are undertaken with a strong appreciation of how technical bias shapes such data, their capacity to meaningfully influence policy making in the economic arena will be undermined. This is particularly the case given that the *Guiding Principles* presume a role for economic methodologies in assessing human rights impact of economic reforms; these, we argue, are riddled with technical biases – both overt and subtle.

The politics of evidence in the context of economic policymaking

Assessing the human rights impact of economic reforms in a way that can influence policy decisions necessitates engagement with economic methodologies – and the overt and subtle technical biases embedded in them. In the case of mainstream or 'orthodox' economics, these biases are pronounced. In fact, they are so pronounced, we argue, they may skew the objectives of an assessment back to a narrower and more traditional range of concerns, which would end up reinforcing issue biases that the *Guiding Principles* seek to move away from. This section explains how economics and economists have come to play a prominent, and often dominant, role in policymaking and introduces a frame for unpacking how technical bias plays out in the context of economic policymaking. Key methodological elements of neoclassical economics are then explained using this frame.

While economics is not homogenous, particular schools of thought have come to dominate economic theory, teaching and practice. The mainstream of economics today is underpinned by the neoclassical school of thought, although it has partially incorporated (some argue bastardised) other schools, most notably Keynesian economics. This theoretical basis has, to varying degrees, underpinned free-market economic reforms. As James Curtis notes, following a series of interviews with Ha-Joon Chang,[37] Radhika Balakrishnan,[38] and Margaret Summers,[39] 'for the last three decades this body of theory has dominated the economic field, while this field has in turn dominated society; systematically privileging markets, finance and abstruse mathematical conceptions of human life over social values of solidarity, distributive justice, substantive equity and democracy'.[40]

There is a substantial body of mostly sociological literature concerned with the 'increasing authority granted to economists' in debates about how to organise economies and societies.[41] Daniel Hirschman and Elizabeth Popp Berman describe how economics has come to shape the 'cognitive infrastructure' of policymaking, for example. They identify two ways through which this occurs. The first is through spreading an *economic style of reasoning*. That is, by teaching policymakers to think about problems as economists do. The second is by helping them establish economic *policy devices*. These are the sociotechnical tools that allow policymakers to see the world in certain ways (like GDP, or the unemployment rate) or that assist them in making decisions (like cost–benefit analysis).[42] In other words, through the spread of ideas and the spread of tools, economics reshapes how non-economists understand an issue – what others have referred to as 'economics imperialism'.[43]

This framing casts new light on Parkhurst's idea of technical bias, highlighting how it plays out in the context of economic policymaking. Indeed, a classic example of subtle technical bias shared by Parkhurst is a popular case study from the early 1990s. The study compared original data sources to a World Bank assessment of Lesotho's economy. It concluded that mistakes made by the Bank's analysts in their assessment 'were always of a particular kind', which reflected 'a stereotypical idea of a 'less developed' country' and 'fit within the World Bank's existing models' of African development.[44]

Given their influence on how reforms are understood and analysed, economic styles of reasoning and policy devices must be addressed by those advancing human rights impact assessments. As discussed further below, both have particular assumptions embedded within them about how economies work, which, once they solidify, tend to obscure their own partiality. Further, both styles of reasoning and policy devices 'restructure the political relations around them',[45] circumscribing what are seen as legitimate ways of evaluating economic policies. Assessments of the impact of a particular economic reform will be influenced by these realities.

Economic styles of reasoning – welfare, utility and efficiency

The bedrock of mainstream economic reasoning is *homo economicus*. This concept describes the individual who, behaving rationally, seeks to maximises his 'utility' given the constraints he faces.[46] This entails a commitment to methodological individualism and to rationality. Only the preferences of the individual matter and the individual anticipates the consequences of all his possible actions, makes internally consistent choices, and maximises self-interest. Within this paradigm, the atomistic individual is socially disembedded, described without reference to social characteristics, relations, or how personal preferences may be shaped by society.[47]

On the collective level, mainstream economics evaluates economic decisions by reference to human 'welfare'. The most prevalent notion is that welfare is maximised by reaching a 'situation in which no one can be made better off without making anyone else worse off – irrespective of who would be affected or to what extent'.[48] This is known as a state of 'Pareto efficiency' or 'Pareto optimality'. This means that welfare is maximised by making people 'better off' without causing harm to anyone else in the process. The most immediate problem with this is that finding a common measure of 'better off' or 'worse off', across a disembedded set of individuals, is a 'prerequisite to coherent policy assessment'.[49]

The 'solution' to this measurement problem is to equate welfare with 'utility'. Within neoclassical economics, utility has been distanced from its original usage as a measure of satisfaction or pleasure. Now, utility is linked to individual preferences and is maximised when individual preferences are satisfied.[50] However, determining preferences is also difficult, as is judging their relative intensity. Economists could, in theory, rely on some form of survey data in which individuals report their preferences. Instead, they have opted to equate preferences with 'revealed preferences'. In other words, simply the choices that individuals make in reality (to the extent that these can be systematically measured). This proxy for welfare is three steps removed from the original concept:[51]

Welfare ⇔ utility ⇔ preferences ⇔ choices

This string of assumptions is riddled with problems and does not provide any viable measures for comparing the actual welfare effects of policies on different individuals. What results is 'nothing more than an ordinal ranking of each individual's preferences',[52] which are exogenously given and unrelated to the social environment within which the individual is embedded.[53] Further, it does not account for the fact that such preferences can be based on imperfect information or cognitive limitations, and may themselves have been shaped by existing public policy, changed over time, or be in conflict with one another.[54] In response to this, it is sometimes argued that policies should maximise 'actual' welfare of individuals, rather than their revealed choices. In this case, actual preferences means those that are 'rational', 'self-interested', and 'well-informed'.[55] This does not solve the problem of determining these. Further, it embeds normative assumptions into what actual preferences are, or should be.

Returning to the definition of Pareto efficiency – a situation that is 'optimal' because no one can be made better off without making anyone else worse off – we spot other problems. In particular, Pareto efficiency assumes distributional neutrality – maintaining or increasing utility matters, not its distribution.[56] A policy in which the wealthy are made worse off through high taxation but the poor better off through public spending would not be a 'Pareto improvement'. Equity is therefore portrayed as a trade-off with efficiency.

This alleged trade-off features regularly in assessments of economic reforms. The IMF, for example, notes that the 'conventional belief' has been 'that taxing income entails a higher welfare (efficiency) cost than taxing consumption',[57] despite the fact that consumption taxes make tax systems less progressive. That is, it shifts a greater share of taxation onto poor and low-income earners. This approach reinforces the status quo distribution of resources, irrespective of actual efficiency,[58] not to mention equity, in the real word. Further, an economic reform that made some worse off would not be Pareto efficient, even if the policy leads to the economy expanding in a way that its capacity to satisfy preferences increased; that is, if it made the 'pie' larger.[59]

In an attempt to overcome this narrowness, welfare economists argue that a Pareto improvement would still occur if it was possible for the 'winners' to compensate the 'losers' in a way that left the losers no worse off than at the outset, and the winners better off.[60] This allows one to argue that welfare can be enhanced by pursuing a situation of maximising total utility.[61] This is the theoretical basis of widely used cost–benefit analysis.[62]

But, a focus on total utility ignores distribution even further. First, how an individual's relative position in society affects their preferences is not considered. It is irrelevant whether the worse off are the wealthiest or the poorest. As Amartya Sen notes:

> The utility calculus can be deeply unfair to those who are persistently deprived [...] The deprived people tend to come to terms with their deprivation because of sheer necessity of survival, and they may, as a result, lack the courage to demand any radical change, and may even adjust their desires and expectations to what they unambitiously see as feasible. The mental metric of pleasure or desire is just too malleable to be a firm guide to deprivation and disadvantage.[63]

Second, there is no imperative that compensation actually occur. This means that a policy is a Pareto improvement if it is *possible* for the winners to sufficiently compensate the losers.

These understandings of welfare feature in how economics understands desired states of the economy. In general, economics aims for situations of 'equilibrium'. A classic depiction of supply and demand in economics would show that when the price goes up for fish, the demand falls (and vice versa). The point at which demand equals supply is the 'equilibrium'. This is an example of 'partial equilibrium' analysis, as it refers to only one market: the market for fish. 'General equilibrium' analysis refers to attempts to depict the economy as a whole, to establish points – equilibria – at which supply and demand balance in all markets. This informs how economists think of optimal economic conditions.

In general equilibrium theory, the first and second 'fundamental theorems of welfare economics' state, respectively, that market equilibria are Pareto efficient and that there are a set of market prices at which every Pareto efficient allocation of resources is also in equilibrium. Under these assumptions, markets are *de facto* efficient and, given some redistribution of initial resources, the market can be left alone to do its work. Any insufficiencies that arise are not due to the market system, but to market failures or imperfections. The manner in which this theoretical position underpins structural adjustment programmes and the Washington Consensus – policy prescripts that present the market as a paragon of efficiency – is clear in the Lesotho example above.

These theorems rely on highly restrictive – even patently absurd – assumptions. These include, but are not limited to: perfectly competitive markets with no externalities (all economic costs, even things like pollution, are reflected in prices); no economies of scales (products don't get cheaper the more of them that are produced); preferences taken as fixed; no uncertainty; and goods exchanged directly, with no role for money.[64] Even accepting these assumptions, the volumes of ink that has been spilled by neoclassical economists has failed to mathematically prove the existence, uniqueness or stability of such equilibria.[65] This indicates how, while economics' legitimacy rests of its claims of scientific rigour, it is, in the words of Somers 'a radically anti-empirical project', which 'expresses itself as a disdain for the epistemic validity of dis-confirming evidence'.[66] What matters most is whether the theory – or policy assessment – conforms to predetermined theoretical premises and views of the economy.

The consequence is that these styles of reasoning have embedded a pro-market bias that may run counter to rights claims. Humans are conceptualised as competing, selfish, individuals – with competition the expression of individuals pursuing their own interests. Perfectly competitive markets are therefore considered 'good' institutions because the outcomes of interactions therein are Pareto efficient.[67] Adherence to these mainstream economic approaches therefore implies that prioritising human rights could reduce, rather than enhance, welfare.[68] This is because doing so would demand policies that interfere with market operations and are therefore likely to introduce inefficiencies.

These theoretical premises shape mainstream economics' *a priori* outlook on policy choices and therefore how mainstream economists would assess the impact of particular economic reforms. Take for example, an assessment of whether a government should directly provide healthcare or provide a cash transfer with which healthcare can be purchased. Standard economic practice would present this choice as a trade-off between the quantity of healthcare, and the quantity of everything else that an individual would be able to purchase given a particular budget. The direct provision of healthcare would relieve some constraint on her budget, but, on the basis of standard utility calculations (using 'indifference curves'), the cash payment satisfies her preferences 'at least as well as the in-kind health-care benefit, and will typically satisfy her preferences better'. Further, the cash payment is regarded as Pareto superior, because, within this framework, it is shown that 'no one will prefer the in-kind provision and many will prefer the cash payment'.[69] Daniel Hausman and Michael McPherson note:

> Although the value of freedom lurks within the standard argument for cash benefits, the argument remains within the terms set by orthodox economic theory. There is no mention of needs, of the presuppositions of individual dignity, of opportunity, of rights, or of fairness. There is no concern with the moral reasons that make individuals willing to pay taxes to provide such benefits.[70]

Economic policy devices – seeing and taking decisions in the economic world

Economic styles of reasoning have shaped commonly used policy devices – both for perceiving the world and for making decisions. The dominant economic perception of the world is one which reduces social and economic reality to a series of numbers and uses mathematical formulas to make decisions. Incorporating these devices helps assess the economic reforms discussed in the *Guiding Principles*. But, if these policy devices are reliant on unsustainable assumptions, then, in the words of Parkhust, they may result in 'problematic use of evidence from the perspective of scientific best practice',[71] that is, a technical bias.

While numbers and mathematical formulas can be of value, in many instances, they have become an end in itself. As Paul Krugman contended, in the wake of the 2007/8 global financial crisis, 'the economics profession went astray because economists, as a group, mistook beauty, clad in impressive-looking mathematics, for truth'.[72] This has been aptly labelled by Ben Fine and Dimitris Milonakis as 'the triumph of form over substance'.[73] Unfortunately, as Sen notes, such a narrow basis of analysis has considerably undermined the predictive power of economics.[74] This results, as we see below, in policy devices producing predictions out of sync with empirical reality.

In mainstream economics, mathematical formulae which result from the styles of reasoning discussed above, regularly produce pro-market, pro-business, or pro-elite policy recommendations, irrespective of historical evidence to the contrary. Examples include: the so-called Laffer Curve, which purports to demonstrate that cuts in tax rates will increase overall revenue; the 'natural rate of unemployment' literature, which supports contractionary monetary policy when unemployment becomes 'too low'; and the 'efficient market hypothesis', which posits that asset prices reflect all available information. While the latter hypothesis is both untested and untestable, it is part of the reason why mainstream economic models not only failed to predict the 2007/8 global financial crisis but considered it to be *a priori* impossible.

Devices for making decisions would also need to be deployed to assess economic reforms. One we have already mentioned is cost–benefit analysis. This is a widely used policy device. It gives preference to policies with the lowest cost–benefit ratio (those that that minimise costs and maximise benefits) because these would be regarded as a Pareto improving. The US government, for example, requires a cost–benefit analysis to be conducted when it issues regulations over product safety or environmental protection. Introducing a rights-based lens to this device conflicts with its basic assumptions. As Irene van Staveren notes, 'even if cost–benefit analysis is applied at the aggregate level, including a wide variety of social costs and benefits for a large group of people, its outcome may have very unequal distributional effects […] A net benefit accruing to one group may jeopardize human rights […] for another group'.[75] Hausman and McPherson note poignantly that economists 'have managed to salvage a practical method of evaluation – cost–benefit analysis – but it rests on shaky foundations precisely because the fundamental evaluative apparatus of contemporary normative economics is so narrow'.[76]

Turning back to the *Guiding Principles*, a particular policy device proposed therein is economic modelling.[77] Macroeconomic models are particularly relevant to the policy concerns of the *Guiding Principles*. These are essentially a series of mathematical equations representing relationships within the economy. To model the impact of economic reforms you change one variable (e.g. level of wages) and watch how this impacts the other variables in the model (e.g. employment levels). The *Guiding Principles*' encouragement to make use of such models reflects the broader literature on human rights impact assessments, which encourages the use of predictive modelling and other forms of econometric analysis in *ex ante* assessments. It does this because these methods 'can provide important information towards determining the direction of change of human rights in a particular country',[78] which, in turn, takes the debate further 'in a more empirical way'.[79] Despite the *Guiding Principles* urging that 'contingencies in the use of quantitative models are recognized and, if possible, avoided',[80] and other commentators cautioning that 'it is essential to bear in mind the underlying assumptions and heuristic limitations of the models used',[81] these assumptions and limitations remain unexplored within the *Guiding Principles* and broader literature.

The use of these models has important consequences for assessing the human rights impact of economic policy reforms. A recent example from South Africa illustrates this. The predictions of such models played a prominent role in debate over whether to move from a system of sectorally-differentiated minimum wages (i.e. different minimum wages in agriculture, retail, mining, clothing, domestic work, etc.) to a unitary national minimum wage. During this debate, which raged between 2015 and 2018, the South African National Treasury made use of a Computable General Equilibrium (CGE) model to estimate the impact of implementing this policy at different wage levels. This type of model, together with Dynamic Stochastic General Equilibrium (DSGE) models, are the most common macroeconomic modelling tools. They're used by National Treasuries; by multilateral institutions, such as the IMF, World Bank, and OECD; and by central banks world over.[82] They rely on some, but not all, of the general equilibrium theory outlined above.

In practice, like in general equilibrium theory, the mechanisms through which these models reach equilibria are adjustments in prices; equilibrium for the demand and supply of fish will only be reached through an adjustment in the price of fish, for example. Giving price adjustments this role determines how results that the model spits out are interpreted. The example of wages is instructive. In neoclassical theory, the implementation of statutory minimum wages lifts the 'price of labour' (wages) above its equilibrium point. This means the demand for labour falls. The results of this in the model – together with other neoclassical assumptions commonly made – is that a rise in wages causes a contraction in investment, a fall in GDP, rising unemployment and general economic deterioration.

This is precisely the prediction South Africa's National Treasury made. Their CGE model showed that even minimum wages as low as $90 per month (an amount one-third *below* the lowest sectoral minimum wage at the time) would result in significant job losses and economic deterioration.[83] Such dire projections are ubiquitous prior to the implementation of, or significant increase, in minimum wages.[84] This is despite the empirical evidence that has amassed over the last three decades showing that the impact of minimum wages on employment is negligible, and that raising wages can have positive macroeconomic effects through increasing demand in the economy.[85] In the South African case, this international evidence was marshalled; the architecture of these models was challenged; and alternative models presented,[86] in order to debunk these claims.[87] This latter evidential base prevailed and the national minimum wage was implemented at a level that would lift wages for approximately 30% of the formal sector workforce.

Such neoclassical CGE models are commonly used in other spheres of policy analysis. A few examples of the results derived therefrom – particularly relevant to the economic reforms addressed in the *Guiding Principles* – are worth highlighting.[88] These include that consumption taxes are less distortionary and more efficient than income taxes or taxes on capital;[89] that fiscal consolidation can have limited growth impacts; that trade liberalisation de facto leads to welfare gains,[90] as well as poverty reduction;[91] and that structural adjustment programmes should be beneficial.[92] This is a poignant caution that in mainstream macroeconomic models – underpinned by the assumption of efficient markets and the potential for Pareto efficient equilibria – it is market adjustments that are seen as leading to efficient outcomes.

Addressing bias and contesting economic orthodoxies

These neoclassical styles of reasoning and policy devices dominant in mainstream economics systematically produce technical biases. But they also circumscribe what questions are asked, answered, and answerable. This may very well skew concerns towards a narrow range of issues, reinforcing the issue biases that the *Guiding Principles* try to move away from.

This is because mainstream economics overwhelmingly views rights as instrumental to achieving other ends, in particular the maximisation of utility. As Sen argued almost 30 years ago, it is 'fair to say that the view that rights cannot be intrinsically important is fairly ingrained in the economic tradition now established'.[93] Little has changed. The realisation of rights is neither seen by mainstream economists as a legitimate outcome to seek to achieve, nor a motivating factor to human behaviour. For this reason, neoclassical economists either exclude human rights from their analysis or limit their inclusion to a narrow set of 'market friendly' rights.[94] Chang goes further and argues that 'the division between civil and political rights on the one hand and socio-economic rights on the other [...] buys into the neoclassical world'.[95] Where rights do feature in mainstream economics, property rights are uncritically centred – predominately as a means to ensure initial ownership of resources and thereby facilitate market exchange. More substantive rights may fall foul of being welfare enhancing. This is because '[s]ecuring these entitlements is likely to require either increased government expenditures or increased governmental regulation of the economy, measures that generally run counter to the existing preferences of some portion of the population for lower taxes and limited government'.[96]

How does deepening understanding of these biases help strengthen human rights impact assessments of economic reforms? In answering this question, it is useful to return to Parkhurst. He concludes that having a deeper appreciation of 'the origins and manifestations of bias' makes it 'more understandable and, indeed, predicable'; this, in turn, 'enables reflection on where to target strategies to reduce or mitigate the bias that is expected to arise'.[97] We argue that biases like those unpacked in the preceding part can only meaningfully be mitigated if human rights impact assessments are embedded in a broader project to contest the political and ideological exclusion of human rights in the economic policy arena in the first place.

Human rights impact assessment should be seen as being about political prioritisation as much as, if not more than, they are about evidence. In other words, the purpose of economic reforms must be contested, not just the way in which such reforms are evaluated. The *Guiding Principles* do this to an extent, stressing that 'the economy should serve the people, not vice versa' and calling for policy coherence to protect all human rights.[98] Impact assessments are presented as the means of achieving policy coherence. But if impact assessments are approached in a technocratic manner, a danger arises that 'a fundamentally normative debate over social values' becomes conflated with 'an evaluation of evidence'.[99] To avoid this, contestation is needed in three areas.

To begin with, how the relationship between human rights and the economy is conceptualised needs to be deepened. A number of paragraphs in the *Guiding Principles* suggest that human rights may conflict with other economic policy goals.[100] As Perelman argues, this 'trade-off consciousness' is problematic because it absorbs human rights into a risk assessment framework decided upon according to existing priorities, as opposed to interrogating the legitimacy of those priorities.[101] To genuinely transcend this consciousness, a more precise reframing of economic questions in human rights terms and vice versa is necessary.

Reframing economic questions in human rights terms challenges the manner in which mainstream economics has attempted to define itself as a 'neutral science', devoid of imprecise and inherently subjective ethical reasoning. This gives us a broader perspective about the purpose of the economy 'whereby the market is repositioned as just one institution among many in society, including a number of others deserving equal or greater power in many contexts'.[102] Similarly, reframing human rights questions in economic terms, expands the traditionally state-centric lens, to better see the interrelated social processes concerned with the generation and distribution of resources that facilitates the fulfilment of rights.

This expanded perspective on the economy and on human rights calls for interdisciplinary methodologies that can generate evidence, which, in turn, should be judged on its 'appropriateness', rather than relying on hierarchies of evidentiary 'quality'.[103] This approach recognises that evidence can be constructed in a number of different ways that would be considered technically valid. The *Guiding Principles* endorses this kind of methodological pluralism – noting the need for 'a diverse range of both quantitative and qualitative data' as well as 'a wide range of economic theory and evidence'.[104]

As discussed above in part one, however, what constitutes 'relevant' evidence for assessing the human rights impact of economic reform has yet to be systematised. Caution is necessary when drawing on mainstream economic theory, economic tools, and economists themselves for such systematisation. Economic knowledge production 'is organized according to a clearly perceived hierarchy', of which neoclassical styles of reasoning and policy devices sit at the top.[105] Efforts to 'professionalise' assessment through more 'rigorous' methodology risk reinforcing this hierarchy if they rely on particular policy devices because they are considered influential. As Hirschman and Berman explain, as policy devices solidify, the political choices in them get hidden.[106] For example, a number of human rights treaty bodies have adopted the official development assistance target of 0.7 percent of GDP as a benchmark to define the obligation of international assistance. This target is a political commitment from the 1970s that has been reaffirmed in subsequent international declarations. However, how that figure is calculated continues to be controversial.[107]

The manner in which various heterodox, alternative, or non-mainstream schools of thought, such as, post-Keynesian, Marxist, and feminist, have come to see rights as instructive and beneficial to economic theory shows what disrupting evidentiary hierarchies and working across disciplines can look like. Some within these schools have come to recognise the relevance and importance of the positive obligations that rights – especially socioeconomic rights – place on states and markets.[108] These are the schools of thought that, as Chang notes, have 'the greatest affinity to progressive human rights lawyers' as they 'see the individual as a product of society, rather than something that fell from the sky in a complete form'.[109] As Balakrishnan notes, 'the norms and standards of human rights offer heterodox economists a widely accepted ethical language in which to pose economic questions without reducing them to simple questions of economic calculus'.[110]

A promising example of working across disciplines is research commissioned by the Equality and Human Rights Commission in the United Kingdom, which assessed the cumulative distributional impacts of tax and spending decisions on people sharing different characteristics protected under the Commission's mandate. The research used relative income poverty measures and the Minimum Income Standard as proxy indicators to examine the impact of government policy on the right to an adequate standard of living. It also used a microsimulation tool called the tax-transfer model (TTM) to simulate changes in disposable income after a series of policy changes affecting taxation and social security transfers have been considered. Importantly, this produced results at the individual level, which enabled a more detailed focus on gendered impacts of these changes. The modelling revealed that changes have a disproportionately negative impact on several protected groups, including disabled people, certain ethnic groups, and women.[111]

Finally, it is important to understand the institutions through which competing interests, as well as competing evidence, are mediated in the economic policy arena. The *Guiding Principles* call for the 'engagement of affected communities' in conducting assessments, as well as for 'genuine public debate' in the consideration of policy options, facilitated through the dissemination of evidence 'expressed in language accessible to the public'.[112] Achieving this would necessitate a major shift in the status quo of 'policy advisory systems', meaning the networks of actors and organisations 'that provide decision-makers with policy advice'.[113]

Economists often play a central role in such networks – becoming policymakers themselves, staffing international financial institutions, and providing policy advice from think tanks or consultancy firms. The construction of such systems as 'ostensibly depoliticized' has been an important channel for sustaining 'the rise of economic knowledge to power around the world'.[114] As Dena Freeman argues, this move to de-politicise policymaking has been accompanied by an emphasis on the constitutional component of democracy – ensuring appropriate checks and balances across institutions and role for courts. But the popular component – namely accountability to the people – has been de-emphasised. Economic policy decisions are increasingly made in multi-stakeholder networks, in which government officials participate alongside representatives from the private sector and civil society.[115] Power asymmetries in such networks are immense. While it is important to see impact assessments as one tool that can be leveraged to address such asymmetries, complementary efforts will also be needed.

A joint assessment on the impact of potential electricity price rises on children's rights in Bosnia and Herzegovina led by UNICEF in 2007 – often cited as good practice – is a good example of the way power asymmetries affect the success of a human rights impact assessment. An evaluation of the assessment notes that while it was 'well appreciated' by gatekeepers within the energy sector, it had 'no influence on the electricity sector reform'.[116] A key factor affecting policymaking was the process of accession to the European Union, which 'determined' socio-economic reform priorities. In this context, the 'influence and leverage' of the government directorate leading the assessment was 'limited'.[117]

Conclusion

Relying on economic ways of thinking and economic policy devices to shape the cognitive infrastructure for evaluating economic reforms in human rights terms is double-edged. On the one hand, it provides an opening for collaboration, one which spurs us to 'reformulate the whole debate, through a basic refusal to accept some evidently false premises', without which 'we will never win it'.[118] As Chang concludes, '[i]n this reformulation the combination of economic discourse with legal discourse is essential, and, within this combination, the merging of certain heterodox economic viewpoints and progressive strands of human rights will similarly be crucial'.[119] On the other, it risks allowing room for a series of propositional assumptions and evaluative tools riddled with bias that systematically disregard the value of rights and produce policy recommendations that undermine rights concerns.

The way evidentiary challenges are addressed in the emerging field of human rights impact assessments remains limited. Assessments are seen as a way to improve evidence-based policymaking. But, as Parkhurst cautions, evidence-based policymaking is an 'extremely malleable' term that gives 'no obvious indication of which evidence is the right evidence upon which to base particular policies'.[120] For impact assessments to advance the goals of the *Guiding Principles*, closer attention needs to be paid to the political dynamics at play in shaping the methodologies through which evidence is created, selected and interpreted. If it is not, neoclassical economics could easily come to dominate, with the result that assessments get co-opted and narrowed into a technocratic box ticking exercise, stripping out political context and local concerns or justifying policies which limit rights as 'welfare enhancing'.

In certain respects, heterodox economists and socioeconomic rights activists and scholars have fought similar battles. For human rights scholars and activists, the *Guiding Principles* challenge them to articulate economic harms in human rights terms that can then be used to shape economic policy. For heterodox economists, the imperative to audit economic reforms according to human rights standards opens up space for contesting economic orthodoxies. The orthodoxy of efficiency, in particular, has had devastating consequences – as COVID-19 has laid bare. A rights-based approach, which values resilience over efficiency, means explicitly designing economics that can protect everyone in worst-case scenarios.

As the economic fallout of the global coronavirus pandemic unfolds, conversation between economics and human rights is more important than ever and the *Guiding Principles* advance this considerably. This conversation pushes the disciplines of economics and human rights in positive directions. Despite all its pretence, economics is not ethically neutral and the avowed absence of any normative foundation serves to reinforce the economic status quo. But human rights should not strive to be economically neutral either. While a range of economic policies may allow for rights fulfilment, this is not true of all possible policy choices. Importantly, not all forms of economic analysis will assess these policies in the same way.

Notes

1. Amartya Sen, *On Ethics and Economics* (Wiley, 1991), 71.
2. This and the preceding quotations are from Juan Pablo Bohoslavsky, *Guiding Principles on Human Rights Impact Assessments of Economic Reforms: Report of the Independent Expert on the Effects of Foreign Debt and Other Related International Financial Obligations on the Full Enjoyment of Human Rights, Particularly Economic, Social and Cultural Rights*, Report to the Human Rights Council, December 2018 paras 6, 7, 17(2).
3. Ibid., para. 20(4).
4. Gillian MacNaughton, 'Human Rights Impact Assessment: A Method for Healthy Policymaking', *Health and Human Rights* 17, no. 1 (2015): 64.
5. Richard Boele and Christine Crispin, 'What Direction for Human Rights Impact Assessments?' *Impact Assessment and Project Appraisal* 31, no. 2 (2013): 133.
6. Bohoslavsky, *Guiding Principles*, para. 11(6) and Principle 20.
7. This and previous quotation from Jeremy Perelman, 'Human Rights, Investment and the Rights-Ification of Development', in *The Future of Economic and Social Rights*, ed. Katherine G. Young (2019), 467, 446.
8. Oliver Hudson and Jefferson Nascimento, 'Human Rights Impact Assessments Must Be Part of Economic Reforms: Interview with Juan Pablo Bohoslavsky', *Sur International Journal on Human Rights* 15, no. 27 (2018): 165.
9. Nora Götzmann, 'Human Rights Impact Assessment of Business Activities: Key Criteria for Establishing a Meaningful Practice', *Business and Human Rights Journal* 2, no. 1 (2017): 92–3.
10. See e.g. Center for Economic and Social Rights, 'Assessing Austerity: Monitoring the Human Rights Impacts of Fiscal Consolidation', February 2018.
11. Paul Cairney, *The Politics of Evidence-Based Policy Making* (Springer, 2016), 5.
12. Simon Walker, 'Human Rights in the Trade and Sustainability Impact Assessment of the EU–Tunisia Free Trade Agreement', *Journal of Human Rights Practice* 10, no. 1 (2018): 121.
13. James Harrison, 'Human Rights Measurement: Reflections on the Current Practice and Future Potential of Human Rights Impact Assessment', *Journal of Human Rights Practice* 3, no. 2 (2011): 172.
14. Fabiane Baxewanos and Werner Raza, 'Human Rights Impact Assessments as a New Tool for Development Policy?' (ÖFSE, January 2013), 17.
15. Ibid.
16. World Bank, 'Human Rights Impact Assessments: A Review of the Literature, Differences with Other Forms of Assessments and Relevance for Development', 1 February 2013, 30, citing Simon Walker, *The Future of Human Rights Impact Assessments of Trade Agreements* (Intersentia, 2009).
17. Bohoslavsky, *Guiding Principles*, paras 20(3) and 20(5).

18. Baxewanos and Raza, 'Human Rights Impact Assessments as a New Tool for Development Policy?' 17.
19. Bohoslavsky, *Guiding Principles*, paras 20(4) and 18(6).
20. See e.g. Carmel Williams and Paul Hunt, 'Neglecting Human Rights: Accountability, Data and Sustainable Development Goal 3', in *The Sustainable Development Goals and Human Rights: A Critical Early Review*, ed. Carmel Williams and Inga Winkler (Routledge, 2018).
21. World Bank, 'Human Rights Impact Assessments', 31.
22. For a proposed framework for identifying indicators related to the normative standards and principles underpinning states' obligations regarding fiscal consolidation see Center for Economic and Social Rights, 'Assessing Austerity'.
23. Harrison, 'Human Rights Measurement', 167.
24. Center for Economic and Social Rights, 'Assessing Austerity', 35.
25. World Bank, 'Human Rights Impact Assessments', 34.
26. Jason Hickel, 'The True Extent of Global Poverty and Hunger: Questioning the Good News Narrative of the Millennium Development Goals', *Third World Quarterly* 37, no. 5 (2016): 758.
27. Alex Cobham, *The Uncounted* (Cambridge, UK: Polity, 2020), 49.
28. Cobham, *The Uncounted*, 58.
29. See e.g. Bohoslavsky, *Guiding Principles*, paras 7, 17(1), 18(3).
30. This and the preceding two quotations are from Alan Bond and Jenny Pope, 'The State of the Art of Impact Assessment in 2012', *Impact Assessment and Project Appraisal* 30, no. 1 (2012): 2.
31. Harrison, 'Human Rights Measurement', 183.
32. Justin Parkhurst, *The Politics of Evidence: From Evidence-Based Policy to the Good Governance of Evidence* (Routledge, 2017), 23.
33. Parkhurst, *The Politics of Evidence*, 24.
34. Ibid., 6.
35. Ibid., 42–3.
36. Bohoslavsky, *Guiding Principles*, para. 18(4).
37. Ha-Joon Chang in Conversation with Joshua Curtis, 'History, Law and the Myth of Economic Neutrality', Series on Economics and Law in Conversation (Laboratory for Advanced Research on the Global Economy, Centre for the Study of Human Rights, LSE, July 2016), http://www.lse.ac.uk/sociology/assets/documents/human-rights/HR-SO-3.pdf.
38. Radhika Balakrishnan in Conversation with Joshua Curtis, 'Advancing Human Rights through Economics', Series on Economics and Law in Conversation (Laboratory for Advanced Research on the Global Economy, Centre for the Study of Human Rights, LSE, January 2016), http://www.lse.ac.uk/sociology/assets/documents/human-rights/HR-SO-5.pdf.
39. Margaret Somers in Conversation with Joshua Curtis, 'Socially Embedding the Market and the Role of Law', Series on Economics and Law in Conversation (Laboratory for Advanced Research on the Global Economy, Centre for the Study of Human Rights, LSE, March 2016), http://www.lse.ac.uk/sociology/assets/documents/human-rights/HR-SO-4.pdf.
40. Joshua Curtis, 'Merging Socio-Economic Rights and Heterodox Economics: Emancipatory and Transformative Potentials', Series on Economics and Law in Conversation (Laboratory for Advanced Research on the Global Economy, Centre for the Study of Human Rights, LSE, October 2016), 2.
41. Johan Christensen, 'Economic Knowledge and the Scientization of Policy Advice', *Policy Sciences* 51, no. 3 (2018): 293.
42. Daniel Hirschman and Elizabeth Popp Berman, 'Do Economists Make Policies? On the Political Effects of Economics', *Socio-Economic Review* 12, no. 4 (2014): 790, https://doi.org/10.1093/ser/mwu017 emphasis in original.
43. Ben Fine and Dimitris Milonakis, *From Economics Imperialism to Freakonomics*, 1 ed. (London; New York: Routledge, 2009).
44. Parkhurst, *The Politics of Evidence*, 90.

45. Hirschman and Berman, 'Do Economists Make Policies?' 799.
46. As feminist economists have stressed, homo economicus is very much a he. See e.g. Martha Fineman and Terence Dougherty, eds., *Feminism Confronts Homo Economicus: Gender, Law, and Society*, 1 ed. (Ithaca, NY: Cornell University Press, 2005).
47. John B. Davis, 'Individualism', in *Handbook of Economics and Ethics*, ed. Jan Peil and Irene van Staveren (Edward Elgar Publishing, 2009).
48. Irene van Staveren, 'Efficiency', in *Handbook of Economics and Ethics*, ed. Jan Peil and Irene van Staveren (Edward Elgar Publishing, 2009), 107; See also Sen, *On Ethics and Economics*.
49. Louis Kaplow and Steven Shavell, 'Fairness Versus Welfare', *Harvard Law Review* 114, no. 4 (2001): 1368, https://doi.org/10.2307/1342642.
50. Daniel M. Hausman and Michael S. McPherson, *Economic Analysis, Moral Philosophy and Public Policy*, 2 ed. (New York: Cambridge University Press, 2006).
51. Philip Harvey, 'Human Rights and Economic Policy Discourse: Taking Economic and Social Rights Seriously', *Columbia Human Rights Law Review* 33 (1 January 2002): 421.
52. Harvey, 'Human Rights and Economic Policy Discourse'.
53. Carlos Rodriquez-Sickert, 'Homo Economicus', in *Handbook of Economics and Ethics*, ed. Jan Peil and Irene van Staveren (Edward Elgar Publishing, 2009), 226.
54. Harvey, 'Human Rights and Economic Policy Discourse'; Hausman and McPherson, *Economic Analysis, Moral Philosophy and Public Policy*.
55. Kaplow and Shavell, 'Fairness Versus Welfare'; Hausman and McPherson, *Economic Analysis, Moral Philosophy and Public Policy*, 128–29.
56. Sen, *On Ethics and Economics*, 33; van Staveren, 'Efficiency', 107.
57. Vito Tanzi and Howell Zee, 'Tax Policy for Emerging Markets Developing Countries', *National Tax Journal* 53 (1 March 2000): 305.
58. As van Staveren notes 'This leads to the conclusion that Pareto efficiency is not really about maximum efficiency, but rather about relative maximum utility, that is total utility constrained by a strong no-harm principle. In other words, Pareto efficiency allows for the wage of resources - land, food or health care - by the affluent'. van Staveren, 'Efficiency'.
59. Hausman and McPherson, *Economic Analysis, Moral Philosophy and Public Policy*, 144.
60. Ibid.
61. van Staveren, 'Efficiency'.
62. Such empirical welfare analysis relies on monetary measures of welfare, using incomes and prices. This has its own shortcomings: income is a poor indicator of well-being across different income classes; some valued subjective goods cannot be measured in monetary terms; and monetary compensation is not always possible.
63. Amartya Sen, *Development as Freedom* (OUP Oxford, 2001), 62.
64. Fine and Milonakis, *From Economics Imperialism to Freakonomics*, 280; Sen, *On Ethics and Economics*, 34.
65. Alan Kirman, 'General Equilibrium: Problems, Prospects, and Alternatives', in *General Equilibrium, Capital and Macroeconomics: A Key to Recent Controversies in Equilibrium Theory*, ed. Fabio Petri and Carl H. Hahn (Edward Elgar Publishing, 2004); Carl H. Hahn, 'On the Notion of Equilibrium in Economics', *Recherches Économiques de Louvain/ Louvain Economic Review* 40, no. 4 (1974): 447–68; Frank Ackerman, 'Still Dead After All These Years: Interpreting the Failure of General Equilibrium Theory', (working papers, Tufts University, Global Development and Environment Institute, 2000).
66. Margaret Somers in Conversation with Joshua Curtis, 'Socially Embedding the Market and the Role of Law', 3.
67. Hausman and McPherson, *Economic Analysis, Moral Philosophy and Public Policy*, 139.
68. An argument made by Kaplow and Shavell, 'Fairness Versus Welfare' for example.
69. Hausman and McPherson, *Economic Analysis, Moral Philosophy and Public Policy*, 142, see pages 141–3 for a lengthier and more technical explanation.
70. Hausman and McPherson, *Economic Analysis*, 143.
71. Parkhurst, *The Politics of Evidence*, 42–3.

72. Paul Krugman, 'How Did Economists Get It So Wrong?' *The New York Times*, September 6, 2009, sec. Magazine, 1, http://www.nytimes.com/2009/09/06/magazine/06Economic-t.html.
73. Ben Fine and Dimitris Milonakis, '"Useless but True": Economic Crisis and the Peculiarities of Economic Science', *Historical Materialism* 19, no. 2 (2011): 13.
74. Sen, *On Ethics and Economics*, 79.
75. van Staveren, 'Efficiency', 111.
76. Hausman and McPherson, *Economic Analysis, Moral Philosophy and Public Policy*, 152–3.
77. Bohoslavsky, *Guiding Principles*, para. 20.
78. Baxewanos and Raza, 'Human Rights Impact Assessments as a New Tool for Development Policy?' 18.
79. Edward Anderson and Marta Foresti, 'Assessing Compliance: The Challenges for Economic and Social Rights', *Journal of Human Rights Practice* 1, no. 3 (2009): 471.
80. Bohoslavsky, *Guiding Principles*, para. 20(7).
81. Baxewanos and Raza, 'Human Rights Impact Assessments as a New Tool for Development Policy?' 18.
82. For a history, see Lance Taylor, 'CGE Applications in Development Economics' (SCEPA working paper, Schwartz Center for Economic Policy Analysis (SCEPA), The New School, 2011), https://ideas.repec.org/p/epa/cepawp/2011-1.html.
83. Catherine MacLeod, 'Measuring the Impact of a National Minimum Wage'; Servaas Storm and Gilad Isaacs, 'Modelling the Impact of a National Minimum Wage in South Africa: Are General Equilibrium Models Fit for Purpose?', Research Brief, National Minimum Wage Research Initiative (University of the Witwatersrand, Johannesburg: CSID, 2016).
84. Storm and Isaacs, 'Modelling the Impact of a National Minimum Wage in South Africa'
85. Hansjorg Herr and others, 'The Theoretical Debate About Minimum Wages', (working papers, Global Labour University, February 2009), http://www.global-labour-university.org/fileadmin/GLU_Working_Papers/GLU_WP_No.6.pdf; Bernhard Boockmann, 'The Combined Employment Effects of Minimum Wages and Labor Market Regulation – A Meta-Analysis', IAW Discussion Paper (Institut für Angewandte Wirtschaftsforschung (IAW), 2010), https://ideas.repec.org/p/iaw/iawdip/65.html; Arindrajit Dube, 'Minimum Wages', *Journal of Economic Literature* 49, no. 3 (September 2011): 762–66; John Schmitt, 'Why Does the Minimum Wage Have No Discernible Effect on Employment?' (Center for Economic and Policy Research, 2013). Availability Note: Information provided in collaboration with the RePEc Project: http://repec.org; Dale Belman and Paul Wolfson, *What Does the Minimum Wage Do?* (Kalamazoo, MI: W.E. Upjohn Institute, 2014); Megan Linde Leonard and others, 'Does the UK Minimum Wage Reduce Employment? A Meta-Regression Analysis', *British Journal of Industrial Relations* 52, no. 3 (2014): 499–520; Stijn Broecke and others, 'The Effect of Minimum Wage on Employment in Emerging Economies: A Literature Review' (OECD Social, Employment and Migration working papers, OECD Publishing, 2015); Gilad Isaacs, 'A National Minimum Wage for South Africa', Summary Report, National Minimum Wage Research Initiative (University of the Witwatersrand, 2016).
86. Asghar Adelzadeh and Cynthia Alvillar, 'The Impact of a National Minimum Wage on the South Africa Economy' (working paper series, National Minimum Wage Research Initiative, University of the Witwatersrand, 2016).
87. Isaacs, 'A National Minimum Wage for South Africa'.
88. CGE models do not unanimously have these conclusions and there is variation over the types of models, the assumptions made, and time and location. Nevertheless, given that we know that these outcomes seldom hold, it is illustrative that a substantial number of CGE models would yield these results.
89. B. Douglas Bernheim and others, 'Consumption Taxation in a General Equilibrium Model: How Reliable Are Simulation Results?', in *National Saving and Economic Performance*, ed. B. Douglas Bernheim and John B. Shoven (University of Chicago Press, 1991), 131–62, https://www.nber.org/chapters/c5990; Keshab Bhattarai and others, 'The Economic Effects of the Fair Tax: Analysis of Results of a Dynamic CGE Model of the US Economy',

International Economics and Economic Policy 13, no. 3 (1 July 2016): 451–66, https://doi.org/10.1007/s10368-016-0352-4; Dale W. Jorgenson and Kun-Young Yun, 'Chapter 10 - Taxation, Efficiency and Economic Growth', in *Handbook of Computable General Equilibrium Modeling*, ed. Peter B. Dixon and Dale W. Jorgenson, vol. 1, Handbook of Computable General Equilibrium Modeling SET, Vols. 1A and 1B (Elsevier, 2013), 659–741, https://doi.org/10.1016/B978-0-444-59568-3.00010-9.

90. Lance Taylor and Rudiger von Amin, 'Modelling the Impact of Trade Liberalisation: A Critique of Computable General Equilibrium Models', *Policy & Practice*, 1 July 2006, http://policy-practice.oxfam.org.uk/publications/modelling-the-impact-of-trade-liberalisation-a-critique-of-computable-general-e-112547.
91. Asian Development Bank, *Using Macroeconomic Computable General Equilibrium Models for Assessing Poverty Impact of Structural Adjustment Policies* (Asian Development Bank, 2004), https://www.adb.org/publications/using-macroeconomic-computable-general-equilibrium-models-assessing-poverty-impact.
92. Lorenzo Maio and others, 'Computable General Equilibrium Models, Adjustment and the Poor in Africa', *World Development* 27 (1 February 1999): 453–70, https://doi.org/10.1016/S0305-750X(98)00143-0; Shantayanan Devarajan et al., 'Simple General Equilibrium Modeling', in *Applied Methods for Trade Policy Analysis: A Handbook*, ed. Joseph F. Francois and Kenneth A. Reinert (Cambridge University Press, 1997).
93. Sen, *On Ethics and Economics*, 49.
94. See Jessica Whyte, *The Morals of the Market: Human Rights and the Rise of Neoliberalism* (Verso, 2019).
95. Ha-Joon Chang in Conversation with Joshua Curtis, 'History, Law and the Myth of Economic Neutrality', 8.
96. Harvey, 'Human Rights and Economic Policy Discourse', 368.
97. Parkhurst, *The Politics of Evidence*, 76.
98. Bohoslavsky, *Guiding Principles*, para. 2.
99. Parkhurst, *The Politics of Evidence*, 71.
100. They note, for example, that efforts directed at trying to stabilise the economcy comes with the 'risk of disregarding' human rights obligations, that states need to 'balance competing priorities and make approriate trade-offs'. Bohoslavsky, *Guiding Principles*, paras 2(3), 17(6).
101. Perelman, 'Human Rights, Investment and the Rights-Ification of Development', 467–68.
102. Curtis, 'Merging Socio-Economic Rights and Heterodox Economics', 5–6.
103. Parkhurst, *The Politics of Evidence*, 108.
104. Bohoslavsky, *Guiding Principles*, para. 11(6) and Principle 20.
105. Christensen, 'Economic Knowledge and the Scientization of Policy Advice', 294.
106. Hirschman and Berman, 'Do Economists Make Policies?' 798–99.
107. Olivier De Schutter, 'Public Budget Analysis for the Realization of Economic, Social and Cultural Rights: Conceptual Framework and Practical Implementation', in *The Future of Economic and Social Rights*, ed. Katherine G. Young (Cambridge University Press, 2019), 585–86.
108. Harvey, 'Human Rights and Economic Policy Discourse'.
109. Ha-Joon Chang in Conversation with Joshua Curtis, 'History, Law and the Myth of Economic Neutrality', 8.
110. Radhika Balakrishnan in Conversation with Joshua Curtis, 'Advancing Human Rights through Economics', 3.
111. Jonathan Portes and Howard Reed, 'The Cumulative Impact of Tax and Welfare Reforms' (Equality and Human Rights Commission, 2018).
112. Bohoslavsky, *Guiding Principles*, paras 22(2) and 11(6).
113. Ibid., paras 22(2) and 11(6).
114. Marion Fourcade, 'Economics: The View from Below', *Swiss Journal of Economics and Statistics* 154, no. 1 (2018): 5.
115. Dena Freeman, 'De-Democratisation and Rising Inequality: The Underlying Cause of a Worrying Trend' (International Inequalities Institute, May 2017), 19–20.

116. Yulia Privalova Krieger and Erna Ribar, 'Child Rights Impact Assessment of Economic Policies: A Case Study from Bosnia and Herzegovina', 2008, 32.
117. Ibid., 40–41.
118. Ha-Joon Chang in Conversation with Joshua Curtis, 'History, Law and the Myth of Economic Neutrality', 9.
119. Ibid.
120. Parkhurst, *The Politics of Evidence*, 76.

Disclosure statement

No potential conflict of interest was reported by the authors.

Human rights and democracy in economic policy reform: the European COVID-19 response under scrutiny

Matthias Goldmann

ABSTRACT

This article argues that the impact of economic policy reforms on democratic institutions might compromise the enjoyment of human rights, especially economic, social, and cultural rights (ESC rights). This impact is twofold: First, economic reform policies driven by international and supranational institutions compromise democratic self-determination. Second, economic reform policies driven by the need to reduce public expenditure might put marginalised groups at risk and hamper their democratic participation. Since the realisation of ESC rights requires a framework for legitimate redistributive decisions, any such impairment of democratic institutions poses a risk to the realisation of ESC rights. Courts are unlikely to fully compensate for this risk. The *Guiding Principles on Human Rights Impact Assessments of Economic Reforms* (the *Guiding Principles*) devise a way for jointly strengthening human rights and democracy. Crucially, they urge states to subject economic policy reforms to democratic control. Human rights impact assessments may empower the public sphere and shift economic policy reforms from the Arcanum of high-level international negotiations back to democratic processes. Moreover, the *Guiding Principles* oblige states to design comprehensive and participatory economic policy reforms. The article shows the potential of the *Guiding Principles* by probing the European Union's response to COVID-19 and suggests improvements.

A. Introduction

In 2015, when thousands of Greek citizens took their outrage against European austerity policies to the streets, it became evident that economic policy reforms carry risks for both democracy and human rights. Motivated, amongst other factors, by fears of the adverse impact of austerity on human rights,[1] the resounding rejection of the economic policy reforms agreed at European level in a referendum was ultimately shattered by the European Council's tenacious insistence on the terms of the negotiated agreement. At that point, austerity inflicted damage on both human rights and democratic self-determination.[2] International intervention in economic reform, it seemed, not only amplified pre-existing inequalities and increased the lot of vulnerable groups of society, but ignored democratic self-determination and subjected Greece to what one could perceive as a contemporary form of economic colonialism.[3] Importantly, the assaults on human rights and democracy are related, for it is improbable that the former could have passed without the latter.

The Greek crisis of 2015 may appear as an extreme example of the intricate relationship between democracy and human rights in the context of economic policy reform. However, things may only have escalated in the Greek context because austerity affected a developed economy with a well-educated population possessing the ability to raise their voice. In other cases, the impact of economic policy reforms on democracy and human rights is more subtle, silencing, rather than inciting, the voice of those affected. Such effects might derive from imbalanced economic policy reforms that deprive disadvantaged individuals and groups of the means and capabilities necessary for effective political participation. In the contemporary COVID-19 context, the economic recovery programmes adopted in response to the public health crisis might fail to adequately support the poorer and marginalised parts of society, which are disproportionately affected by the crisis.[4] This would further decrease their financial, social, and cultural capital to raise their voices and make themselves heard in the public. Moreover, while the full social and political effects of the COVID-19 crisis in every country still remain to be seen, it cannot be excluded that the related risks to human rights enjoyment might even increase acceptance of authoritarian solutions.[5]

This article argues that the *Guiding Principles* on human rights impact assessments of economic reforms, adopted by the Human Rights Council in 2019,[6] enable the negative feedback loops between risks to democracy and human rights caused by economic policy reform to be addressed. This is because they aim at strengthening the self-determination of the affected societies. In fact, one of their major strengths is that they use the nexus between human rights and democracy to strengthen the former through the latter. Part B specifies the feedback loop between democracy and human rights in economic policy reforms. For this purpose, one needs to distinguish between primary and secondary negative effects on human rights. Primary affects are caused by economic reform policies directly, usually in the form of deregulation, cuts to public spending on budget items crucial for the realisation of human rights, especially ESC rights, or privatisation of public services and related access restrictions. Secondary negative effects arise from the dependence of ESC rights realisation on democracy for the purpose of legitimate redistributive decision-making. While democratic forms of government do not constitute a guarantee for legitimate decision-making, they seem a necessary condition for there to be at least some form of decision-making representing the public interest and highly responsive to the views and needs of the different groups of society. The subsequent part briefly sets out how the *Guiding Principles* seek to shortcut negative feedback loops and safeguard human rights by strengthening democratic self-determination (Part C). To test these provisions, the following part uses the *Guiding Principles* to assess the economic reforms adopted and envisaged by the European Union in response to the COVID-19 crisis (Part D). Specifically, it focusses on the impact of human rights impact assessments (HRIA) on democratic decision-making; on the participation requirements of the *Guiding Principles* and their relation with constitutional provisions; and ultimately on the provision regarding policy coherence, including its relationship with the separation of powers. In conclusion, the article argues that the *Guiding Principles* contribute to resolving the current crisis of democratic capitalism.

B. The feedback loop between human rights and democracy in economic policy reforms

Economic policy reforms may cause both primary and secondary negative effects on human rights. Only the latter thrive on the negative feedback loop between declining democracy and declining levels of human rights enjoyment. For reasons of conceptual clarity, however, I shall begin by briefly restating primary risks to human rights created by economic policy reforms (I), before distinguishing them from secondary risks and explaining the negative feedback loop (II).

I. Primary risks

Economic reforms can have a direct impact on human rights. Many, if not all, human rights require some kind of state activity for their full realisation. This also applies to civil and political rights. For instance, the prohibition of torture requires adequate training of police and military forces. Concerning ESC rights, economic policy reforms are likely to affect the revenue and expenditure of a state. Tax rates might increase or decrease and, depending of the impact of such measures on growth, the revenue of the state will change accordingly. Increasing expenditure might lead to growth at some point in the future, while decreasing expenditure might stifle it. Sovereign debt might enable productive, future-oriented investments, or enable expenditures that only increase debt.[7]

The precise results are often difficult to project. However, by now there is ample knowledge that economic policy reforms centred on expenditure cuts, commonly known as austerity, will often fall short of expectations and therefore have a negative impact on human rights.[8] Past growth projections have often been exaggerated as the models failed to sufficiently take into account negative effects deriving from decreasing public expenditure.[9] The Eurozone debt crisis provides a textbook example, causing a slow economic recovery, high unemployment and dire social conditions in the affected states.[10] Moreover, the effects of tax cuts on growth are all but clear.[11]

Unfortunately, such policies have been at the centre of many supply-side oriented economic reform policies in the past decades. The IFIs contributed to their popularisation from the late 1970s onwards.[12] The impact of such policies on human rights enjoyment did not take long to emerge. For example, in the early 1980s, UNICEF realised that there were rising rates of malnutrition amongst children in states affected by such economic reform policies. It called upon the IMF to better safeguard basic human needs.[13] Nevertheless, it took a while for this critique to be formulated in terms of human rights.[14] In the wake of the debt crisis in the Global South and related austerity policies, the United Nations Commission on Human Rights was among the first institutions to articulate its criticism in terms of human rights in a series of documents dating from the late 1980s.[15] A 1989 report by Danilo Türk identifies structural adjustment and poverty eradication as two key issues requiring a new approach to ESC rights and elaborates on the human rights responsibilities of the IMF in this regard.[16] This work informed the Human Rights Commission's Open-Ended Working Group on Structural Adjustment Programmes and Economic, Social and Cultural Rights established in 1997.[17] It appointed an Independent Expert in 2000[18] and intended to draft guidelines on structural adjustment programmes and economic, social and cultural rights, which the Human Rights Council adopted in 2009.[19]

In contrast to the United Nations, the IFIs have been much more hesitant to admit the human rights impact of the economic policy reforms they encouraged.[20] In the 1990s, the World Bank took an important step in this direction by recognising that its policies contribute to the realisation of human rights, including social rights by providing access to, amongst other, health, education, food, or water.[21] Accordingly, the mandate of the World Bank allows promoting human rights as long as they do not conflict with economic considerations.[22] Despite the devastating human rights record of its economic reform policies, which some argue to have contributed to catastrophic events like the Rwandan genocide,[23] the IMF took some time to recognise the relation. To UNICEF's plea to respect human needs, it responded with policies targeting human capital.[24] The IMF over time became more responsive to calls for social protection, but avoided human rights language until 2017, when an evaluation of its policies on social spending considered them to be aligned with human rights.[25] In addition, the IMF has developed increasing attention for the lot of vulnerable groups.[26]

Reducing primary human rights risk requires economic policy reforms that allow for sufficient social spending especially on crucial services with either devastating or long-term impacts (e.g. social protection, water supply, education).[27] Moreover, mitigating measures should cushion the impact of economic policy reform on vulnerable parts of society.[28] The *Guiding Principles* address the relevant duties of the IFIs as well as of bilateral lenders in Principle 15, including the duty to refrain from undermining the ability of a state to fulfil its human rights obligations. Human Rights Impact Assessments are a useful tool to frame policy-making in this respect.[29]

Unfortunately, the COVID-19 crisis has revealed that not only expenditure cuts, but also increases in expenditure can be a cause of human rights violations. The principal concern in this regard is equality. The stimulus packages adopted by the US government disproportionately benefit large corporations.[30] Human Rights Impact Assessments can provide comparative data and project the impact of a stimulus package on employment or social security.

II. Secondary risks

This paper is essentially about secondary risks to human rights, which accrue from negative feedback loops between damage caused by economic policy reforms to democratic decision-making and consequential deficits in human rights enjoyment, which further impact democratic decision-making. One can distinguish two scenarios in which such feedback loops operate. In the first scenario, the feedback loop is set in motion by the transfer of decision-making to the international level. In the second scenario, it emerges from primary risks, i.e. from economic policy reforms that disempower underrepresented groups.

The first scenario parts from the observation that economic reform policies requested by international institutions often leave countries with no meaningful democratic control over such policies. This has been the shared experience of countries undergoing IFI sponsored austerity, also known as structural adjustment, to address an impending sovereign debt crisis.[31] While the IFIs do not formally oblige their member states to adopt structural adjustment, it is effectively a requirement for access to their resources. It therefore hardly matters that the letters of intent and memoranda of understanding specifying such policies lack binding legal effect.[32] As the Greek experience of 2015 amply demonstrated, debtor states often have no effective choice in terms of rejecting the conditions and may only marginally influence them. This damages the integrity of such states' domestic decision-making processes.[33] In the view of Wolfgang Streeck, market citizenship, understood as the power of creditors, replaces political citizenship in such scenarios.[34] In extreme cases, like Chile in the 1970s, governments went so far as to use force to break resistance against their economic reforms.[35] In the 1990s, the involvement of the IFIs in such economic reforms intensified as conditionalities became more demanding, obliging countries to liberalise their markets and privatise public services.[36] Ironically, this occurred precisely at a time when democracy, along with human rights, was elevated to the level of a global constitutional principle.[37]

Beyond conditionalities, a diverse field of economic policy reforms originates at the international level. As a consequence, economic and social policies in Western welfare states have developed along similar lines since the postwar era,[38] and they have more often than not spilled over to the Global South.[39] Venues and procedures include Article IV consultations by the IMF, World Bank programmes, or membership in the Basel Committee and the Organization for Economic Cooperation and Development (OECD). Examples include the obsolescence of capital controls,[40] shifts in tax policy such as lower rates on direct taxes together with broader tax bases,[41] the trend towards balanced budget requirements and fiscal policy constraints,[42] the introduction of weighted capital requirements,[43] and even education, to the extent that one reduces it to an economic factor.[44] While each of these reform proposals primarily relies on learning and voluntary adaptation by member states for ensuring compliance, a number of factors lend teeth to them, including market reactions. Such proposals are especially influential if combined with any sort of indexation or ranking. Their power reveals itself especially in case of conflicts, such as the clash of the World Bank Doing Business Indicator with international labour standards,[45] or the intransigence of the Danish government in relation to the OECD Jobs Study.[46]

In the second scenario, the negative feedback loop emerges from primary risks, i.e. via economic reforms which negatively impact the human rights enjoyment of disadvantaged groups.[47] Economic reforms may strip them of the material basis necessary for democratic participation and disempower the economically powerless a second time in their role as political citizens. It is well-known today that citizens' participation in democratic states cannot be taken for granted. Ideally, the public sphere, where democratic decision-making takes place, is accessible to everyone on equal terms.[48] In reality, not all citizens have equal access to it as it depends on status and material requirements.[49] Political participation among poorer and disadvantaged segments of society is therefore lower.[50] Hence, as the late Judge Böckenförde held, democracy is unable to ensure the social conditions of its operation.[51] Democracy hinges on a high level of ESC rights enjoyment, a fact that has long been ignored by international human rights debates due to an exclusive focus on civil and political rights.[52]

Both scenarios might trigger negative feedback loops that endanger human rights enjoyment. The reason for this lies in the deep entanglement between human rights and democracy. This entanglement is not so much a matter of positive law, including the highly debated question of a human right to democracy,[53] than it is of the political theories corroborating the idea of liberal democracy. The entanglement derives from the paradox of combining collective self-determination with individual liberty, a core problem of political theory in modernity. According to Kant's definition of right, individual liberty finds its limit in the categorical imperative.[54] Kant held the categorical imperative to be accessible to reason. As trust in individual reason to reach universally acceptable decisions waned during the nineteenth century, the reach of individual rights needed to be determined by a political decision, ideally a democratic one respectful of collective autonomy. Democracy was therefore to be combined with bills of rights.[55] Jürgen Habermas in his reconstruction of twentieth century liberal democracy elaborates the ensuing 'equiprimordiality' of democracy and human rights. Human rights define the framework for democratic decision-making, while democratic decision-making is the way to guarantee and implement value-charged, open-ended, and oftentimes programmatic human rights norms that defy any mechanical application.[56] As there is simply no objective standard for deciding such redistributive questions,[57] it is preferable to consign the concretisation of human rights to representative parliaments or comparable majoritarian institutions with the capacity to achieve broad consensus on the public interest based on an inclusive process that takes into account a wide range of perspectives. If these institutions function well, they are in the best position to concretise contingent terms such as the duty to realise ESC rights to the 'maximum of the available resources', as Article 2(1) of the International Covenant on Economic, Social and Cultural Rights (ICESCR) famously holds.[58] This applies even though tensions do arise between human rights and majoritarian democratic decisions.[59]

Consequently, the full realisation of human rights, particularly ESC rights, benefits to an important extent from well-oiled processes of democratic decision-making. If economic policy reforms damage democratic procedures, either by foisting controversial policies popular in international organisations upon a country, or by decreasing the level of political participation of disadvantaged segments of society, then one can expect human rights to suffer, too. Deficits in democratic decision-making and representation will most probably contort the needs and interests of the population of the affected state, particularly those of its disadvantaged segments.

One might argue that courts could and should compensate for such deficits in democratic decision-making with courageous ESC rights adjudication. Many theorists of liberal democracy have cautioned against judicial review of legislative measures, arguing that democracy requires courts to defer to majoritarian institutions, particularly on redistributive issues.[60] But one could equally argue that the crisis of representative democracy suggests a stronger role for courts. This crisis, which manifests itself not least in numerous turns to authoritarian forms of government around the globe, is first and foremost a crisis of majoritarian institutions.[61] For example, it seems difficult to explain the strikingly uneven design of the stimulus package adopted by the US to address COVID-19 without pointing to dysfunctionalities in American democracy.[62] Economic reforms were a contributing factor to the decline of representative democracy insofar as they paid insufficient heeds to ESC rights and alienated large parts of the population.[63] As a result, majoritarian institutions are no longer necessarily the more democratic site for bottom-up, inclusive decision-making. Moreover, there are ways to control for the discretion of courts other than by confining them to the role of bystanders. For example, the use of cross-country comparative data helps to establish a sound basis for determining whether a country has met its human rights obligations.[64]

On a practical level, however, one might have doubts whether courts can play such an activist role. The historical record shows that court activism in the realisation of ESC rights is the exception rather than the rule. In the interwar and postwar decades, ESC rights bore the character of programmatic norms, rather than of actionable entitlements.[65] This only changed in the 1990s, when a new brand of transformative constitutionalism put courts, particularly constitutional courts, into the first line for the progressive realisation of ESC rights, pitching them against the perceived inertia of specific parliaments with highly fragmented and polarised composition,[66] or against the risks of economic transformation.[67]

But even then, courts tended to avoid decisions involving considerable budgetary implications or challenging the hardship involved in the transition to capitalism.[68] Moreover, in the aftermath of the financial crisis, many courts called upon to balance ESC rights against austerity and economic reform, found it difficult to review non-binding international commitments to economic reform,[69] or granted governments wide margins of discretion allegedly required by the urgency of the situation.[70] It stands to reason that courts may have faced backlash for intervening in carefully crafted conditionalities. Certainly, the multiple interventions of the Portuguese Constitutional Court in the implementation of austerity measures adopted in response to the Eurozone sovereign debt crisis demonstrates that courts can make a difference without major risks to their institutional integrity.[71] But for the most part, problems of standing, general restraints in causing budgetary consequences, and the sense of urgency surrounding many economic reforms leads to trepidant court reactions. It is therefore unlikely that courts can fully set off the impact of democratic decline on human rights enjoyment.

At this point, a disclaimer about the concept of democracy as used in this article seems necessary. One might get the impression that the nexus between democracy and human rights is primarily based on the European experience and might not necessarily apply elsewhere. This appears problematic as the principle of democracy has given rise to numerous intrusions by Western democracies into the sovereignty of less powerful states.[72] But the endorsement of democracy as a structural principle for government is widespread today and by no means confined to the West. The duty of states to respect democracy has become part of the legal framework of non-European regional organisations.[73] Moreover, the present framework ties in with human rights approaches that emerged in the context of post-war decolonisation. Newly independent states insisted on their right to self-determination, the foundational right of both human rights covenants, because they saw it as the key to improving human rights enjoyment.[74] Stressing democracy in the context of economic reform equals promoting self-determination. Finally, there is a wide variety of possible forms of democratic government to ensure the full enjoyment of human rights. One might even go so far as to argue that 'democracy' does not require regular elections, provided there are other mechanisms in place that ensuring the responsiveness of government vis-à-vis the governed, such as a functioning public sphere.[75] It is in this sense that I use the concept of democracy in this article.

C. Redeeming human rights and democracy: the *Guiding Principles*

The diagnosis of the negative feedback loops between human rights and democracy raises the question of potential remedies. Some might argue, though, that one should not even try. John Tasioulas advocates restricting the ambit of international human rights protection to essential civil and political rights and minimum core ESC rights.[76] This would reduce human rights to a supposedly apolitical core and therefore avoid the negative feedback loops altogether. The full realisation of ESC rights, in Tasioulas's account, is a matter for domestic politics, not for international human rights law.

I do not find this position convincing for two reasons. First, one does not have to imagine the core of human rights obligations to be any less controversial.[77] Many of the measures adopted in the frame of the 'war against terrorism' touched upon the core of fundamental rights, yet their judicial scrutiny provoked enormous political controversy.[78] Second, this position is mistaken in suggesting an antagonism between human rights and democracy. A different understanding of human rights would take the equiprimordiality of human rights and democracy seriously. It would imagine the relationship of human rights with democracy as complementary and mutually supportive, emphasising the role of human rights for the political process. To break the negative feedback loop, human rights need to ensure the proper functioning of democratic processes. Human rights theory and practice therefore needs to focus on strengthening the public sphere and enabling free and fair deliberation which ensures a voice and sufficient practical respect for the needs and interests of marginalised groups. The means of choice to reach this end comprise the whole spectrum of procedural rights and requirements, including transparency, participation, justification, and accountability. The role of judicial control would be to ensure the proper functioning of these procedural devices.[79]

This, of course, does not imply that human rights exhaust themselves in procedural principles. Rather, the latter are necessary requirements for policies to come forward which are respectful of human rights, including ESC rights, and for moving effectively beyond minimum requirements towards the full realisation of ESC rights to the maximum of the available resources. This reasoning stands behind the trend to procedural approaches in ensuring ESC rights.[80] A good example for how procedural changes might impact substantive outcomes is the recent IMF adjustment programme for Barbados, which put particular emphasis on social spending and allowed countries to set their priorities in larger independence, allowing for a fresh start and independent growth perspectives.[81]

The *Guiding Principles* provide a helpful framework for strengthening democratic decision-making. In fact, this seems to be their main purpose and contribution: human rights impacts assessments are all about establishing a high degree of transparency and access to robust information necessary for public deliberations.[82] Moreover, the *Guiding Principles* stress the need for participation at every stage of economic policy-making.[83] And they provide the right procedural incentives for encouraging high levels of respect for human rights in substance, including the duty to coordinate the generation and allocation of resources across different policy fields,[84] and emphasising that the burden of proof is on the state,[85] in conformity with general human rights law.

While specific enough to make a difference, the General Principles are abstract enough to be compatible with different constitutional frameworks. In fact, one should not understand them as superseding binding constitutional provisions, e.g. on procedure or on the separation of powers, but rather as complementing them and serving as interpretative guidelines. At no point do they impose a specific institutional choice that would likely render them incompatible with the constitutional law of many states.

D. The European COVID-19 response: testing the *Guiding Principles*

The potential of the *Guiding Principle* reveals itself best through their concrete application. In fact, being phrased in rather abstract terms, the *Guiding Principles* are in need of concretisation whenever they are applied, taking into account the challenges of the specific situation and the state of the political entity adopting them. This section will show how that process of concretisation might work in respect to the measures adopted by the European Union in response to the COVID-19 crisis.

The Union measures comprise a wide range of different programmes. They range from monetary interventions announced by the European Central Bank (ECB),[86] a fund for labour market support policies guaranteed by the Union and the Member States,[87] to a whole set of measures aimed at medium and long term recovery and pandemic prevention, to be financed by debt issued and guarantees backed by the Union alone.[88] The details of these acts are still under deliberation at the time of writing. In light of this, it seems apposite to use the *Guiding Principles* as a standard for assessing the decision-making process for these reform policies. The question is whether this process corresponds to the *Guiding Principles* and how the latter may enrich and enhance the former to ensure democratic decision-making and, ultimately, the conformity of EU economic policy responses to COVID-19 with human rights. The principles are clearly applicable in this case, as their scope covers economic reforms adopted in response to acute economic and financial crises.[89]

I. Transparency: human rights impact assessments

One of the foremost purposes of HRIAs is to establish transparency about the potential consequences of economic policy reforms. To this end, the General Principles specify important requirements for HRIAs in Principles 17–22. Measuring the impact on human rights requires two steps: first a projection of actual results, and second a quantification of the enjoyment of specific human rights affected by these results. In light of the uncertainty surrounding such projections, the *Guiding Principles* require a diverse range of qualitative and quantitative data, including data on vulnerable groups.[90] Assessing the implications of such data requires the use of reliable methodologies and full transparency about them.[91] To prevent narrowing rather than widening the range of potential measures, different scenarios should be considered.[92] As economic policy reform is a process, HRIAs have to be carried out at different stages in the political process, including during implementation. In case of acute crisis, there is still ample opportunity for carrying out HRIAs at a later stage.[93]

The European Union has adopted a solid framework for ensuring transparency and the right to access information.[94] By contrast, its practice of conducting HRIAs is more fragmented. The introduction of environmental impact assessments was a major step in the development of environmental regulation and is now common practice. For some years, environmental impact assessments have required governments to study the social impacts of their projects and policies.[95] Apparently, this aspect of environmental impact assessment still shows some potential for improvement.[96] In recent years, the European Union has taken recourse to distributional impact assessments, for example for measuring the outcomes of structural adjustment[97] as part of its initiative to establish a social rights pillar for the EU.[98] Nevertheless, social and distributional impact assessments, whether in the context of environmental impact assessments, trade or adjustment policies,[99] generally do not use human rights language. While quantifying the effects of proposed measures, they do not quantify the normative yardstick by which they should be judged. For example, the social impact assessment carried out by the Commission on the highly controversial 2015 Greek structural adjustment programme does not mention human or social rights even once.[100] Without any clearly defined standard, it should hardly surprise that the document does not criticise the adjustment programme, but buys into the logic that further economic liberalisation, especially labour market reforms and collective dismissals, will improve social conditions by allowing growth and jobs creation in the long run. Only a brief review of the then-experimental Greek guaranteed minimum income scheme provides a certain counter-weight and takes account of the need for short-term relief. Existing social and distributional impact assessments therefore cannot replace HRIAs and should not be confused with them. Moreover, the above-mentioned existing EU impact assessments are too specific and do not cover economic policy reforms as such. While specific projects to be financed from the funds put at the disposal of the Member States through the COVID-19 rescue measures might entail specific impact assessments such as environmental impact assessments obligatory for project financing, the entire ensemble of rescue measures does not.

The European Union should therefore carry out a holistic HRIA for the entirety of their measures adopted and proposed to address the COVID-19 crisis. This should ideally happen before adoption in order to ensure a balanced result. This is all the more important as intergovernmental negotiations on budgetary matters, which will also play a major role in the COVID-19 response, tend to favour national interests, rather than focusing on human rights.[101]

In the implementation of the rescue measures, the European Semester will play a key role, the annual budgetary surveillance process enabling the Commission to ensure that Member States respect their obligations under the Stability and Growth Pact.[102] The Commission proposed that the Member States should identify projects for the allocation of funds from the COVID-19 financing package in their draft budgets in response to calls from the Commission. The disbursement of the funds would be integrated into the recommendations for the European semester.[103] The European Union in fact expects its Member States to include distributional impact assessments in their draft budgets.[104] These assessments should be further developed into fully-fledged HRIAs, paying particular attention to the need to identify potential discrimination of vulnerable groups.[105]

As to the content of the proposed HRIAs, the *Guiding Principles* demand that they provide justification for potential regressions in human rights enjoyment and identify potential mitigating measures.[106] In case of the European measures to address the COVID-19 crisis, the measures are unlikely to lead directly and immediately to regressions. In fact, their purpose is to mitigate the negative impact of the COVID-19 crisis. However, there might be risks further down the road when the support measures are phased out or when debt repayment begins. These risks should also be taken into account in the policy design. In this way, the *Guiding Principles* would help ensuring the sustainability of the recovery measures. To ensure the reliability of the projections,[107] it might be advisable to use historical data from past fiscal expansions or contractions as a basis for calculation.

II. Participation

Along with transparency, participation is the second fundamental principle pervading the *Guiding Principles*. They urge states to ensure the participation of the affected population at all stages of the policy-making process.[108] This is crucial to ensure the legitimacy of economic policy reforms vis-à-vis the holders of human rights. Moreover, participation might help governments to discover specific needs and vulnerabilities that would otherwise not be evident to them. The *Guiding Principles* do not seek to replace constitutional requirements for participation, but rather complement them and encourage their further development. This is especially important if one considers that in the context of economic policy reforms, existing democratic procedures might suffer from the negative feedback loops described above.[109] Full respect for human rights might therefore require a different quality and quantity of participation than the indispensable procedures required by the applicable constitutional framework. Many constitutional frameworks and legislative procedures will be flexible enough to integrate additional participation to reduce and mitigate potential democratic deficits.

In this respect, it is important that participation is included in the process of making a HRIA.[110] For Europe's COVID-19 response, this means that the European Commission should not only insist that Member States submit HRIAs in relation to their funding applications in the frame of the European Semester, but also that such HRIAs integrate the input of different segments of society, including representatives of vulnerable groups. Governments should not simply produce HRIAs at the green table based on econometric data. Their whole design, including the question of the data to be included, should be participatory.

Moreover, the *Guiding Principles* require participation in the formulation of economic policy, especially of groups at risk, of groups affected by potential retrogressive effects, and of debt restructurings.[111] Policy-makers should know precisely what is at stake before making decisions. These requirements seem somehow difficult to reconcile with Europe's policy-making process in general, and with the COVID-19 process specifically, for a number of reasons.

First, in general, European competencies in economic and social matters are rather limited.[112] With the exception of the common currency, these matters are essentially left to the Member States. Even though the European Union could be more specific in defining how it will spend its funds, the COVID-19 response follows the existing repartition of competences in matters of economic policy and leaves the Member States with considerable discretion regarding the purposes and amounts it wishes to spend through the various sectoral policies funded by it. For the most part, the (envisaged) legislative or regulatory framework only sketches out some basic requirements that the funding would need to meet.[113] Nevertheless, the European Union might encourage participation by continuously monitoring the human rights performance of the member states.[114]

Second, decisions on the financial framework of the European Union do not feature a high level of participation. While the EU budget requires the consent of the European Parliament,[115] the crucial decision on revenue, the so-called Own Resources Decision, requires a unanimous vote by the Council and only attributes a consultative role to the European Parliament. The competencies of the European Parliament therefore do not equal the budgetary rights of most domestic parliaments. In the case of the COVID-19 recovery package, the situation is even worse as the European Union intends to base its borrowing on Article 122(2) TFEU, an emergency clause which does not even attribute a consultative role to the European Parliament.[116] The reason for this choice of a legal basis is that the normal EU budget does not allow the Union to borrow funds,[117] rather than to undercut parliamentary participation. Nevertheless, the result is not very encouraging. It might be worthwhile considering Article 352 TFEU as a potential legal basis as it would make the borrowing dependent on the consent of the European Parliament, which would arguably be the best way of enhancing participation.

Third, since the COVID-19 response ushers in a new phase in the constitutional development of the European Union by attributing a significant budgetary function to the European Union,[118] the political process midwifing that response so far has been strongly characterised by a top-down process. The European Council, composed of the heads of state or government, took the decisive steps, after informal consultations among its financially most powerful members, especially Chancellor Merkel and President Macron. The Council in the composition of the ministers for finance concretised the proposals, and the Commission developed drafts of the legislative acts, while the financial envelope became the subject of considerable bickering among the Heads of State and Government in the European Council in July 2020. Thus, very much unlike in the ordinary legislative procedure, where the Commission sets the agenda, the process originates at the intergovernmental level, and the whole package has then been deployed in a top-down fashion, involving many backroom deals and arm wrestling among governments. Even though the European Union has seen worse scenarios,[119] such a process is simply not very participatory. To litigate some of the resulting acts would not help from the participation angle since courts in the European legal framework cannot replace broad participatory decision-making. It therefore seems all the more important that participation is realised during the further concretisation and implementation of the programme. In this respect, it is highly unfortunate that the European Semester will play a key role, which stands for the attempt to depoliticise economic reform policies. Perhaps the COVID-19 response would provide a reason to overhaul the European Semester, making it less technocratic and more participatory.[120] This would also raise the chances that undue influence and special interests at Member State level would get discovered.

III. Policy coherence

Principle 11 of the *Guiding Principles* requires a holistic approach to economic policy reform. It is based on the idea that the standard relevant for human rights implementation, the duty to use the 'maximum of the available resources', has a revenue and an expenditure component, and that both sides depend on many different factors. In analogy to what I stated above in relation to the participatory requirements, the point of this provision is not to upset the constitutional separation of powers as the *Guiding Principles* do not call for constitutional reform. Rather, I read it as a recommendation to use existing leeway to ensure the comprehensive coordination of different economic policies, including fiscal policy, tax, and monetary policy. In this respect, the *Guiding Principles* move away from an economic model that put economic policy-making into the hands of a series of independent actors with specific, clearly defined mandates.[121] Distributive justice requires coordination of various policies.

In this respect, the COVID-19 measures originally proposed by the European Commission is remarkable. For the most part, they constitute one comprehensive package which spreads the entire financing volume available for crisis response across a variety of sectoral policies. Only the mentioned division of the financing volume into different national appropriations deflects from the requirement to maximise the positive impact on human rights.[122] Unfortunately, the need to find consensus on the financing envelope shifted allocations from sectoral policies to the central recovery instrument, the so-called Recovery and Resilience Facility, which gives member states larger discretion over the ultimate use of the funds.[123] One can only hope that the Commission will ensure coherence at the implementation stage.

Another aspect is the plan to fund the brunt of the financial burden through new taxes levied at EU level, including taxes on emissions, a carbon border adjustment, and a new digital tax.[124] These taxes are in tune with the purposes of the programme. The only difficulty is that they will be highly controversial. Given that their adoption requires unanimity, the outcome of any future decision on this point is uncertain. Perhaps human rights might serve as an argument to bring such common taxes on their way, even though the discretion of the Member States in defining their tax policy is very wide.[125]

Lastly, the actor that is perhaps least integrated into the decision-making process is the ECB. There is no doubt that the ECB has always been attentive to developments in the field of fiscal policy. Over the last decade or so, it only announced its various unorthodox policies when the lack of a fiscal policy response had an impact on monetary policy that justified its intervention. Moreover, the ECB does in fact conduct assessments of its social impact.[126] Nevertheless, the review of its monetary policy strategy currently under deliberation might provide the ECB with the opportunity to more closely and more explicitly coordinate its policy with other economic and social policies.[127] This would also please the German Federal Constitutional Court.[128]

E. Conclusion

On the whole, the General Principles turn out as a set of guidelines allowing states to ensure conformity with human rights law in their economic policy-making. Their most innovative aspect lies in my eyes in their capacity to strengthen democratic decision-making in states wishing to undertake economic policy reforms. As economic policy reforms potentially lead to a negative feedback loop between democratic deficits and a decline in human rights enjoyment, the *Guiding Principles* target a key mechanism for sustainable economic policy reforms.

The review of the European Union's COVID-19 response has demonstrated that the *Guiding Principles* do not stand in contradiction to constitutional rules on transparency, participation, and the separation of powers, but provide useful recommendations for using existing leeway and for the further development of institutional frameworks. It is difficult to fathom why the EU Member States represented in the Human Rights Council chose to reject the *Guiding Principles*, especially since the European Union likes to portrait itself as a defender of human rights and democracy.[129]

The need for a profound reorientation of the current global economic order is imminent. The climate crisis underlined that the current model of democratic capitalism oriented towards aggregate growth not only brings the planet near collapse, but also human society due to persisting inequalities and exclusion. The COVID-19 crisis accelerates the process of change. Nevertheless, as in the past with the introduction of neoliberal financial capitalism, change is more likely to be incremental and to occur in a myriad of small steps. The *Guiding Principles* are one of them, and certainly not the least important one.

Notes

1. Angelique Chrisafis et al., 'Greek No Voters Protest against Pain of Austerity but Concerns for Future Remain', *The Guardian*, July 5, 2015, https://www.theguardian.com/world/2015/jul/05/greek-referendum-no-voters-pain-austerity-concerns-future-euro (accessed July 27, 2020).
2. Cf. Ilias Bantekas, 'Sovereign Debt and Self-Determination', in *Sovereign Debt and Human Rights*, ed. Ilias Bantekas and Cephas Lumina (Oxford: Oxford University Press, 2018), 271; Emilios Christodoulidis, 'Europe's Donors and Its Supplicants: Reflections on the Greek Crisis', in *Constitutional Sovereignty and Social Solidarity in Europe*, ed. J. van der Walt and J. Ellsworth (Baden-Baden: Bloomsbury Academic, 2014), 241.
3. Ashoka Mody, 'The IMF abetted the European Union's subversion of Greek democracy', openDemocracy, September 1, 2018, https://www.opendemocracy.net/en/can-europe-make-it/imf-abetted-european-union-s-subversion-of-greek-democracy/ (accessed July 15, 2020).
4. Cf. Davide Furceri, Prakash Loungani, Jonathan D. Ostry, and Pietro Pizzuto, 'COVID-19 Will Raise Inequality if Past Pandemics Are a Guide', VoxEU, comment posted May 8, 2020, https://voxeu.org/article/covid-19-will-raise-inequality-if-past-pandemics-are-guide (accessed July 24, 2020).
5. Francesc Amat et al., 'Pandemics Meet Democracy. Experimental Evidence from the COVID-19 Crisis in Spain', *Working Paper* (2020). Available at https://osf.io/dkusw/download (accessed July 24, 2020). But see Damien Bol et al., 'The Effect of COVID-19 Lockdowns on Political Support: Some Good News for Democracy?', *European Journal of Political Research* 59 (2020, forthcoming).
6. Human Rights Council, *Guiding Principles on Human Rights Impact Assessments of Economic Reforms: Report of the Independent Expert on the Effects of Foreign Debt and Other Related International Financial Obligations of States on the Full Enjoyment of Human Rights, Particularly Economic, Social and Cultural Rights*, UN Doc. A/HRC/40/57, December 19, 2018 (hereinafter '*Guiding Principles*'). The Human Rights Council adopted the *Guiding Principles* with Resolution 40/8 of March 21, 2019, U.N. Doc. A/HRC/RES/40/8.
7. For many: Mariana Mazzucato, *The Value of Everything: Making and Taking in the Global Economy* (Hachette UK, 2018), 233–35.
8. Juan Pablo Bohoslavsky, 'Complicity of International Financial Institutions in Violation of Human Rights in the Context of Economic Reforms', *Colum. Hum. Rts. L. Rev.* 52 (2020, forthcoming).
9. Cf. Olivier Blanchard and Daniel Leigh, 'Growth Forecast Errors and Fiscal Multipliers', *IMF Working Paper*, no. WP/13/1 (2013).
10. Mark Blyth, *Austerity: The History of a Dangerous Idea* (Oxford University Press, 2013), 252; David Stuckler and Sanjay Basu, *The Body Economic: Why Austerity Kills* (Basic Books (AZ), 2013), 77.
11. William G. Gale and Andrew A. Samwick, 'Effects of Income Tax Changes on Economic Growth', available at SSRN (2014), https://doi.org/10.2139/ssrn.2494468.
12. Alexander E. Kentikelenis and Sarah Babb, 'The Making of Neoliberal Globalization: Norm Substitution and the Politics of Clandestine Institutional Change', *American Journal of Sociology* 124, no. 6 (2019), https://doi.org/10.1086/702900.
13. On this episode and the IMF response, see Richard Jolly, 'Adjustment with a Human Face: A UNICEF Record and Perspective on the 1980s', *World Development* 19, no. 12 (1991/12/01/1991), https://doi.org/10.1016/0305-750X(91)90026-E.
14. For a full account, see Matthias Goldmann, 'Contesting Austerity: Genealogies of Human Rights Discourse', *Max Planck Institute for Comparative Public Law & International Law*

(MPIL) Research Paper, no. 2020-09 (2020), https://doi.org/10.2139/ssrn.3561660. Early examples from the scholarly literature include Daniel D. Bradlow, 'The World Bank, the IMF, and Human Rights', *Transnational Law and Contemporary Problems* 6 (1996).

15. E.g. U.N. Commission on Human Rights, The New International Economic Order and the Promotion of Human Rights, Draft resolution of the Sub-Commission on Prevention of Discrimination and Protection of Minorities, U.N. Doc. E/CN.4/Sub.2/1987/L.57, August 28, 1978; U.N. Commission on Human Rights, Foreign debt, economic adjustment policies and their effects on the full enjoyment of human rights and, in particular, on the implementation of the Declaration on the Right to Development, Resolution 1989/15, March 2, 1989 (this resolution added the topic to the Commission's agenda).
16. U.N. Commission on Human Rights, *The New International Economic Order and the Promotion of Human Rights, Realization of Economic, Social and Cultural Rights, Preliminary report prepared by Mr. Danilo Türk, Special Rapporteur*, U.N. Doc. E/CN.4/Sub.2/1989/19, June 28, 1989, para. 52 et seq., 77 et seq.
17. Cf. U.N. Commission on Human Rights, Report of the open-ended working group on structural adjustment programmes and economic, social and cultural rights on its first session, U.N. Doc. E/CN.4/1997/20, March 10, 1997.
18. Radhika Balakrishnan, James Heintz, and Diane Elson, *Rethinking Economic Policy for Social Justice: The Radical Potential of Human Rights* (Routledge, 2016), 71.
19. Human Rights Council, Guiding principles on foreign debt and human rights, Annex to the Report of the Independent Expert on the effects of foreign debt and other related international financial obligations of States on the full enjoyment of all human rights, particularly economic, social and cultural rights, Cephas Lumina, U.N. Doc. A/RES/20/23, April 10, 2011, paras 10–20. The Human Rights Council endorsed the *Guiding Principles* by majority with Resolution 20/10, U.N. Doc. A/HRC/RES/20/10, July 18, 2012.
20. For a full account, see Matthias Goldmann, 'Financial Institutions and Social Rights: from the Washington Consensus to the Lagarde Concord?', in *Research Handbook on International Law and Social Rights*, ed. Christina Binder et al. (Cheltenham: Elgar, 2020), 452.
21. U.N. General Assembly, Report of the Special Rapporteur on extreme poverty and human rights, Philip Alston, UN Doc. A/20/ 274, August 4, 2015, 5; Willem Van Genugten, *The World Bank Group, the IMF and Human Rights: A Contextualised Way Forward* (Intersentia, 2015), 4, https://www.cambridge.org/core/books/world-bank-group-the-imf-and-human-rights/41235D9987C4A890F9E536448C608611.
22. Ibrahim FI Shihata, *The World Bank in a Changing World: Selected Essays and Lectures*, vol. 2 (Martinus Nijhoff Publishers, 1991), 70.
23. Cf. Michel Chossudovsky and Pierre Galand, 'The 1994 Rwandan Genocide – The Use of Rwanda's External Debt (1990–1994). The Responsibility of Donors and Creditors.' CADTM Website, comment posted April 7, 2016, http://www.cadtm.org/The-1994-Rwandan-Genocide-The-Use (accessed July 24, 2020).
24. Cf. Goldmann, 'Contesting Austerity: Genealogies of Human Rights Discourse', 15.
25. IMF Independent Evaluation Office, The IMF and Social Protection, 2017 Evaluation Report (2017), 13 (footnote 40). This evaluation triggered policy changes, see IMF, A Strategy for IMF Engagement on Social Spending, IMF Policy Paper, June 2019. See also the letter by the IMF to Mr Juan Pablo Bohoslavsky, July 27, 2017, https://www.ohchr.org/Documents/Issues/IEDebt/impactassessments/IMF.pdf (accessed July 24, 2020).
26. Viljam Engström, 'The IMF and Protection of Vulnerable Groups', *Nordic Journal of International Law* 89 (2020): 209.
27. Many of these issues are discussed in Council of Europe, Commissioner for Human Rights, 'Safeguarding Human Rights in times of economic crisis', Issue Paper (2013).
28. Engström, 'The IMF and Protection of Vulnerable Groups,' 221.
29. On framing in this context, see Hannah Miller, 'From 'Rights-Based' to 'Rights-Framed' Approaches: A Social Constructionist View of Human Rights Practice', *The International Journal of Human Rights* 14, no. 6 (2010): 915, https://doi.org/10.1080/13642987.2010.512136.

30. Robert Brenner, 'Escalating Plunder', *New Left Review* 123 (2020): 5.
31. Devesh Kapur and Moises Naim, 'The IMF and Democratic Governance', *Journal of Democracy* 16, no. 1 (2005): 91.
32. Armin von Bogdandy and Matthias Goldmann, 'Sovereign Debt Restructurings as Exercises of Public Authority: Towards a Decentralized Sovereign Insolvency Law', in *Responsible Sovereign Lending and Borrowing: The Search for Common Principles*, ed. Carlos Espósito, Juan Pablo Bohoslavsky, and Yuefen Li (Oxford University Press, 2013), 39.
33. See Yusuf Bangura, Peter Gibbon, and Arve Ofstad, 'Adjustment, Authoritarianism and Democracy: An Introduction to Some Conceptual and Empirical Issues', in *Authoritarianism, Democracy, and Adjustment: The Politics of Economic Reform in Afriak*, ed. Yusuf Bangura and Peter Gibbon (Uppsala: Nordiska Afrikainstitutet, 1992), 8; Bantekas, 'Sovereign Debt and Self-Determination'; Matthias Goldmann and Silvia Steininger, 'A Discourse Theoretical Approach to Sovereign Debt Restructuring: Towards a Democratic Financial Order', *German Law Journal* 17 (2016): 709, https://doi.org/10.1017/S207183220002143X; Federico Reho, 'European Union after the Sovereign Debt Crisis: A Post-Democratic Polity', *The Public Sphere* 2 (2014): 83.
34. Wolfgang Streeck, *Gekaufte Zeit: Die vertagte Krise des demokratischen Kapitalismus* (Berlin: Suhrkamp Verlag, 2013), 91. See also Commentary 6(1) to *Guiding Principle* 6, which recognises the implications of economic reforms on political rights.
35. James H. Mittelman and Will Donald, 'The International Monetary Fund, State Autonomy and Human Rights', *Africa Today* 34, no. 1/2 (1987): 49, 63, www.jstor.org/stable/4186408.
36. Benedicte Bull, Alf Morten Jerfe, and Erlend Sigvaldsen, 'The World Bank's and the IMF's Use of Conditionality to Encourage Privatization and Liberalization: Current Issues and Practices. Report prepared for the Norwegian Ministry of Foreign Affairs as a Background for the Oslo Conditionality Conference', *SUM Report No. 13* (2006), https://www.duo.uio.no/bitstream/handle/10852/32692/Bull.pdf (accessed July 24, 2020).
37. Cf. Mattias Kumm, 'The Cosmopolitan Turn in Constitutionalism: On the Relationship between Constitutionalism in and Beyond the State', in *Ruling the World? International Law, Global Governance, Constitutionalism*, ed. Jeffrey L. Dunoff and Joel P. Trachtman (Cambridge: Cambridge University Press, 2009), 258. 258.
38. E.g. Poul F. Kjaer, 'The Transnational Constitution of Europe's Social Market Economies: A Question of Constitutional Imbalances?', *JCMS: Journal of Common Market Studies* 57, no. 1 (2019), https://doi.org/10.1111/jcms.12811, https://onlinelibrary.wiley.com/doi/abs/10.1111/jcms.12811.
39. On the global impact of austerity after 2010, see Isabel Ortiz et al., 'The Decade of Adjustment: A Review of Austerity Trends 2010–2020 in 187 Countries', *ESS Working Paper*, no. 53 (2015), https://doi.org/10.2139/ssrn.2685853.
40. Andreas Busch, 'National Filters: Europeanisation, Institutions, and Discourse in the Case of Banking Regulation', *West European Politics* 27, no. 2 (2004): 310. On the role of the IMF, cf. Joseph P. Joyce, *The IMF and Global Financial Crises. Phoenix Rising?* (Cambridge: Cambridge Univ. Press, 2013), 72 et seq.
41. Hugh J. Ault, 'Reflections on the Role of the OECD in Developing International Tax Norms Symposium: Ruling the World: Generating International Legal Norms', *Brooklyn Journal of International Law* 34, no. 3 (2008–2009 2008): 757, 782, https://heinonline.org/HOL/P?h=hein.journals/bjil34&i=750; Tony Porter and Michael Webb, 'The Role of the OECD in the Orchestration of Global Knowledge Networks', *Canadian Political Science Association Annual Meeting* (2007), http://www.cpsa-acsp.ca/papers-2007/Porter-Webb.pdf (accessed July 20, 2020).
42. Thomas Biebricher, 'Neoliberalism and Law: The Case of the Constitutional Balanced-Budget Amendment', *German Law Journal* 17 (2016): 835, https://doi.org/10.1017/S2071832200021489; Matthias Goldmann, 'On the Comparative Foundations of Principles in International Law: The Move towards Rules and Transparency in Fiscal Policy as Examples', in *Sovereign Financing and International Law*, ed. Carlos Espósito, Juan Pablo Bohoslavsky, and Yuefen Li (Oxford: Oxford University Press, 2013), 113.

43. David Zaring, 'Informal Procedure, Hard and Soft, in International Administration', *University of Chicago International Law Journal* 5 (2005): 547.
44. Armin von Bogdandy and Matthias Goldmann, 'Taming and Framing Indicators: A Legal Reconstructon of the OECD's Programme for International Student Assessment (PISA)', in *Governance by Indicators. Global Power through Classification and Rankings*, ed. Kevin E. Davis et al. (Oxford University Press, 2012), 52.
45. Kevin E. Davis and Michael B. Kruse, 'Taking the Measure of Law: The Case of the Doing Business Project', *Law & Social Inquiry* 32, no. 4 (2007): 1095, https://doi.org/10.1111/j.1747-4469.2007.00088.x.
46. Kerstin Jacobsson and Niklas Noaksson, 'From Deregulation to Flexicurity? The Makeover of the OECD Jobs Strategy', in *Mechanisms of OECD Governance*, ed. Kerstin Martens and Anja P. Jakobi (Oxford University Press, 2012), 119.
47. On austerity and inequality, see Juan Pablo Bohoslavsky, 'Economic Inequality, Debt Crises and Human Rights', *Yale Journal of International Law Online* 42 (2016): 177, https://campuspress.yale.edu/yjil/files/2016/10/J-Bohoslavsky-Special-Edition-11nf9v3.pdf.
48. On the concept of the public sphere, cf. Jürgen Habermas, *Strukturwandel der Öffentlichkeit. Untersuchungen zu einer Kategorie der bürgerlichen Gesellschaft*, Politica; 4, (Neuwied: Luchterhand, 1962). The concept was further refined in his later writings. The concept is related to public reason, which John Rawls considers an essential aspect of deliberative democracy. See John Rawls, 'The Idea of Public Reason Revisited', *University of Chicago Law Review* 64 (1997): 772.
49. Nancy Fraser, 'Rethinking the Public Sphere: A Contribution to the Critique of Actually Existing Democracy', *Social Text* 25/26 (1990): 59–60, https://doi.org/10.2307/466240.
50. UN General Assembly, Report of the Special Rapporteur on Extreme Poverty and Human Rights, UN Doc. A/72/502, 4 October 2017, 10.
51. Ernst-Wolfgang Böckenförde, *Recht, Staat, Freiheit: Studien zur Rechtsphilosophie, Staatstheorie und Verfassungsgeschichte* (Suhrkamp, 1991), 112–3.
52. Richard Burchill, 'Democracy and the Promotion and Protection of Socio-Economic Rights', in *Economic, Social, and Cultural Rights in Action*, ed. Mashood Baderin and Robert McCorquodale (Oxford: Oxford University Press, 2007), 362.
53. Cf. Johannes Hendrik Fahner, 'Revisiting the Human Right to Democracy: A Positivist Analysis', *The International Journal of Human Rights* 21, no. 3 (2017/03/24 2017): 321, https://doi.org/10.1080/13642987.2017.1298735; Niels Petersen, *Demokratie als teleologisches Prinzip. Zur Legitimität von Staatsgewalt im Völkerrecht* (Heidelberg: Springer, 2009); Thomas M. Franck, 'The Emerging Right to Democratic Governance', *American Journal of International Law* 86 (1992): 46; Gregory H. Fox and Brad R. Roth, *Democratic governance and international law* (Cambridge University Press, 2000).
54. Immanuel Kant, 'Die Metaphysik der Sitten', in *Akademie-Ausgabe* (Berlin: Preußische Akademie der Wissenschaften, 1900 (1797)), 230.
55. Thomas Jefferson, 'Letter to James Madison', in *The Papers of Thomas Jefferson*, vol. 12, 7 August 1787 – 31 March 1788, (ed. Julian P. Boyd. Princeton: Princeton University Press 1955), 438–43.
56. Jürgen Habermas, *Between Facts and Norms. Contributions to a Discourse Theory of Law and Democracy*, trans. William Rehg, Repr. ed. (Cambridge: Polity Press, 2008), 89–94. Reaching the same conclusion with regard to international human rights: David Beetham, *Democracy and Human Rights* (Polity Press Cambridge, 1999), 91–2. From the perspective of children's rights: Aoife Nolan, *Children's Socio-Economic Rights, Democracy and the Courts* (Bloomsbury Publishing, 2011), 93 et seq. Popular is also a more one-sided view that sees human rights as a precondition to democracy, yet without stressing the reverse relationship. E.g. Robert A. Dahl, *Democracy and Its Critics* (New Haven: Yale University Press, 1989), 219–20.
57. Instructive on the limitations of non-majoritarian institutions such as international organisations: Jürgen Habermas, 'The Constitutionalization of International Law and the Legitimation Problems of a Constitution for World Society', *Constellations* 15 (2008): 451.
58. It is widely recognised that Article 2(1) ICESCR does not stipulate an objective standard. Comprehensively on the development of this debate: Sigrun Skogly, 'The Requirement of

Using the 'Maximum of Available Resources' for Human Rights Realisation: A Question of Quality as Well as Quantity?', *Human Rights Law Review* 12, no. 3 (2012): 398 et seq., https://doi.org/10.1093/hrlr/ngs022.

59. Cf. Michael P. Donnelly, 'Democracy and Sovereignty vs International Human Rights: Reconciling the Irreconcilable?', *The International Journal of Human Rights* (2018): 1, https://doi.org/10.1080/13642987.2018.1454904; on direct democracy and human rights, see Matthias Goldmann, 'Völkerrechtliche Vereinbarungen und direkte Demokratie', *Zeitschrift für ausländisches öffentliches Recht und Völkerrecht (ZaöRV)* 78, no. 2 (2018): 281.
60. E.g. Jeremy Waldron, 'Judicial Review and the Conditions of Democracy', *Journal of Political Philosophy* 6, no. 4 (1998): 335, https://doi.org/10.1111/1467-9760.00058; John Hart Ely, *Democracy and Distrust. A Theory of Judicial Review* (Cambridge, MA: Harvard University Press, 1980), 43 et seq; Habermas, *Between Facts and Norms. Contributions to a Discourse Theory of Law and Democracy*, chapter 5. See, however, Ronald Dworkin, *Freedom's Law: The Moral Reading of the American Constitution* (OUP Oxford, 1999). Specifically on ESC rights: Aoife Nolan, Bruce Porter, and Malcolm Langford, 'The Justiciability of Social and Economic Rights: An Updated Appraisal', *CHRGJ Working Paper*, no. 15 (2009), https://ssrn.com/abstract=1434944 (accessed July 27, 2020).
61. Kári Hólmar Ragnarsson, 'The Counter-Majoritarian Difficulty in a Neoliberal World: Socio-Economic Rights and Deference in Post-2008 Austerity Cases', *Global Constitutionalism* 8, no. 3 (2019): 605, https://doi.org/10.1017/S2045381719000212; sceptical also Lin Chun, 'Human Rights and Democracy: The Case for Decoupling', *The International Journal of Human Rights* 5, no. 3 (2001): 19, https://doi.org/10.1080/714003726.
62. See Brenner, 'Escalating Plunder.' On the dysfunctionalities of US democracy, see Steven Levitsky and Daniel Ziblatt, *How democracies die* (Broadway Books, 2018).
63. The analysis of the factors for democratic decay is complex and in flux. Emphasising economic decline: Oliver Nachtwey, *Die Abstiegsgesellschaft. Über das Aufbegehren in der regressiven Moderne* (Berlin: Suhrkamp, 2016).
64. Katharine G Young, 'Waiting for Rights: Progressive Realization and Lost Time', in *The Future of Economic and Social Rights*, ed. Katharine G. Young (Cambridge University Press, 2019), 654.
65. On the example of the Weimar Constitution, see Brun-Otto Bryde, 'Fundamental Rights as Guidelines and Inspiration: German Constitutionalism in International Perspective Lead Article', *Wisconsin International Law Journal* 25, no. 2 (2007–2008, 2007): 193, 208, https://heinonline.org/HOL/P?h=hein.journals/wisint25&i=199. For the postwar period: Samuel Moyn, *Not Enough. Human Rights in an Unequal World* (Cambridge, MA: Harvard University Press, 2018), 41 et seq.
66. Manuel José Cepeda-Espinoza, 'Transcript: Social and Economic Rights and the Colombian Constitutional Court', *Tex. L. Rev.* 89 (2010): 1699; Karl E. Klare, 'Legal Culture and Transformative Constitutionalism', *South African Journal on Human Rights* 14, no. 1 (1998): 146. For a comprehensive assessment and further case studies, see Roberto Gargarella, Pilar Domingo, and Theunis Roux, eds., *Courts and Social Transformation in New Democracies: An Institutional Voice for the Poor?* (Aldershot: Ashgate, 2006).
67. Wiktor Osiatynski, 'Rights in New Constitutions of East Central Europe', *Colum. Hum. Rts. L. Rev.* 26 (1994): 138 et seq.
68. On Colombia: David Landau, 'The Promise of a Minimum Core Approach: The Colombian Model for Judicial Review of Austerity Measures', in *Economic and Social Rights after the Global Financial Crisis*, ed. Aoife Nolan (Cambridge: Cambridge University Press, 2014), 267. On Central and Eastern Europe: Osiatynski, 'Rights in New Constitutions of East Central Europe.'
69. From a European perspective: Margot E. Salomon, 'Of Austerity, Human Rights and International Institutions', *European Law Journal* 21 (2015): 521, https://doi.org/10.1111/eulj.12138.
70. Overview: Claire Kilpatrick, 'Constitutions, Social Rights and Sovereign Debt States in Europe: A Challenging New Area of Constitutional Inquiry', in *Constitutional Change*

through Euro-Crisis Law, ed. Bruno de Witte, Claire Kilpatrick, and Thomas Beukers (Cambridge: Cambridge University Press, 2017), 279. See also Ragnarsson, 'The Counter-Majoritarian Difficulty in a Neoliberal World: Socio-Economic Rights and Deference in Post-2008 Austerity Cases.'

71. Mariana Canotilho, Teresa Violante, and Rui Lanceiro, 'Austerity Measures under Judicial Scrutiny: The Portuguese constitutional Case-law: Portuguese Constitutional Court Decision 399/2010 (Surtax on Personal Income Tax 2010) Decision 396/2011 (State Budget 2011) Decision 353/2012 (State Budget 2012) Decision 187/2013 (State Budget 2013) Decision 474/2013 (Public Workers Requalification) Decision 602/2013 (Labour Code) Decision 794/2013 (40-Hour Work Week) Decision 862/2013 (Pensions Convergence) Decision 413/2014 (State Budget 2014) Decision 572/2014 (Special Solidarity Contribution 2014) Decision 574/2014 (Pay cuts 2014–2018) Decision 575/2014 (Special Sustainability Contribution)', *European Constitutional Law Review* 11, no. 1 (2015): 155, https://doi.org/10.1017/S1574019615000103.
72. Constance G. Anthony, 'American Democratic Interventionism: Romancing the Iconic Woodrow Wilson', *International Studies Perspectives* 9, no. 3 (2008): 239; Mark J. L. McClelland, 'Exporting Virtue: Neoconservatism, Democracy Promotion and the End of History', *The International Journal of Human Rights* 15, no. 4 (2011/05/01 2011): 520, https://doi.org/10.1080/13642987.2011.561984.
73. Carlos Closa, 'Institutional Design of Democratic Conditionality in Regional Organizations', *EUI Working Paper*, no. 2013/45 (2013).
74. RP Anand, 'Sovereign Equality of States in International Law—II', *International Studies* 8, no. 4 (1966): 406.
75. Amartya K. Sen, *The Idea of Justice* (Cambridge, MA: Harvard University Press, 2009), 324 et seq.
76. John Tasioulas, 'Minimum Core Obligations: Human Rights in the Here and Now', *World Bank Nordic Trust Fund Research Paper* (2017).
77. Many of these controversies, and possible ways of overcoming them, are addressed in Toomas Kotkas, Ingrid Leijten, and Frans Pennings, eds., *Specifying and Securing a Social Minimum in the Battle Against Poverty* (Bloomsbury Publishing, 2019).
78. E.g. CJEU, Joined Cases C-402/05 P & C-415/05, Kadi & Al Barakaat International Foundation v Council and Commission, judgment of 3 September 2008, ECLI:EU:C:2008:461; ECtHR, Application No. 27021/08, Al-Jedda v UK, judgment of 7 July 2011.
79. Cf. Ely, *Democracy and Distrust. A Theory of Judicial Review*, 105 et seq; Habermas, *Between Facts and Norms. Contributions to a Discourse Theory of Law and Democracy*, chapter 9.3, calls this the procedural paradigm.
80. Yota Negishi, 'The Proceduralization of Social Rights: Access to Information, Justice and Remedies', in *Research Handbook on International Law and Social Rights*, ed. Christina Binder et al. (Celtenham: Elgar, 2020), 311.
81. Myrvin Anthony, Gregorio Impavido, and Bert van Selm, 'Barbados' 2018–19 Sovereign Debt Restructuring–A Sea Change?', *IMF Working Paper WP/20/34* (2020).
82. James Harrison, 'Human Rights Measurement: Reflections on the Current Practice and Future Potential of Human Rights Impact Assessment', *Journal of Human Rights Practice* 3, no. 2 (2011): 179, https://doi.org/10.1093/jhuman/hur011.
83. See, especially, *Guiding Principles*, Principle 19.
84. Principle 11, *Guiding Principles*.
85. Principle 3, *Guiding Principles*.
86. Decisioni (EU) 2020/440 of the European Central Bank of 24 March 2020 on a temporary pandemic emergency purchase programme (ECB/2020/17).
87. European Commission, Proposal for a Council Regulation on the establishment of a European instrument for temporary support to mitigate unemployment risks in an emergency (SURE) following the COVID-19 outbreak, COM(2020) 139 final, April 2, 2020.
88. For an overview, see Francesco Costamagna and Matthias Goldmann, 'Constitutional Innovation, Democratic Stagnation? The EU Recovery Plan', *Verfassungsblog*, May 30, 2020, https://doi.org/10.17176/20200530-133220-0.

89. Commentary 1(2) to Principle 1, *Guiding Principles.*
90. Principle 20, *Guiding Principles.*
91. Ibid., Commentary 20(4).
92. Commentary 17(4) to Principle 17, *Guiding Principles.*
93. Principle 18, *Guiding Principles.*
94. Art. 15, TFEU.
95. Directive 2011/92/EU (known as 'Environmental Impact Assessment' – EIA Directive), Annex IV No. 3; Directive 2001/42/EC (known as 'Strategic Environmental Assessment' – SEA Directive), Annex I lit. f.
96. Sanne Larsen et al., 'Social Impact Assessment in Europe: A Study of Social Impacts in Three Danish Cases', *Journal of Environmental Assessment Policy and Management* 17 (01/04 2016): 1550038, https://doi.org/10.1142/S1464333215500386.
97. Werner Roeger, Janos Varga, Jan in 't Veld and Lukas Vogel, 'A Model-Based Assessment of the Distributional Impact of Structural Reforms', (2019) European Commission Discussion Paper No. 91.
98. Communication from the Commission to the European Parliament, the Council, the European Economic and Social Committee and the Committee of the Regions on Establishing a European Pillar of Social Rights, COM(2017) 250 final, April 26, 2017.
99. E.g. impact assessments in the area of trade, see https://ec.europa.eu/trade/policy/policy-making/analysis/policy-evaluation/impact-assessments/ (accessed July 24, 2020).
100. European Commission, Commission Staff Working Document: Assessment of the Social Impact of the new Stability Support Programme for Greece, August 8, 2015, SWD(2015) 162 final, https://ec.europa.eu/info/sites/info/files/economy-finance/ecfin_assessment_social_impact_en_0.pdf (accessed July 27, 2020).
101. This is related to the 'juste retour' principle, which has been much criticised. Cf. High Level Group on Own Resources, 'Future of Financing the EU', Final report and recommendations (2016).
102. Article 2(a), Regulation (EC) No 1466/97; cf. Kenneth Armstrong, 'The New Governance of EU Fiscal Discipline', *European Law Review* 38, no. 5 (2013): 601; on the relation of the Stability and Growth Pact with social rights, see Mark Dawson, 'New Governance and the Displacement of Social Europe: The Case of the European Semester', *European Constitutional Law Review* 14, no. 1 (2018): 191.
103. European Commission, Proposal for a Regulation of the European Parliament and of the Council establishing a Recovery and Resilience Facility, COM(2020) 408 final, May 28, 2020.
104. Article 6(3)(d), Regulation (EU) No 473/2013 of the European Parliament and of the Council on common provisions for monitoring and assessing draft budgetary plans and ensuring the correction of excessive deficit of the Member States in the euro area, May 21, 2013.
105. Principle 17(b) in conjunction with Principles 7 and 8, *Guiding Principles.*
106. Principle 17, *Guiding Principles.*
107. Cf. Principle 20, *Guiding Principles.*
108. Cf. Commentary 4.2 to Principle 4; Commentary 6.1 to Principle 6; Commentary 7.3 to Principle 7; Commentary 8.3 to Principle 8; Principle 10(h); Commentary 11.5 to Principle 11; Principle 14; Commentary 15.2 to Principle 15; Principle 19.
109. Section B.II.
110. Principle 19, *Guiding Principles.*
111. *Guiding Principles*, Commentaries 7(3) and 8(3) to Principles 7 and 8, Principle 10(h), Commentary 15(2) to Principle 15.
112. Cf. Art. 121, TFEU.
113. Communication from the Commission to the European Parliament, the European Council, the Council, the European Economic and Social Committee and the Committee of the Regions, 'Europe's moment: Repair and Prepare for the Next Generation', COM(2020) 456 final, May 27, 2020.
114. Cf. Principle 18, *Guiding Principles.*
115. Art. 314, TFEU.

116. Costamagna and Goldmann, 'Constitutional Innovation, Democratic Stagnation? The EU Recovery Plan'.
117. Art. 310(1), TFEU; cf. Siegfried Magiera, Article 310 AEUV, in Eberhardt Grabitz, Meinhard Hilf, and Martin Nettesheim, *Das Recht der Europäischen Union* (69th edn, Beck, Munich 2020), no. 40.
118. Situating the COVID-19 response in the context of European constitutional law: Matthias Goldmann, 'The European Economic Constitution after the PSPP Judgment: Towards Integrative Liberalism?', *German Law Journal* 21, no. 4 (forthcoming).
119. Some might recall the negotiations leading to the Comprehensive Economic and Trade Ageement between the European Union and Canada.
120. Cf. Francesco Costamagna, 'The Impact of Stronger Economic Policy Coordination on the European Social Dimension: Issues of Legitimacy', in *The Constitutionalization of European Budgetary Constraints*, ed. Maurice Adams, Federico Fabbrini, and Pierre Larouche (Oxford: Hart, 2014), 359.
121. One of the intellectual godfathers of the separation theory is Jan Tinbergen, *Centralization and Decentralization in Economic Policy*, Contributions to economic analysis (Amsterdam,: North Holland Pub. Co., 1954). See comprehensively Matthias Goldmann, 'United in Diversity? The Relationship between Monetary Policy and Prudential Supervision in the Banking Union', *European Constitutional Law Review* 14, no. 2 (2018): 288 et seq, https://doi.org/10.1017/S1574019618000184.
122. See above, text accompanying n 75.
123. European Council, Special meeting of the European Council (17, 18, 19, 20 and 21 July 2020) – Conclusions, EUCO 10/20, July 21, 2020, https://www.consilium.europa.eu/media/45109/210720-euco-final-conclusions-en.pdf (accessed July 27, 2020).
124. European Commission, Factsheet: Financing the Recovery Plan for Europe, May 27, 2020, https://ec.europa.eu/info/sites/info/files/factsheet_3_04.06.pdf (accessed July 24, 2020).
125. See Olivier De Schutter, Nicholas Lusiani, and Sergio Chaparro, in this issue; see also the contributions in Philip Alston and Nikki Reisch, *Tax, Inequality, and Human Rights* (Oxford University Press, 2019).
126. Introductory statement by Christine Lagarde, President of the ECB, at the ECON committee of the European Parliament, June 8, 2020, https://www.ecb.europa.eu/press/key/date/2020/html/ecb.sp200608~4225ba8a1b.en.html (accessed July 27, 2020).
127. ECB, 'ECB launches review of its monetary policy strategy, Press Release, January 23, 2020, https://www.ecb.europa.eu/press/pr/date/2020/html/ecb.pr200123~3b8d9fc08d.en.html (accessed July 24, 2020).
128. BVerfG, 2 BvR 859/15 et al. (*Weiss*), Judgment of the Second Senate, May 5, 2020, ECLI:DE:BVerfG:2020:rs20200505.2bvr085915.
129. See, e.g., https://www.europarl.europa.eu/about-parliament/en/democracy-and-human-rights/global-democracy (accessed July 27, 2020).

Acknowledgement

Thanks to Aoife Nolan and Juan Pablo Bohoslavsky for highly valuable advice, and to Benjamin Arens for research assistance.

Disclosure statement

No potential conflict of interest was reported by the author(s).

Economic inequality and human rights impact assessments of economic reforms

Gillian MacNaughton

ABSTRACT
For over a decade, activists and scholars have sounded alarms over the extreme and growing economic inequalities in the world. In 2020, Forbes reported that there were 2095 billionaires in the world, while the World Bank recorded that 3.5 billion people lived on less than the poverty line of $5.50 per day. Such inequalities prevent the full realisation of human rights, undermine democracy and threaten peace. Economic inequalities are not inevitable however. They are the result of policy choices. As governments are obligated to respect, protect and fulfil human rights, they must take steps to ensure that their actions are consistent with their human rights obligations. Human rights impact assessment is an evidence-based method to aid governments in considering the potential human rights effects of policy options. The UN Independent Expert on Debt and Human Rights recently issued *Guiding Principles on Human Rights Impact Assessment of Economic Reforms*. This article reviews the *Guiding Principles* and argues for including a *Guiding Principle* on economic inequality in order to ensure that governments consider the impact of economic reforms on income and wealth inequality as critical causes of human rights violations.

1. Introduction

For over a decade, activists and scholars have sounded alarms over the extreme and growing economic inequalities in the world. Inspired by the Arab Spring and the Spanish Indignados movements, among others, the global Occupy movement, launched by Occupy Wall Street in New York City in 2011, protested rising social and economic inequality and its impact on democracy.[1] Occupy spread to 82 countries and almost 1,000 cities, seeking to unify the power of 99% of the population against that of the wealthiest 1%.[2] In the same period, economists, including Thomas Piketty and Anthony Atkinson, published work documenting the extreme and growing global economic inequality and its negative impacts.[3] They also established the World Inequality Lab to promote research on global inequality,[4] and published the *World Inequality Report 2018* to inform global debate on rising economic inequality and the potential for related political, economic and social catastrophes.[5] Scholars in other fields, such as social epidemiologists Richard Wilkinson and Kate Pickett, have also documented the negative impacts of economic inequality on a range of social indicators, including infant mortality and political participation rates.[6] Further, nongovernmental organisations such as Oxfam, previously focused on poverty and social justice, have also expanded their work to examine economic inequality, thereby acknowledging extreme wealth as a critical issue as well.[7]

The current crisis of extreme economic inequality is the result of four decades of neoliberal policies, which reduced individual and corporate taxes, repealed labour protections, reduced social benefits, deregulated markets, and privatised public functions, including public education, water systems and prisons.[8] In April 2020, Forbes reported that there were 2,095 billionaires in the world,[9] while the World Bank reported that 3.5 billion people live on less than the poverty line of $5.50 per day.[10] In 2018, CEOs in the 350 largest firms in the US received an average annual compensation of $17.2 million while the average worker in these companies earned $62,000.[11] This is a ratio of 278 to 1.[12] In 1978, that ratio was 30 to 1.[13] Since 1978, CEO compensation has grown 940%, while worker compensation has grown only 12%.[14] The current COVID-19 pandemic has drastically widened this gap. In June 2020, the Institute for Policy Studies reported that as the pandemic spread across the US from March to June 2020, 45 million people filed for unemployment benefits, while 'the combined wealth of the 614 US billionaires increased by $584 billion'.[15] Such inequalities in income and wealth result in inequalities in social outcomes, including disparities in educational achievement and life expectancy.[16] Further, income and wealth inequalities often translate into political inequalities as wealthy groups are able to influence policymaking in their favour.[17] As the *Human Development Report 2019* explains, 'Those privileged can capture the system, moulding it to fit their preferences, potentially leading to even more inequalities.'[18]

Since 2010, several UN entities – including the International Labour Organization, UNESCO and the UN Department of Economic and Social Affairs – have issued reports on economic inequality.[19] The *2019 Human Development Report* published by UNDP is about inequalities in human development, and it addresses both vertical (income and wealth) and horizontal (status-based) inequalities.[20] Even the World Bank and the International Monetary Fund (IMF) have acknowledged that economic inequality is a pressing global issue.[21] Indeed, according to the IMF, 'Research indicates that increased inequality can erode social cohesion, lead to political polarization, and ultimately lower economic growth.'[22] Most importantly, the UN General Assembly recognised the crisis of growing economic inequality when it adopted the 2030 Agenda for Sustainable Development by including a goal on inequality.[23] Sustainable Development Goal (SDG) 10 calls for reducing inequalities within and between countries.[24] SDG 10 aims to address both vertical (income and wealth) and horizontal (status-based) inequalities, as well as inequalities at the global and domestic levels. The adoption of SDG 10 ensures that inequalities will remain on the global agenda, as well as domestic agendas, for the next decade, bringing attention, expertise, monitoring and funding to this crucial issue.

The human rights community has also participated in global discussions on economic inequality, particularly since the adoption of SDG 10.[25] Indeed, many human rights bodies and experts recognise that extreme economic inequalities are one of the most pressing human rights challenges in the world today. In her keynote statement at the Expert Meeting on SDG 10 in April 2019,[26] UN High Commissioner for Human Rights Michelle Bachelet stated:

> [T]he growing gap between rich and poor is undermining the fight against poverty and fuelling public anger across the globe. High levels of inequality correlate with underfunding of public services and low levels of access to essential services such as education, healthcare, safe water, decent housing and social protection. As these fundamental rights are diminished, dismantled, commodified and privatized, more and more people are pushed to the margins. Political and economic instability are the logical outcomes, because inequalities deprive people of their rightful voice in decision-making – their power.[27]

The UN Committee on Economic, Social and Cultural Rights has also recognised economic inequality as a critical human rights issue.[28] A key concern of the Committee is that poverty cannot be eradicated when there are widening economic disparities between rich and poor people both within and across countries.[29] Several UN Special Procedures, including Philip Alston, formerly Special Rapporteur on Extreme Poverty and Human Rights, and Juan Pablo Bohoslavsky, formerly Independent Expert on Debt and Human Rights, have also recognised the linkages between economic inequalities and human rights.[30] Specifically, they have maintained that current levels of economic inequality have negative impacts on civil, political, economic, social and cultural rights. Further, economic inequalities are not an inevitable result of market economies. As High Commissioner Bachelet asserts, 'They stem from policy choices.'[31]

In this light, this article argues that human rights have a role to play in government decision-making on policy choices that impact on economic inequality. As governments are obligated to respect, protect and fulfil human rights, they must take steps to ensure that their actions (and inactions) are consistent with and do not violate their human rights obligations. Indeed, governments have the obligation to take deliberate, concrete and targeted steps, and to use the maximum of their available resources to achieve progressively the full realisation of economic and social rights.[32] They should therefore elect from among policy options those policies that will most effectively ensure the full enjoyment of human rights for all. Human rights impact assessment (HRIA) is an evidence-based method to aid governments, as well as nongovernmental organisations, in ensuring that governments carefully consider the potential human rights effects of policy options prior to making decisions on which policies to adopt.[33] As increased economic inequality makes it difficult for governments to reduce poverty and to ensure realisation of human rights – and may indeed result in violations of human rights – governments should assess the impact of policy options on economic inequality as part of their process of decision-making.

Juan Pablo Bohoslavsky, formerly UN Independent Expert on Debt and Human Rights, recently issued *Guiding Principles on Human Rights Impact Assessment of Economic Reforms*, providing a framework of human rights principles and standards for States and others to apply to systematically assess proposed economic reforms, ensuring that States do not violate their international legal obligations.[34] In the preamble to the *Guiding Principles*, Bohoslavsky states, 'Obligations under human rights law should guide all efforts to design and implement economic policies. The economy should serve the people, not vice versa.'[35] The *Guiding Principles* then draw on international human rights law to propose 21 principles for human rights impact assessment of economic reforms. Curiously, although the UN recognises economic inequality as one of the major challenges of our time, the *Guiding Principles* do not include a principle on economic inequality. This article, therefore, argues for the addition of a *Guiding Principle* on economic inequality to ensure that governments consider the impact of their reforms on income and wealth inequality as critical causes and consequences of human rights violations.

Following this introduction, Part 2 discusses vertical (income and wealth) and horizontal (status-based) inequalities and their relationship to both SDG 10 and international human rights. Part 3 provides a brief overview of UN work on human rights impact assessment, focusing on some of the key developments in order to provide context for the *Guiding Principles on Human Rights Impact Assessment of Economic Reforms*. Part 4 reviews the *Guiding Principles* in light of the earlier discussion on vertical and horizontal inequalities and then argues for integrating reduction of vertical inequalities – as recognised by SDG 10 and the CESCR – as a new *Guiding Principle*. The article concludes that human rights scholars and practitioner should make every effort to link the global discussion on economic inequality with human rights to squarely bring to light the necessity of greater vertical equality to progressively realise human rights for all.

2. Vertical (wealth and income) inequalities and horizontal (status-based) inequalities

To understand the relationship of human rights and inequalities, it is helpful to distinguish two types of inequalities, horizontal and vertical inequalities. Discrimination or status-based inequality – that is inequality between status-based groups – is also called *horizontal* inequality.[36] Balakrishnan, Heintz, and Elson explain, 'Horizontal inequality is defined as inequality between culturally defined or socially constructed groups. Inequalities with respect to gender, race, ethnicity, religion, caste, and sexuality are all examples of horizontal inequalities.'[37] SDG 5, for example, addresses horizontal inequality as it aims to '[a]chieve gender equality and empower all women and girls'. On the other hand, *vertical* inequalities are inequalities of wealth or income between individuals or households.[38] Common measurements of vertical inequality include, for example, the Gini coefficient (a measure between 0 and 1 of the income distribution among a population) and the Palma ratio (the ratio of the richest 10% of the population's share of gross national income to the poorest 40% of the population's share).[39] This article focuses on vertical inequalities and uses the terms 'vertical inequalities' and 'economic inequalities' interchangeably.

Over the past 40 years, horizontal inequalities have attracted much attention, and significant progress has been made in reducing these inequalities in many countries. In contrast, the dominance of neoliberal ideology and policy over this period has led to extreme and increasing vertical inequalities, which have not attracted much attention until the past decade. At the global level, Oxfam reported that in 2019, the 2153 billionaires had more wealth than 4.6 billion people, 60% of the global population.[40] In the same report, Oxfam found that the combined wealth of the 22 richest men is more than the wealth of all the women in Africa.[41] Further, the richest 1% have more than twice as much wealth as 6.9 billion people.[42] Oxfam concludes that '[extreme] wealth is a sign of a failing economic system' and calls for an end to extreme wealth in order to end poverty.[43]

Moreover, in recent decades income inequality has increased in almost all countries.[44] The *World Inequality Report 2018* indicates that since 1980, income inequality has increased swiftly in North America, China, India and Russia, moderately in Europe, and remained relatively stable at extremely high levels in the Middle East, Sub-Saharan Africa and Brazil.[45] In terms of outcomes, in 2016, the top 10% national income share in Europe was 37%. In contrast, this share was 41% in China, 46% in Russia and 47% in the US–Canada. Inequality was even more extreme in Sub-Saharan Africa where the top 10% share of national income was 54%, in Brazil and India where it was 55%, and in the Middle East, the most unequal region of the world, where it was 61%.[46] Notably, in 1980, the United States and Europe had similar levels of inequality; the top 1% income share was about 10%. By 2016, this had doubled in the United States to 20% but grew to only to 12% in Europe.[47] The *World Inequality Report 2018* concludes that inequality is not inevitable but is the result of institutions and policies.[48]

These economic inequalities are also closely related to social inequalities. For example, in the United States, the gap in life expectancy between the top 1% of the income distribution and the bottom 1% is 15 years for men and 10 years for women.[49] And these disparities are growing.[50] In middle-income countries, the poorest 20% of children may have the same life expectancy as children in a low-income country.[51] Gaps in education are also higher for children in the lower income quintiles, and they also drop out of school more frequently.[52] In economic crises, people in lower income quintiles are also hardest hit.[53] In addition to health and education disparities between income groups, concentration of wealth at the top has numerous negative impacts. For example, more unequal societies experience slower growth than more equal ones.[54] And more egalitarian countries tend to reduce poverty more quickly.[55] Inequality can also lead to market instability; both the Great Depression (1930s) and the great Recession (2007–2008) followed steep increases in income and wealth inequality.[56]

Further, high inequality undermines trust and contributes to social instability.[57] It often results in residential segregation, and in turn, the wealthy become less aware of the impact of inequality across society and less inclined to want to contribute to improving it.[58] As a result, the quality of public goods and services declines, the wealthy turn to purchase private alternatives, and the divide between rich and poor expands into education, health care, utilities and other areas of public goods and services.[59] Moreover, the wealthy have greater political influence and thereby influence adoption of policies that increase economic inequality, resulting in greater economic and financial instability.[60] High economic inequality is also associated with elite capture of the media and reduced media freedom, as well as lower political participation.[61]

In light of the research on the extreme and growing economic inequalities and their negative impacts on reducing poverty, the UN General Assembly adopted SDG 10 – on reducing inequalities within and among countries – in the 2030 Development Agenda. SDG 10 is a promising turn after the Millennium Development Goals (2001–2015), which did not address inequalities except those based on gender. Within countries, SDG 10 targets include two indicators on horizontal inequalities, addressing (1) promotion of inclusion of status-based groups, such as race, ethnicity, sex, age, etc.; and (2) eliminating discriminatory laws, policies and practices.[62] At the global level, SDG 10 targets call for improvement of the regulation and monitoring of global financial markets and institutions, enhanced representation and voice for developing countries, regular and responsible migration of people, encouraging official development assistance and foreign direct investment where there is the greatest need, and reduction of transaction costs of migrant remittances.[63]

Nonetheless, the SDG 10 targets fail to include any benchmark for the reduction of economic inequality.[64] In particular, target 10.1 calls upon states to, '[b]y 2030, progressively achieve and sustain income growth of the bottom 40 per cent of the population at a rate higher than the national average'.[65] This 'target' is actually a 'means' for inclusive growth rather than a benchmark for reduced inequality. Like other targets for SDG 10, it ignores the concentration of wealth and income at the top that have been central in global debates on the crisis of economic inequality.[66] Target 10.4 is similarly a 'means' rather than a 'target'. It calls for adopting 'policies, especially fiscal, wage, and social protection policies, and progressively achiev[ing] greater equality'.[67] While these may be effective means for achieving greater equality – both vertical and horizontal – target 10.4 does not aim for any specific level of equality and does not set a deadline to achieve it. In short, the SDG 10 targets focus largely on means to reduce poverty and discrimination, not on setting benchmarks for reduced wealth and income inequalities by 2030.

The absence of an SDG 10 target on the reduction of economic inequalities received considerable attention.[68] In her keynote statement at the Expert Meeting on SDG 10 in April 2019, High Commissioner Bachelet recommended that, when the SDG indicators are reviewed in 2020, it would be important to add a clearer indicator of inequality, such as the Gini Coefficient or the Palma Ratio, so that progress on reducing economic inequality can be measured.[69] As she explained, 'Measuring the incomes of the bottom 40%, as the SDG indicator 10.1 does, can get us to a certain point, but it will be impossible to address inequality without also shining a light on the top 1%.'[70] Indeed, in 2020 a new indicator was adopted under target 10.4: 'Redistributive impact of fiscal policy', calling for reporting of the Gini Coefficient as one component of this indicator.[71] Thus, the change in economic inequality is now incorporated into the SDG framework, yet there remains no target for greater equality and no deadline to achieve it. In sum, SDG 10 is a considerable improvement over the MDGs, which overlooked inequality (except gender inequality), however, the targets and indicators need improvement to serve the purposes of monitoring and encouraging States to adopt policies that will result in reduced vertical inequalities by 2030.

Like the SDGs, international human rights law, as interpreted to date, has been similarly inadequate in addressing vertical inequalities. It addresses horizontal inequality (non-discrimination) directly but it does not (yet) address vertical inequality – at least directly. The right to nondiscrimination is actually the only human right that is specifically spelled out in the Charter of the United Nations. Article 1 of the Charter provides that one of the four purposes of the UN is to achieve international co-operation 'in promoting and encouraging respect for fundamental freedoms for all without distinction as to race, sex, language, or religion'.[72] The right to nondiscrimination is similarly set out in Article 2 of the Universal Declaration of Human Rights (UDHR), which states: 'Everyone is entitled to all the rights and freedoms set forth in this Declaration, without distinction of any kind, such as race, colour, sex, language, religion, political or other opinion, national or social origin, property, birth or other status.'[73] Both the International Covenant on Economic, Social and Cultural Rights (ICESCR) and the International Covenant on Civil and Political Rights (ICCPR) also include a provision almost identical to Article 2 in the UDHR.[74] Further, several international treaties focus specifically on nondiscrimination, including the Convention on the Elimination of All forms of Racial Discrimination (1965) and the Convention on the Elimination of All Forms of Discrimination Against Women (1979).[75]

The right to nondiscrimination – the prohibition of status-based inequality – is widely recognised in international human rights law and has been widely adopted in domestic constitutional and statutory law as well. Moreover, the concept of 'equality' in international human rights is generally understood to be the achievement of nondiscrimination. Many scholars and practitioners of human rights use the two words 'nondiscrimination' and 'equality' interchangeably, often referring to them as 'two sides of the same coin'.[76] This merger of equality with nondiscrimination, as well as the dominance of neoliberalism over the past 40 years, has contributed to a narrowing of the potential of the right to equality in international law.[77] Vertical inequality is an area that calls for greater attention from the human rights community.[78]

Unlike horizontal inequalities, which are explicitly prohibited by numerous provisions and treaties, human rights scholars and practitioners generally agree that vertical inequalities are not expressly prohibited (yet) by international human rights law.[79] To date, the international human rights bodies have registered concern over growing economic inequalities but have not recognised specific norms or established standards for vertical inequalities in international human rights law.[80] Further, in contrast to horizontal inequalities, with few exceptions, vertical inequalities have only recently garnered attention from scholars and practitioners of human rights.[81] Indeed, some human rights scholars maintain that the dominant human rights framework since the 1970s, narrowly addressing only individual civil and political rights and hostile to the State and the social realm, has aligned remarkably with the global neoliberal policy regime that has caused these extreme inequalities.[82] Thus, even extreme vertical inequalities are not (yet) recognised to be violations of human rights. More recently, however, a growing number of human rights scholars and practitioners have acknowledged that reducing the current extreme vertical inequalities between individuals and households within and between countries will be essential to realising human rights for all.[83]

Balakrishnan, Heintz, and Elson, for example, recognised that economic inequalities have negative impacts on human rights, such as the rights to education, health, housing and a life free from violence. Therefore, in their view,

> There is an implicit obligation within the human rights framework for states to consider the impact of inequality on the realization of rights and, where inequality impedes the realization of rights, to take steps to move toward a more just distribution of income.[84]

Similarly, Bohoslavsky maintains that '[s]evere economic inequality frequently affects the effective enjoyment of particular human rights, both civil and political rights, as well as social, economic and cultural ones'.[85] In his view, '[h]uman rights law therefore imposes certain legal obligations on States to address economic inequalities affecting human rights'.[86] Consistent with this view, in 2019, the Committee on Economic, Social and Cultural Rights stated:

> In the context of the periodic reporting system, the Committee requires States parties to provide information on the impact of income and wealth inequalities on the enjoyment of economic, social and cultural rights. This reflects the common understanding that the eradication of poverty will not be achieved in the context of widening gulfs between rich and poor both within and between countries.[87]

By requiring State parties to report on the impact of income and wealth inequalities on these rights, the CESCR has begun to develop human rights standards on vertical inequalities.[88] In short, reducing vertical inequalities, whether or not explicitly recognised in international human rights law, is instrumentally crucial to realising human rights. As a result, governments have obligations to monitor and respond to vertical inequalities that prevent the full enjoyment of human rights.[89]

3. The obligation to conduct human rights impact assessment

Governments are responsible for respecting, protecting and fulfilling human rights, and must take 'all appropriate means' to ensure that human rights are fully realised.[90] One appropriate means (method or tool) is human rights impact assessment (HRIA). In a 2007 report, Paul Hunt, then UN Special Rapporteur on the right to health, defined HRIA:

> Human rights impact assessment is the process of predicting the potential consequences of a proposed policy, programme or project on the enjoyment of human rights. The objective of the assessment is to inform decision makers and the people likely to be affected so that they can improve the proposal to reduce potential negative effects and increase positive ones.[91]

Thus, as High Commissioner Navanethem Pillay reported, HRIA helps 'Governments to adopt and implement policies, programmes and projects that will best meet their obligations to take deliberate and concrete steps towards progressive realization of human rights.'[92] In terms of policymaking, HRIA serves as an evidence-based method for policymakers to choose, from among policy options, those options that will most effectively ensure the full realisation of human rights. It also serves to make the policymaking process transparent and allows for people who are potentially affected by the policy to participate in decision-making.[93] Further, HRIA is a means by which people can hold decision-makers to account for the decisions that they make as it is a systematic method to collect and evaluate evidence based on human rights standards.[94] Thus, HRIA promotes the human rights principles of transparency, participation and accountability.

At the UN level, the idea of HRIA was raised by Kurt Waldheim, the Secretary-General, in a report to the Commission on Human Rights in 1979. He maintained that, for the right to development, it was of major importance to consider, among other issues,

> the practicability of requiring a 'human rights impact statement', which might be similar in concept to an environmental impact statement, to be undertaken prior to the commencement of specific development projects or in connexion with the preparation of an overall development plan or programme.[95]

It was not until the 1990s, however, when economic and social rights gained greater traction, that this idea was taken up and put into practice. Experts in the field of economic, social and cultural rights have been central to promoting and conducting research on HRIA.[96] In 1990, for example, the Committee on Economic, Social and Cultural Rights asserted in General Comment 2, 'Consideration should be given by United Nations agencies to the proposal made by the Secretary-General in a report of 1979 that a "human rights impact statement" be required to be prepared in connection with all development activities.'[97] During the 1990s, scholars at the Harvard School of Public Health took this idea further by developing and implementing an HRIA methodology to assess the impacts of proposed public health policies on human rights in the context of the HIV pandemic.[98]

On economic policy specifically, HRIA was recommended as early as 1998. Katarina Tomasevski, then UN Special Rapporteur on the right to education, recommended, 'A procedural approach can become an effective method of challenging disregard of human rights in macroeconomic policies through a requirement that a human rights impact assessment be carried out before such policies are developed and adopted.'[99] Subsequently, in 2007, Paul Hunt, then UN Special Rapporteur on the right to health, published a report on HRIA methodology that focused on poverty and health. It included seven principles for performing HRIA, and a six-step process for integrating the right to health into other forms of impact assessment (such as social impact assessment) that governments were already undertaking.[100] This was followed in 2011 by Olivier De Schutter, then UN Special Rapporteur on the right to food, publishing *Guiding Principles on Human Rights Impact Assessments of Trade and Investment Agreements.*[101] Later, in 2017, Juan Pablo Bohoslavsky, the Independent Expert on Debt and Human Rights, also asserted, 'States and international financial institutions have a duty to assess the impact of proposed and implemented economic reform measures, in particular, when significant adverse human rights are expected.'[102]

Indeed, as Hunt maintained, for any new proposal, a State party must ensure that it is consistent with its existing international and national legal obligations, including its human rights obligations.[103] HRIA is an aid to doing so. It also contributes to 'equitable, inclusive, robust and sustainable policymaking'.[104] In short, the UN Special Rapporteurs and other experts working on economic and social rights have taken a leading role in unpacking the obligation of governments to conduct HRIA, especially in relation to economic policies, and in developing principles and guidelines for them to do so.

At this point, a number of UN human rights mechanisms have recognised a State obligation to conduct HRIA before adopting and implementing policies, including economic policies. For example, in 2003 the Committee on the Rights of the Child stated in General Comment 5 that ensuring 'that all the provisions of the Convention are respected in legislation and policy development and delivery at all levels of government demands a continuous process of *child impact assessment* (predicting the impact of any proposed law, policy or budgetary allocation which affects children and the enjoyment of their rights) and child impact evaluation (evaluating the actual impact of implementation)'.[105] Similarly, for decades, the CESCR has recommended to State parties in its concluding observations that they employ human rights impact assessment as 'an integral part of every proposed piece of legislation or policy initiative on a basis analogous to environmental impact assessments'.[106] More recently, in the context of public debt and austerity measures, the CESCR has indicated that both lending and borrowing states are required to carry out HRIA prior to issuing a loan to ensure that the conditions of the loan do not negatively impact on economic and social rights or discriminate against marginalised or disadvantaged groups.[107]

HRIA includes several steps. While there is no consensus on the precise number of steps on HRIA, many methodologies include the following six steps.[108]

(1) *Screening*: The screening step involves identifying the State's human rights obligations, the people most likely to be affected by the proposed policy and the resources

available to carry out the HRIA. It then requires carrying out a 'mini-assessment' of the policy's likely impacts to determine if a full assessment is warranted.

(2) *Scoping*: The scoping step involves identifying the questions, indicators, data collection methods, and analysis techniques to be used, as well as the stakeholders to be consulted.

(3) *Data Collection*: The data collection step involves collecting evidence on the potential impacts of the proposal, ensuring participation of those most likely to be affected.

(4) *Analysis*: The analysis step involves analysing the evidence on potential impacts of the proposal in comparison to the State's human rights obligations spelled out during the screening step.

(5) *Conclusions and Recommendations*: This step involves drafting a statement that spells out the impacts of the proposed policy, identifies modifications to the policy that would increase the enjoyment of human rights and mitigate any negative impacts on human rights, makes recommendations from among the options, and makes public the results of the assessment.

(6) *Monitoring and Evaluation*: This step involves both (a) evaluating the HRIA process to determine the extent to which it promoted and respected human rights, and (b) monitoring the implementation the policy adopted to ensure that measures are continually taken to be most effective in realising human rights for all.

All HRIA methodologies include a step on setting out explicitly the normative content of the human rights at issue.[109] Once data is collected, it is then analysed in comparison to the human rights obligations or standards and recommendations can be made on the best avenue forward to ensure realisation of human rights. The human rights obligations that are identified in the initial step in an HRIA are spelled out in international human rights treaties, the general comments of the human rights treaty bodies, and other human rights instruments. For example, nondiscrimination, horizontal inequality, is a human rights obligation that is often incorporated in an HRIA because every UN member recognises the right to nondiscrimination and therefore must consider this obligation in adopting policies.

On the other hand, because there is no explicit obligation in international human rights law (to date) on vertical inequalities, and no instrument (to date) detailing the human rights obligations of States parties with respect to vertical inequalities, the screening process will not unveil any such obligations. As a result, an assessment of the impact of vertical inequalities on human rights is unlikely to be included as a part of HRIA methodology or tools. There are, at this time, no human rights standards on vertical inequalities that could provide the basis for such an assessment. Yet, many human rights scholars and practitioners, as well as human rights mechanisms, recognise that extreme vertical inequalities have substantial negative impacts on human rights.[110] As a result, it makes sense – even in the absence of any norms or standards on vertical inequalities – to include in HRIA some measure of the impact of the proposed policy on economic inequality, and consequently, on human rights.

4. *Guiding Principles on Human Rights Impact Assessment of Economic Policies*

In this context, in 2017, the Human Rights Council adopted a resolution requesting that Juan Pablo Bohoslavsky, the Independent Expert on Debt and Human Rights, 'develop guidelines for human rights impact assessment for economic reform policies, in consultation with States, international financial institutions and other relevant stakeholders'.[111] Such guidelines would appear to be an important opportunity to step forward in developing both policy processes to address economic inequality and human rights norms and standards on economic inequality. The Human Rights Council's request did not emerge specifically from the global concern over extreme and growing vertical inequalities, however, but rather with a concern over the impacts of foreign debt on State party economic stability, and therefore capacities to progressively realise human rights, as well as a concern that many State parties had failed to take human rights into consideration in designing responses to economic and financial crises such as that experienced in 2008. Indeed, the Council's resolution does not mention SDG 10 on reducing inequality or even include the word 'inequality'.[112]

In response to the request of the Human Rights Council, Bohoslavsky issued two reports. His 2017 report includes background research, the objectives and scope of the guidelines, the process for developing the guidelines, and the key features that the guidelines would need to address. In this report, it is clear that the guidelines would be directed primarily to financial crises, particularly the 2008 crisis, and the austerity measures that governments have adopted in response. It states that government responses failed to adequately consider the lessons learned from previous crises and 'revealed a deep-seated structural neglect of human rights in economic policy formulation'.[113] Although the report recognises that HRIA may be applied to acute crisis situations, medium-term reforms, and annual reviews of budgets, the focus in all three situations is on preventing potentially impermissible retrogressive economic reforms.[114] The overall theme is that 'economic reforms' are in response to economic crises or to prevent or prepare for economic crises. Thus, there is throughout the report an emphasis on limiting negative human rights impacts and mitigating those that cannot be prevented. The report mentions, however, that HRIA should also identify potential positive human rights impacts.[115]

Notably, the 2017 report addresses wealth and income inequalities, noting that they have been 'widening within countries over the two to three decades prior to the latest financial crisis, both in the developing world and among the more developed countries'.[116] It refers to an earlier 2016 report of the Independent Expert that focused specifically on economic inequality and concluded 'that economic inequality was both a result of and a contributor to financial crises'.[117] In the 2016 report, the Independent Expert stated:

> Inequality may also reduce social and political stability. This creates disincentives for investment, disruptions in business activities, disunity, threats to property and policy uncertainty and may even raise the probability of coups and mass violence. The result is a lower level of growth, which consequently provokes higher level of debt.[118]

Consequently, the Independent Expert concluded that policymakers must 'tackle dangerous destabilizing developments in the financial sphere while addressing inequality directly'.[119] In short, he maintained that combating economic inequalities must 'go hand in hand' with preventing and responding to economic crises as both are likely to negatively impact human rights.[120]

His 2018 report sets forth the *Guiding Principles on Human Rights Impact Assessment of Economic Reforms*. The *Guiding Principles* begin by asserting that State parties 'must comply with their international human rights obligations at all times, including during times of economic crisis'.[121] This means that States must ensure, prior to adoption, that their proposed economic policies respect, protect and fulfil human rights for all.[122] Principle 3 then states, in part, 'This implies a duty to carry out human rights impact assessments to evaluate and address any foreseeable effects of their economic policies on human rights.'[123] Principles 5–10 set forth applicable human rights standards, including indivisibility and interdependence of all human rights, nondiscrimination, gender equality, progressive realisation, maximum available resources, and the prohibition of retrogression.[124] As there are, to date, no human rights standards on vertical inequalities – no limits at all on wealth or income inequality and no obligations to limit massive accumulation of wealth – this section of the *Guiding Principles* does not address vertical inequalities.

The next principles are on the articulation of policies and include Principles 11 on policy coherence and Principle 12 on debt sustainability, debt relief and restructuring. With no human rights standards on vertical inequalities, the policy section of the *Guiding Principles* is the place where the *Guiding Principles* could address this human rights issue. The main provision in Principle 11 states:

> States should ensure that governmental departments, agencies and other State-based institutions that take part in and/or shape economic reform policies take into account States' human rights obligations when fulfilling their respective mandates, and that policy coherence is guaranteed for short-, medium- and long-term economic reforms, in order to protect all human rights.[125]

Notably, Principle 11 makes clear that States must consider their human rights obligations whenever they are adopting or implementing economic reforms. Indeed, the *Guiding Principles* are applicable at all times, not just in times of economic crisis. As vertical inequality has been growing for forty years, governments may not see it as an acute crisis – however, it is to people whose human rights are adversely impacted today. Although a long-term problem, States have a duty to develop, propose and adopt economic reforms that will reduce economic inequality where it is adversely impacting human rights.[126]

Principle 11 also sets out guidance for allocation of financial resources, fiscal policy, monetary policy, financial sector regulation, debt policies, and environmental protection.[127] Although Principle 11 does not address vertical inequality, the two-page Commentary on the principle does. Section 11.2 states in part, 'Fiscal policy can play a major role in achieving equality, tackling discrimination and strengthening governance and accountability.'[128] The two provisions that follow state,

> 11.3 Decisions on fiscal policy should not result in expenditure cuts that curtail the guarantee of rights, mainly in sectors such as education, health and social insurance – particularly important for women, children and persons with disabilities – or *in deepening social and economic inequality* and poverty through indirect and regressive taxes.
>
> 11.4 Direct and progressive taxes should be prioritized. Tax policy should promote the redistribution of wealth to overcome the disadvantaged situation of the population in situations of social vulnerability (the poor, minorities and women, among others) and other priority care groups, notably older adults, children and persons with disabilities.[129]

While these two comments on Principle 11 address vertical inequality, they focus more particularly on poverty and nondiscrimination against vulnerable and disadvantaged groups. The idea that vertical inequality alone is a threat to human rights is largely unaddressed. Further, the commentary merely warns against deepening economic inequality rather than calling for States to ensure that economic reforms reduce vertical inequalities where they are adversely impacting on human rights. Additionally, economic reforms to reduce vertical inequalities extend well beyond taxation and other fiscal policies. Labour policies and cash transfers are crucial to reduce inequalities, as well as investment in education and healthcare, as the Independent Expert noted in his 2016 report on economic inequality.[130] While addressing these issues, the *Guiding Principles* do not do so in the context of reducing vertical inequalities.

In sum, the *Guiding Principles* do not set out an agenda for economic policy reforms to address the causes and consequences of extreme vertical inequalities in income and wealth as presented in the Independent Expert's 2016 report. Overall, the *Guiding Principles* focus largely on economic crises, examining the role of economic reforms as both their preventive and reactive functions, as opposed to taking a proactive stance, addressing the current, persistent and growing vertical inequalities within countries. While vertical inequalities have been identified as one of the greatest human rights challenges of our time – as they prevent the full realisation of human rights, cause economic and political instability, and undermine democracy – the *Guiding Principles on Human Rights Impact Assessments of Economic Reforms* say disappointingly little about them.

The Human Rights Council took 'note with appreciation' of the *Guiding Principles*, requested that the High Commissioner for Human Rights disseminate them and encouraged governments, UN entities, NGOs and the private sector to take them into account in formulating and implementing economic reforms. In doing so, the Human Rights Council emphasised 'that inequality continues to increase worldwide, and that it often contributes to social exclusion of certain groups and individuals'.[131]

Both the Human Rights Council and the Independent Expert consider vertical inequalities in conjunction with HRIA of economic reform policies – but just in passing. This is not surprising. As international human rights law has yet to include specific norms and standards on vertical inequality, reducing vertical inequality is not enumerated as a legal obligation of States in the *Guiding Principles* and is only briefly identified as a policy concern for HRIA. Nonetheless, the extreme vertical inequalities today are resulting in economic, social and political instability in many countries, undermining democracy, and preventing the full enjoyment of human rights. An HRIA of economic reforms might, therefore, usefully focus on the progressive realisation of human rights by reducing vertical inequalities, in addition to preventing retrogressive measures. Indeed, the Independent Expert's 2017 report states:

> While the guiding principles will focus on important policies and processes that governments put in place in the immediate aftermath of a crisis, it is equally important to consider the measures that governments take in the medium and longer term to build resilience, even during healthy economic times.[132]

The *Guiding Principles* build on this idea, stating that they apply not just to acute economic crises and medium-term economic reforms, but also to 'longer-term processes, such as systematic review of public budgets and their distributional assessments, cumulative and long-term effects of fiscal consolidation measures on human rights, of the effects of labour market reforms'.[133] Such systematic and regularly scheduled HRIAs should include a focus on reducing the vertical inequalities that prevent the full enjoyment human rights. Indeed, a new *Principle* that focuses specifically on reducing economic inequality would be a helpful addition to the *Guiding Principles*. This *Principle* would propose that State parties measure and track economic inequalities over time, as they are required to do for their reports to the CESCR, and that HRIA of economic reforms include careful consideration of the impact of any proposal on vertical inequalities and their impacts on human rights.

Moving forward, human rights mechanisms, scholars and practitioners must develop human rights norms and standards on vertical inequalities and embed these in HRIA and other human rights methodologies and tools. In many ways, human rights mechanisms, scholars and practitioners lower human rights standards when they demand only that States ensure that situations do not get worse – non-retrogression. For many people around the world, the situation is already dire. Having identified vertical inequality as a pressing human rights challenge in the era of the SDGs, it is incumbent on the human rights community to consider more deeply the role that human rights can play in bringing about an economic, political and social environment more conducive to greater vertical equality, enabling the full enjoyment human rights.

5. Conclusion

The global community has recognised that the extreme and growing vertical inequalities in the world today are alarming – and harmful. They require our full attention. By adopting SDG 10 – reduce inequality within and between countries – the UN General Assembly launched an agenda to address this global challenge. Yet, as High Commissioner Bachelet has pointed out, the SDG 10 targets do not provide any benchmark or deadline for reduction in vertical inequality.[134] International human rights law is also lagging in supporting an agenda to reduce economic inequalities. To date, the human rights mechanisms have not interpreted international human rights law to place any limits on income or wealth inequality. While recognising that extreme economic inequalities adversely impact human rights, they have not ventured to construe any of the multiple equality provisions in the International Bill of Human Rights to address this threat to the full realisation of human rights for all. There is ample language in international human rights law from which such standards might be drawn.[135] As Alston stated, 'Formal recognition of the fact that there are limits of some sort to the degree of inequality that can be reconciled with notions of equality, dignity and commitments to human rights for everyone would be an important step forward.'[136]

The *Guiding Principles on Human Rights Impact Assessments of Economic Reforms* is an opportune place to promote an examination of vertical inequalities that adversely impact on human rights as well as for State parties to find guidance on assessing proposed policies to ensure that (1) they do not increase vertical inequalities, and (2) they reduce vertical inequalities that may be adversely impacting human rights. Like the SDG 10 targets, and the work of the human rights mechanisms on vertical inequality, the *Guiding Principles* fail to provide adequate norms, standards, benchmarks, measures or guidance for State parties on reducing vertical inequality. This missing piece in the *Guiding Principles* – and the SDG framework – calls for States to incorporate an additional *Principle* on reducing vertical inequalities when carrying out HRIA of economic policy reforms.

Since the adoption of SDG 10 in 2015 and the promulgation of the *Guiding Principles* in 2018, economic inequality has worsened considerably due to the COVID-19 pandemic and the consequent massive increase in unemployment and retraction of the economy. There is now an urgent need to improve the SDG 10 framework to address vertical inequalities – beyond the single new indicator added in 2020 – and for human right mechanisms to establish standards on the level of vertical inequalities that can be consistent with 'equal rights and dignity for all'. As former UN Independent Expert Bohoslavsky recently stated, 'the concerted action taken in the face of the COVID-19 crisis demonstrates that coordinated action and a rapid change in policy and practice is possible to face global challenges'.[137] The consequent economic crisis also provides the opportunity to rebuild economies so that promoting greater vertical equality is a central *Guiding Principle* in line with the spirit, if not the targets, of SDG 10. Progress on many other SDGs and on economic and social rights may well result in reducing absolute poverty, however, none of these approaches will address the problem of the great disparity between the 99% and the 1%. It is long overdue to do so.

Notes

1. Micah White, 'Opinion: I Co-Founded Occupy Wall Street. Now I'm headed to Davos. Why?', *The Guardian*, January 18, 2020, https://www.theguardian.com/commentisfree/2020/jan/18/occupy-wall-street-davos (accessed February 24, 2020).
2. Ibid.; see also Martha F. Davis, 'Occupy Wall Street and International Human Rights', *Fordham Urban Law Journal* 39, no. 34 (2012): 931–58; Simon Thorpe, 'Rights, Constitution and Radical Democracy in Occupy Wall Street and Occupy London', *Birkbeck Law Review* 1, no. 2 (2013): 225–80; M. Patrick Yingling, 'Civil Disobediance to Overcome Corruption: The Case of Occupy Wall Street', *Indiana Journal of Law & Social Equality* 4, no. 2 (2016): 121–34.
3. Thomas Piketty, *Capital in the Twenty-First Century* (Cambridge, MA: Harvard University Press, 2013); Anthony Atkinson, *Inequality: What Can be Done?* (Cambridge, MA: Harvard University Press, 2015).
4. World Inequality Lab, https://wid.world/world-inequality-lab/ (accessed February 24, 2020).
5. Facundo Alvaredo, Lucas Chanel, Thomas Piketty, Emmanuel Saez and Gabriel Zucman, *World Inequality Report 2018* (World Inequality Lab), https://wir2018.wid.world/files/download/wir2018-summary-english.pdf (accessed February 25, 2020).
6. Richard Wilkinson, *The Impact of Inequality: How to Make Sick Societies Healthier* (Abingdon: Routledge, 2005); Richard Wilkinson and Kate Pickett, *The Spirit Level: Why More Equal Societies Almost Always Do Better* (London: Allen Lane, 2009).
7. Oxfam, 'Press Release: World's Billionaires Have More Wealth than 4.6 Billion People', January 20, 2020, https://www.oxfam.org/en/press-releases/worlds-billionaires-have-more-wealth-46-billion-people (accessed March 3, 2020).
8. Diane Elson, 'Gender Justice, Human Rights, and Neoliberal Economic Policies', in *Gender Justice, Development, and* Rights, ed. Maxine Molyneux and Shahra Razavi (Oxford; Oxford University Press, 2002), 78–114, 81; David Harvey, *A Brief History of Neoliberalism* (Oxford: Oxford University Press, 2005), 23–6; Gillian MacNaughton and Diane F. Frey, 'Introduction', in *Economic and Social Rights in a Neoliberal World*, ed. Gillian MacNaughton and Diane F. Frey (Cambridge: Cambridge University Press, 2018), 1–23, 6.
9. 'Forbes Publishes 34th Annual List of Global Billionaires', *Forbes*, April 7, 2020, https://www.forbes.com/sites/forbespr/2020/04/07/forbes-publishes-34th-annual-list-of-global-billionaires/#5ec2604f3edf (accessed May 23, 2020).
10. World Bank, *Piecing Together the Poverty Puzzle* (Washington, DC: World Bank Group, 2018), 7. The World Bank has not updated its data on the number of people living below $5.50 since this report. See World Bank, *Povcalnet*, http://iresearch.worldbank.org/PovcalNet/povDuplicateWB.aspx (accessed May 23, 2020).

11. Lawrence Mishel and Julia Wolfe, 'CEO Compensation has Grown 940% Since 1978: Typical Worker Compensation has risen only 12% During that Time' (Washington, DC: Economic Policy Institute, August 14, 2019), 4.
12. Ibid.
13. Ibid., 3.
14. Ibid., 1
15. Chuck Collins, *US Billionaire Wealth Surges to $584 Billion, or 20%, Since the Beginning of the Pandemic* (Washington, DC: Institute for Policy Studies, June 18, 2020), https://ips-dc.org/us-billionaire-wealth-584-billion-20-percent-pandemic/ (accessed August 6, 2020).
16. United Nations Development Program (UNDP), *Beyond Income, Beyond Averages, Beyond Today: Inequalities in Human Development in the 21st Century – Human Development Report 2019* (Pedro Conceição, lead author) (New York: UNDP, 2019), 5–11.
17. Ibid., 11.
18. Ibid.
19. International Labour Organization, *Global Wage Report 2016/2017: Wage Inequality in the Workplace* (Geneva: International Labour Office, 2016); UN Department of Economic and Social Affairs (DESA), *Inequality in a Rapidly Changing World: World Social Report 2020* (New York: United Nations, 2020); UN Department of Economic and Social Affairs (DESA), *Inequality Matters: Report of the World Social Situation 2013* (New York: United Nations, 2013); UNESCO, *Challenging Inequalities: Pathways to a Just World, Social Science Report 2016* (Paris: UNESCO, 2016); see also UNDP, *Humanity Divided: Confronting Inequality in Developing Countries* (New York: UNDP, 2013).
20. UNDP, *Inequalities in Human Development*, chapter 3 (income and wealth) and chapter 4 (gender).
21. World Bank, *Taking on Inequality: Poverty and Shared Prosperity 2016* (Washington, DC: World Bank, 2016); International Monetary Fund (IMF), 'IMF's Work on Inequality', https://www.imf.org/external/np/fad/inequality/ (accessed May 27, 2020).
22. IMF, 'IMF's Work on Inequality'.
23. UNGA, *Transforming Our World: The 2030 Agenda for Sustainable Development*, UN Doc. A/RES/70/1 (October 21, 2015), 14.
24. Ibid.
25. See for example Philip Alston and Nikki Reisch, *Tax, Inequality and Human Rights* (New York: Oxford University Press 2019); Rodrigo Uprimny Yepes and Sergio Chaparro Hernádez, 'Inequality, Human Rights, and Social Rights: Tensions and Complementarities', *Humanity* 10, no. 3 (2019): 376–94; Radhika Balakrishnan and James Heintz, 'Human Rights in an Unequal World: Structural Inequalities and the Imperative for Global Cooperation', *Humanity* 10, no. 3 (2019): 395–403; Samuel Moyn, *Not Enough: Human Rights in an Unequal World* (Cambridge, MA: Belknap Press, 2018); Juan Pablo Bohoslavsky, 'Economic Inequality, Debt Crisis and Human Rights', *The Yale Journal of International Law Online* 41, no. 2 (2016): 177–99; Center for Economic and Social Rights, 'From Disparity to Dignity: Tackling Economic Inequality through the Sustainable Development Goals' (2016), https://www.cesr.org/sites/default/files/disparity_to_dignity_SDG10.pdf (accessed Mary 25, 2020); Samuel Moyn, 'A Powerless Companion: Human Rights in the Age of Neoliberalism', *Law & Contemporary Problems* 77, no. 4 (2014): 147–69; Gillian MacNaughton, 'Beyond a Minimum Threshold: The Right to Social Equality', in *The State of Economic and Social Human Rights: A Global Overview*, ed. Lanse Minkler (Cambridge, UK: Cambridge University Press 2013); Radhika Balakrishnan and Diane Elson, eds., *Economic Policy and Human Rights: Holding Governments to Account* (London: Zed Books, 2011).
26. The Expert Group Meeting on SDG 10 was one of a series of consultations that took place in preparation for the July 2019 session of the UN High-level Political Forum on Sustainable Development, which conducted an in-depth review of SDGs 4, 8, 10, 13, 16 and 17. SDG Knowledge Hub, https://sdg.iisd.org/events/expert-group-meeting-on-sdg-10/ (accessed May 24, 2020).

27. Michelle Bachelet, 'Keynote Statement by UN High Commissioner for Human Rights Michelle Bachelet', Expert Meeting on Reducing Inequalities: SDG 10 Progress and Prospects (Geneva, April 2, 2019).
28. See for example Committee on Economic, Social and Cultural Rights (CESCR), 'Concluding Observations: Bolivia 2008', UN Doc E/C.12/BOL/CO/2 (August 8, 2008), paras 14 and 27 (a); CESCR, 'Concluding Observations: Brazil 2009', UN Doc E/C.12/BRA/CO/2 (June 12, 2009), para. 10; CESCR, 'Concluding Observations: China 2014', UN Doc E/C.12/CHN/CO/2 (June 13, 2014), para. 48; CESCR, 'Concluding Observations: Costa Rica 2016', UN Doc E/C.12/CRI/CO/5 (October 21, 2016), paras 14–5.
29. CESCR, 'The Pledge to Leave No One Behind: The International Covenant on Economic, Social and Cultural Rights and the 2030 Agenda for Sustainable Development', Statement by the Committee on Economic, Social and Cultural Rights, UN Doc. E/C.12/2019/1 (April 5, 2019), para. 5.
30. Philip Alston, 'Report of the Special Rapporteur on Extreme Poverty and Human Rights', UN Doc. A/HRC/29/31 (May 27, 2015); Juan Pablo Bohoslavsky, 'Report of the Independent Expert on the Effects of Foreign Debt and Other Related International Financial Obligations of States on the Full Enjoyment of Human Rights, Particularly Economic, Social and Cultural Rights', UN Doc. A/HRC/31/60 (January 12, 2016). See also Magdalena Sepúlveda Carmona, 'Report of the Special Rapporteur on Extreme Poverty and Human Rights', UN Doc. A/HRC/26/28 (May 22, 2014); Olivier De Schutter, 'Tackling Extreme Poverty in Times of Crisis: Key Challenges Facing the Fight Against Poverty and Priorities for the Special Rapporteur on Extreme Poverty and Human Rights' (May 1, 2020).
31. Bachelet, 'Keynote Statement 2019'.
32. International Covenant on Economic, Social and Cultural Rights (ICESCR) (1966), https://www.ohchr.org/EN/ProfessionalInterest/Pages/CESCR.aspx (accessed February 29, 2020), art. 2(1); Committee on Economic, Social and Cultural Rights, 'General Comment 3: The Nature of the States Parties Obligations (Art 2, par. 1)' (December 14, 1990), para. 2, https://tbinternet.ohchr.org/_layouts/15/treatybodyexternal/Download.aspx?symbolno=INT%2fCESCR%2fGEC%2f4758&Lang=en (accessed March 1, 2020).
33. Navanethem Pillay, 'Report of the High Commissioner for Human Rights on the Implementation of Economic, Social and Cultural Rights' UN Doc. E/2009/90 (June 8, 2009), para. 35.
34. Juan Pablo Bohoslavsky, *Guiding Principles on Human Rights Impact Assessment: Report of the Independent Expert on the Effects of Foreign Debt and Other Related Financial Obligations of States on the Full Enjoyment of Human Rights, Particularly Economic, Social and Cultural Rights*, UN Doc. A/HRC/40/57 (December 19, 2018).
35. Ibid., para. 2.
36. Alston, UN HRC Report 2015, para. 7; Ignacio Saiz and Kate Donald, 'Tackling Inequality Through the Sustainable Development Goals: Human Rights in Practice', *International Journal of Human Rights* 21, no. 8 (2017): 1029–49, 1031.
37. Radhika Balakrishnan, James Heintz, and Diane Elson, *Rethinking Economic Policy for Social Justice: The Radical Potential of Human Rights* (Abingdon: Routledge 2016), 32.
38. Ibid.; Saiz and Donald, 'Tackling Inequality', 1031.
39. The Gini Index is a measure of inequality between 0 (total equality – everyone has the same income or wealth) and 1 (total inequality – one person has all the income or wealth). Although the Gini Index is frequently used by economists, it is not easily understood by the general public or by policymakers, Alvaredo et al, *World Inequality Report 2018*, 27. People do not intuitively understand the difference between a Gini of 0.24 (most equal country – Slovenia) and 0.62 (most unequal country – South Africa). OECD, Income Inequality, https://data.oecd.org/inequality/income-inequality.htm (accessed May 25, 2020). The Palma ratio is more easily understandable, and other similar ratios of income or wealth deciles – such as comparisons of income or wealth deciles to social outcomes – are also useful for measuring and communicating relevant information on changes in vertical inequalities to policymakers and the general public.

40. Oxfam, 'Time to Care: Unpaid and Underpaid work and the Global Inequality Crisis' (Boston: Oxfam, January 2020), 9, https://oxfamilibrary.openrepository.com/bitstream/handle/10546/620928/bp-time-to-care-inequality-200120-en.pdf (accessed March 3, 2020).
41. Ibid., 8.
42. Ibid., 8.
43. Ibid.,19
44. Alvaredo et al, *World Inequality Report 2018*, 9.
45. Ibid., 9–10.
46. Ibid., 9.
47. Ibid., 10.
48. Ibid., 9
49. UNDP, *Human Development Report 2019*, 30.
50. Ibid., 30.
51. Ibid., 7.
52. Ibid., 42, 51.
53. Ibid., 52.
54. DESA, *Inequality Matters*, 63.
55. Ibid., 66.
56. Ibid., 64.
57. Richard Wilkinson and Kate Pickett, *The Inner Level: How More Equal Societies Reduce Stress, Restore Sanity and Improve Everyone's Wellbeing* (New York: Penguin Press, 2019), 41–67.
58. DESA, *Inequality Matters*, 70.
59. Bohoslavsky, 'Economic Inequality, Debt Crisis', 183.
60. DESA, *Inequality Matters*, 70; Balakrishnan, Heintz, and Elson, *Rethinking Economic Policy*, 43.
61. Ibid., 72.
62. UNGA, *The 2030 Agenda*, 21, 21 (targets 10.2 and 10.3).
63. Ibid., 21 (targets 10.5, 10.6, 10.7, 10.b, 10.c).
64. Edward Anderson, 'Equality as a Global Goal', *Ethics and International Affairs* 30, no. 2 (2016): 189–200, 194; Saiz and Donald, 'Tackling Inequality', 1032; Sakiko Fukuda-Parr, 'Keeping Out Extreme Inequality from the SDG Agenda – The Politics of Indicators', *Global Policy* 10, supp. 1 (2019): 61–9, 61.
65. UNGA, *The 2030 Agenda*, 21 (target 10.1).
66. Fukuda-Parr, 'Keeping Out Extreme Inequality', 61.
67. UNGA, The 2030 Agenda, 21 (target 10.4).
68. See, for example, Anderson, 'Equality as a Global Goal'; Saiz and Donald, 'Tackling Inequality'; Fukuda-Parr, 'Keeping Out Extreme Inequality'; Gillian MacNaughton, 'Vertical Inequalities: Are the SDGs and Human Rights Up to the Challenges?' *Journal of International Human Rights* 21, no. 8 (2017): 1050–72; Faiza Shaheen, 'Inequality Within and Among Countries', in *International Norms, Normative Change and the UN Sustainable Development Goals*, ed. Noha Shawki (Landham, MD: Lexington Books, 2016), 99–113; Katja Feistein and Bettina Mahlert, 'The Potential for Tackling Inequalitiy in the Sustainable Development Goals', *Third World Quarterly* 37, no. 12 (2016): 2139–55; Kate Donald, 'Will Inequality Get Left Behind in the 2030 Agenda?' in *Spotlight on Sustainable Development 2016*, Report by the Reflection Group on the 2030 Agenda for Sustainable Development, 80–6, https://www.2030spotlight.org/sites/default/files/contentpix/spotlight/Agenda-2030-en_web_accessible.pdf (accessed May 25, 2020).
69. Bachelet, 'Keynote Statement 2019'.
70. Ibid.
71. Inter-Agency and Expert Group on SDG Indicators, Global Indicator Framework for the Sustainable Development Goals and Targets of the 2030 Agenda for Sustainable Development, UN Doc. A/RES/71/313, as amended by UN Docs, E/C.3/2018/2, E/CN.3/2019/2, E/CN.3/2020/2 (2020), at 10, https://unstats.un.org/sdgs/indicators/indicators-list/.

72. Charter of the United Nations (1945), https://www.un.org/en/sections/un-charter/un-charter-full-text/, (accessed February 29, 2020), art1(3); see also art 55.
73. Universal Declaration of Human Rights (1948), https://www.un.org/en/universal-declaration-human-rights/index.html, art. 2.
74. International Covenant on Economic, Social and Cultural Rights (ICESCR) (1966), https://www.ohchr.org/EN/ProfessionalInterest/Pages/CESCR.aspx, art. 2; International Covenant on Civil and Political Rights (ICCPR) (1966), https://www.ohchr.org/EN/ProfessionalInterest/Pages/CCPR.aspx, art. 2.
75. International Convention on the Elimination of All Forms of Racial Discrimination (1965), https://www.ohchr.org/EN/ProfessionalInterest/Pages/CEDAW.aspx; Convention on the Elimination of All Forms of Discrimination Against Women (1979), https://www.ohchr.org/EN/ProfessionalInterest/Pages/CEDAW.aspx.
76. See for example Johannes Morsink, *The Universal Declaration of Human Rights: Origins, Drafting and Intent* (Philadelphia: University of Pennsylvania, 1999), 45 ('nondiscrimination and equality are two sides of the same coin'); Paul Hunt, *Reclaiming Social Rights: International and Comparative Perspectives* (Aldershot: Dartmouth, 1996), 92 ('these two principles are closely related: they are reciprocal, two sides of the same coin').
77. Gillian MacNaughton, 'Equality Rights Beyond Neoliberal Constraints', in *Economic and Social Rights in a Neoliberal World*, ed. Gillian MacNaughton and Diane F. Frey (Cambridge, UK: Cambridge University Press, 2018), 103–23.
78. Alston, UN HRC Report 2015, para. 55 (the right to equality needs to be given greater attention so that it is able to develop notions of distributive equality); Moyn, *Not Enough*, 10 (challenging human rights advocates to supplement sufficiency with distributive equality in theory and practice); Sakiko Fukuda-Parr, 'It's About Values: Human Rights Norms and Tolerance for Inequality', OpenGlobalRights, https://www.openglobalrights.org/its-about-values-human-rights-norms-and-tolerance-for-inequality/ ('What is needed now is a more coherent articulation of human rights norms and inequality as injustice, which is currently underdeveloped if not entirely absent.')
79. See for example Alston, 'UN HRC Report 2015', para. 54; Balakkrishnan, Heintz, and Elson, *Rethinking Economic Policy*, 47; Uprimny Yepes and Chaparro Hernández, 'Inequality, Human Rights', 382.
80. Alston 'UN HRC Report 2015', para. 54 ('At present, there is no explicitly stated right to equality, as such under international human rights law.').
81. Exceptions include, for example, Danilo Türk, 'The Realization of Economic, Social and Cultural Rights: Final Report Submitted by Mr. Danilo Türk, Special Rapporteur', UN Doc. E/CN.4/Sub.2/1992/16 (July 3, 1992), paras 76–84; Asbjørn Eide, 'Preparatory Document on the Relationship Between the Enjoyment of Human Rights, in Particular Economic, Social and Cultural Rights, and Income Distribution, Prepared by Mr. Asbjørn Eide in Accordance with Sub-Commission Resolution 1993/40', UN Doc. E/CN.4/Sub.2/1994/21 (July 5, 1994); José Bengoa, 'The Relationship Between the Enjoyment of Human Rights, in Particular Economic, Social and Cultural Rights, and Income Distribution: Poverty, Income Distribution and Globalization: A Challenge for Human Rights', UN Doc. E/CN.4/Sub 2/1998/8 (June 10, 1998).
82. Moyn, 'A Powerless Companion'; Mary Nolan, 'Human Rights and Market Fundamentalism in the Long 1970s', in *Toward a New Moral World Order? Menschenrechtspolitik und Völkerrecht seit 1945*, ed. Norbert Frei and Annette Weinke (Göttingen: Wallstein Verlag, 2014), 172–81; MacNaughton and Frey, 'Introduction'.
83. Sepúlveda Carmona, 'UN HRC Report 2014', paras 36–53; Alston, 'UN HRC Report 2015', para. 26; Bohoslavsky, 'UN HRC Report 2016', para. 14; Bachelet, 'Keynote Statement 2019'; Balakrishnan, Heintz, and Elson, *Rethinking Economic Policy*, 39–42; Saiz and Donald, 'Tackling Inequality', 1031–2; Alston and Reisch, *Tax, Inequality*, 24; Daniel Brinks, Julia Dehm and Karen Engle, 'Introduction: Human Rights and Economic Inequality', *Humanity* 10, no. 3 (2020): 363–75.
84. Balakrishnan, Heintz, and Elson, *Rethinking Economic Policy*, 48.
85. Bohoslavsky, 'Economic Inequality, Debt', 177.

86. Ibid.
87. CESCR, 'The Pledge 2019', para. 5.
88. The Harmonized Guidelines for reporting to the UN treaty bodies have called for reporting on the Gini coefficient since at least 2009. Compilation of Guidelines on the Form and Content of Reports to be Submitted by the States Parties to the International Treaties, Report of the Secretary General, UN Doc. HRI/GEN/2/Rev.6 (June 3, 2009).
89. Balakrishnan, Heintz, and Elson, *Rethinking Economic Policy*, 48; Bohoslavsky, 'Economic Inequality, Debt', 177–8.
90. ICESCR, art. 2(1).
91. Paul Hunt, 'Report of the Special Rapporteur on the Right of Everyone to the Enjoyment of the Highest Attainable Standard of Physical and Mental Health', UN Doc. A/62/214 (August 8, 2007), para. 37.
92. Pillay, Report of the High Commissioner 2009, para. 35.
93. Hunt, 'UNGA Report 2007', para. 40; Olivier De Schutter, 'Guiding Principles on Human Rights Impact Assessment of Trade and Investment Agreements', Report of the Special Rapporteur on the Right to Food, Olivier De Schutter, UN Doc. A/HRC/19/59/Add.5 (December 19, 2011), Principle 4.
94. Hunt, 'UNGA Report 2007', para. 40; Gauthier De Beco, 'Human Rights Impact Assessment', *Netherlands Quarterly of Human Rights* 27, no. 2 (2009): 139–66, 147.
95. Kofi Annan, 'Report of the Secretary General: Question of the Realization in All Countries of the Economic, Social and Cultural Rights Contained in the Universal Declaration of Human Rights and the Study of Special Problems which the Developing Countries Face in their Efforts to Achieve these Human Rights', UN Doc. E.CN.4/1334 (January 2, 1979), para. 314.
96. Simon Walker, 'Human Rights Impact Assessment: Emerging Practice and Challenges', in *Economic, Social and Cultural Rights in International Law: Contemporary Issues and Challenges*, ed. Eibe Riedel, Gilles Giacca, and Christophe Golay (Oxford: Oxford University Press, 2014), 391–414.
97. CESCR, 'General Comment 2: International Technical Assistance Measures (Art. 22)', UN Doc. E/1990/23, annex III at 86, February 2, 1990, para. 8(b).
98. Lawrence Gostin and Jonathan M. Mann, 'Towards the Development of a Human Rights Impact Assessment for the Formulation and Evaluation of Public Health Policies', *Health and Human Rights Journal* 1, no. 1 (1994), 58–80; Lawrence Gostin and Zita Lazzarini, 'Human Rights Impact Assessment', in *Human Rights and Public Health in the AIDS Pandemic* (New York: Oxford University Press, 1997), 57–67.
99. Katarina Tomasevski, 'Background Paper submitted by Ms. Katarina Tomasevski, Special Rapporteur on the Right to Education of the Commission on Human Rights', Day of General Discussion: Right to Education (Articles 13 and 14 of the Covenant), Geneva, October 7, 1998, para. 10.
100. Hunt, 'UN GA Report 2007', paras 33–44; see also Paul Hunt and Gillian MacNaughton, 'Impact Assessments, Poverty and Human Rights: A Case Study Using the Right to the Highest Attainable Standard of Health', Health and Human Rights Working Paper Series No. 6, World Health Organization and UNESCO (2006), https://www.who.int/hhr/Series_6_Impact%20Assessments_Hunt_MacNaughton1.pdf (accessed March 7, 2020).
101. De Schutter, 'Guiding Principles'.
102. Juan Pablo Bohoslavsky, 'Developing Guiding Principles for Assessing the Human Rights Impact of Economic Reform Policies', Report of the Independent Expert on the Effects of Debt and Other Related Financial Obligations of States on the Full Enjoyment of All Human Rights, Particularly Economic, Social and Cultural Rights, UN Doc. A/HRC/37/54 (December 20, 2017).
103. Hunt, 'UNGA Report 2007', para. 33; see also De Schutter, 'Guiding Principles', 5 (Principle I: The duty to prepare human rights impact assessments of trade and investment agreements).
104. Hunt, 'UNGA Report 2007', para. 44.

105. Committee on the Rights of the Child (CRC), 'General Comment 5: General Measures of Implementation of the Convention on the Rights of the Child' (Art. 4, 42, and 44, para. 6), UN Doc. CRC?GC/2003/5(2003), para. 45 (emphasis added).
106. CESCR, 'Conclusions and Recommendations, United Kingdom of Great Britain and Northern Ireland', UN Doc. E/C.12/1/Add.19 (1997), para. 33. See also CESCR, 'Concluding Observations: South Africa', UN Doc E/C.12/ZAF/CO/1 (29 November 2018), para. 16; CESCR, 'Concluding Observations: Canada', UN Doc E/C.12/CAN/CO/6 (23 March 2016), para. 54; CESCR, 'Concluding Observations: China', UN Doc. E/C.12/CHN/CO/2 (13 June 2014), para. 12; CESCR, 'Concluding Observations: Austria', UN Doc E/C.12/AUT/CO/4 (13 December 2013), para. 11; CESCR, 'Concluding Observations: Costa Rica', UN Doc E/C.12/CRI/CO/4 (4 January 2008), para. 48; CESCR, 'Concluding Observations: Ecuador', UN Doc. E/C.12/1/Add.100 (7 June 2004), para. 55; CESCR, 'Concluding Observations: Germany', UN Doc E/C.12/1/Add.68 (2001), para. 32.
107. CESCR, 'Public Debt, austerity measures and the International Covenant on Economic, Social and Cultural Rights', Statement by the Committee on Economic, Social and Cultural Rights, UN Doc. E/C.12/2016/1 (July 22, 2016), para. 11.
108. See for example Hunt, 'UNGA Report 2007', para. 41; De Schutter, 'Guiding Principles', 14; Walker, 'Human Rights Impact Assessments', 401; Saskia Bakker, Marieke Van Den Berg, Deniz Düzenli, and Marike Radstaake, 'Human Rights Impact Assessment in Practice: The Case of the Health Rights of Women Assessment Instrument (HeRWAI)', *Journal of Human Rights Practice* 1, no. 3 (2009): 436–58, 444; Center for Economic and Social Rights (CESR), 'Assessing Austerity: Monitoring the Human Rights Impacts of Fiscal Consolidation', Briefing February 2018, 32, https://www.cesr.org/sites/default/files/Austerity-Report-Online2018.FINAL_.pdf (accessed March 7, 2020).
109. See for example De Schutter, 'Guiding Principles', Principle 5(a). In many cases, this will involve setting out the human rights obligations of the State. However, if the State has not ratified the necessary instrument, the normative content of the right may still be used to carry out the assessment. For example, although the United States has not ratified the ICESCR, an HRIA may be done in the United States using the content of the right to health as the human rights standards to demonstrate the extent to which a proposed policy would violate the right to health as set forth in the UDHR upon which all UN members are obliged to report in the Universal Periodic Review. As an advocacy and mobilization tool, the HRIA could still be very effective.
110. See for example Bohoslavsky, 'Economic Inequality, Debt', 177–8; Alston, 'UN HRC Report 2015', para. 16.
111. Human Rights Council (HRC), 'Mandate of the Independent Expert on the Effects of Foreign Debt and Other Related International Financial Obligations of States on the Full Enjoyment of All Human Rights, Particularly Economic, Social and Cultural Rights', Resolution Adopted by the Human Rights Council on 23 Mach 2017', UN Doc. A/HRC/RES/34/3 (April 6, 2017), para. 13.
112. The HRC resolution does not include any of these words: inequalities, inequality, equal, unequal, or equality. Further, it does not address the concept of vertical inequality in other terms – such as disparity between rich and poor.
113. Bohoslavsky, 'UN HRC Report 2017', para. 72.
114. Ibid., paras. 57, 62.
115. Ibid., para. 78(c)(i).
116. Ibid., para. 34.
117. Ibid., para. 34; see Juan Pablo Bohoslavsky, 'Report of the Independent Expert on the Effects of Foreign Debt and Other Related International Financial Obligations of States on the Full Enjoyment of Human Rights, Particularly Economic, Social and Cultural Rights', UN Doc. A/HRC/31/60 (January 12, 2016).
118. Bohoslavsky, 'UN HRC Report 2016', para. 37.
119. Ibid., para. 56.
120. Ibid., para. 56.

121. Bohoslavsky, *Guiding Principles*, Principle 2, 5.
122. Ibid.
123. Bohoslavsky, *Guiding Principles*, Principle 3, 5.
124. Ibid., 6–10.
125. Bohoslavsky, *Guiding Principles*, Principle 11, 11.
126. Balakrishnan, Heintz and Elson, *Rethinking Economic Policy*, 48; Bohoslavsky, 'Economic Inequality, Debt', 177–8; Alston, 'UN HRC Report 2015', para. 16.
127. Bohoslavsky, *Guiding Principles*, Principle 11, 11.
128. Ibid., Commentary, para. 11(2), 11.
129. Ibid., Commentary 11(2) and 11(3), 12 (emphasis added).
130. Bohoslavsky, 'UN HRC Report 2016', paras 58, 66 and 68.
131. Human Rights Council, 'Resolution Adopted by the Human Rights Council on 21 March 2019', UN Doc. A/HRC/RES/40/8 (April 5, 2019).
132. Bohoslavsky, 'UN HRC Report 2017', para. 76.
133. Bohoslavsky, *Guiding Principles*, 4 (Principle 1, Commentary 1(2)).
134. Bachelet, 'Keynote Statement on Reducing Inequalities 2019'.
135. MacNaughton, 'Equality Rights Beyond Neoliberal Constraints', 116–8.
136. Alston, 'UN HRC Report 2015', para. 48.
137. Juan Pablo Bohoslavsky, 'COVID-19: Urgent Appeal for a Human Rights Response to the Economic Recession', Report of the Independent Expert on the Effects of Foreign Debt and Other Related International Financial Obligations of States on the Full Enjoyment of All Human Rights, Particularly Economic, Social and Cultural Rights, Geneva, OHCHR, April 15, 2020.

Acknowledgements

I wish to thank the editors of this special issue and an anonymous reviewer for their helpful comments on an earlier draft of this article.

Disclosure statement

No potential conflict of interest was reported by the author(s).

ORCID

Gillian MacNaughton http://orcid.org/0000-0002-4715-5072

Ex ante children's rights impact assessment of economic policy

Simon Hoffman

ABSTRACT
This article focuses on *ex ante* Child Rights Impact Assessment (CRIA) as a sub-set of Human Rights Impact Assessment (HRIA). CRIA is recommended by the Committee on the Rights of the Child to predict the likely impact of proposals for legislation or policy on children's rights guaranteed by the UN Convention on the Rights of the Child. While *ex post* evaluation of outcomes is also recommended, the Committee emphasises the importance of prospective assessment to help ensure that legislation, policy and delivery of government programmes respect children's rights. This article will demonstrate why CRIA is suitable to predict the likely impact of proposals for economic policy on the human rights of children. It discusses core elements of CRIA procedure and examines CRIA in practice, drawing on experience in seven states where the assessment has been introduced at some level of government: Belgium, Bosnia–Herzegovina, Canada, Ireland, Sweden, New Zealand and the UK. This will provide insights into methodological approaches as well as challenges likely to affect CRIA of economic programmes. The core elements of CRIA and HRIA procedure are comparable, and so the article contributes to better understanding HRIA of economic policy generally.

Introduction

The Human Rights Council (HRC) *Guiding Principles on Human Rights Impact Assessment of Economic Reforms* (*Guiding Principles*) emphasise the importance of systematic Human Rights Impact Assessment (HRIA) to ensuring that economic policy advances human rights, and, in particular, to assessing how economic programmes protect the human rights of the most vulnerable.[1] The *Guiding Principles* refer to both *ex ante* HRIA to assess the 'foreseeable impacts of proposed policy', and *ex post* HRIA to assess the 'actual impacts of policy change and implementation'.[2] This article focuses on Children's Rights Impact Assessment (CRIA) as a sub-set of HRIA. Taking the UN Convention on the Rights of the Child (CRC) as its starting point, CRIA is a procedure to predict the likely impact of policy proposals on the human rights of children aged under 18 years.[3] The UN Committee on the Rights of the Child (the Committee) has recommended that states parties to the CRC carry out predictive *ex ante* 'impact assessment' and retrospective *ex post* 'impact evaluation' to help ensure that legislation, policy and delivery of government programmes respect children's rights.[4] The Committee and other child-rights focussed organisations have sought to emphasise the importance of *ex ante* CRIA to inform the development of policy likely to have a direct or indirect effect on children in order to avoid or mitigate any adverse impact on children's rights.[5]

The article will first introduce CRIA as a procedure to provide government at all levels with advance information to support policy development for the better realisation of children's rights. It will then discuss why CRIA should be applied to economic policy, including budgetary decisions and resource allocation, before turning to the core elements of CRIA procedure, as well as CRIA in practice. While ratification of the CRC is almost universal,[6] adoption of CRIA as a policy tool by government is far from widespread. There are very few states noted in the literature as having adopted CRIA in relation to government policy, whether at national, sub-national or local level. This article therefore examines the experience of CRIA in seven states which are consistently identified as having introduced CRIA at some level to inform policy decision-making: Belgium, Bosnia–Herzegovina, Canada, Ireland, Sweden, New Zealand and the UK. This examination provides a number of insights into methodological approaches and challenges for CRIA of economic policy. As the purpose of and methodological approach to CRIA and HRIA are comparable, the article also contributes to the literature on HRIA of economic policy.

Child rights impact assessment

CRIA is a child-focussed HRIA which pays attention to the rights guaranteed by the CRC as an aspect of the policy development process. While methods vary, CRIA may be described as an in-depth analysis of a proposal for legislation, policy, strategy, programme or budgetary allocation to examine its potential impact on children, to provide an evidential base for policy decision-making, and to develop recommendations for change or adjustment to mitigate or remove any predicted negative impact or to give better effect to children's rights.[7] It is also an opportunity to mainstream consideration of children's rights into policy processes to assist governments (and others) to distinguish children's interests from those of adults.[8] As CRIA is intended to embed the CRC in policy development it should be applied to all policy proposals which are likely to directly or indirectly impact on children introduced by government (at all levels), and should be commenced at an early stage in policy development to allow time for recommendations to be acted on.[9] Proper integration into policy processes will therefore require commitment by government (at all levels) to develop a culture where CRIA is seen as a key aspect of policy decision-making. Government support is also vital to ensure CRIA is properly resourced and that any recommendations which arise from the assessment are given effect.[10]

States parties to the CRC are under no express duty to undertake impact assessment, whether *ex ante* or *ex post*. The *Guiding Principles* suggest that the obligation on states to realise human rights implies a duty to conduct HRIA (Principle 3). This is strongly foregrounded by the work of the Committee which has described 'self-monitoring and evaluation' as an obligation imposed by the CRC, making it abundantly clear that ensuring children's rights are respected in legislation and policy 'demands' a continuous process of CRIA.[11] Concerning economic policy, and in particular budgetary allocation, the Committee urges states to undertake CRIA on public budgeting as an aspect of meeting the obligation under Article 4 of the CRC to give effect to the rights guaranteed to children.[12]

CRIA of economic policy

As a population children are heavily reliant on public services and are therefore likely to suffer adverse impacts when policy fails to protect the most vulnerable groups in society.[13] Despite this, children are often invisible in policy development, and their ability to influence decisions concerning their economic and social rights is limited.[14] This is significant as children as a population group are amongst those most likely to experience hardship and poverty as a result of a reduction in public spending generally, or in discrete policy areas affecting their rights.[15] Children have suffered disproportionately from recent economic reforms driven by austerity and the consequential disinvestment by many states in policy areas such health and education.[16] The Committee is sensitive to the impact of economic policy and reforms on children, and has expressed concern at the negative effects of structural adjustment programmes on children and their families, calling for rigorous monitoring and impact assessment of the effects of economic reforms in order to protect children's economic, social and cultural rights.[17] Consistently, and over an extended period, the Committee has emphasised that economic policies are not child-rights neutral and has urged governments to examine options for reform consistent with the implementation of the CRC.[18] It has emphasised the importance of public budgeting to support the realisation of children's rights and has reminded states of the obligation to 'mobilize, allocate and spend resources' in ways which respect, protect and fulfil those rights.[19] The Committee has also sought to emphasise to states their responsibility to ensure that decisions on resource allocation are taken with the best interests of the child as a primary consideration which should be prioritised at all stages of budgetary decision-making.[20] To protect children from any negative impacts of economic policy or reforms, states will need to examine ways to minimise adverse outcomes and to prioritise the needs of the most vulnerable groups of children, especially where reforms will lead to spending cuts.[21] Where regressive economic measures are contemplated which will have an impact on resource allocation the interests of children should be the last to be affected, especially children in vulnerable situations, and there should not be any compromise of minimum obligations applying to children's rights guaranteed by the CRC, even at times of economic crisis.[22]

In 2007, following a day of general discussion on the responsibilities of states to provide resources for children's rights, the Committee recommended that governments develop 'strong capacity for budget analysis' including CRIA.[23] While there is good reason to assert that the Committee has failed to do enough to link specific budgetary decisions to particular rights,[24] it has sought to offer general guidance on how states should approach public budgeting. In a General Comment on the topic in 2016 the Committee focussed on resource allocation and its impact on children's rights, urging states to adopt rights-based budget analysis and CRIA to examine how (dis)investment in different policy sectors might affect children, recommending that:

> States parties should conduct child rights impact assessments in order to ascertain the effect of legislation, policies and programmes on all children at the national and subnational levels,

> especially children in vulnerable situations who may have special needs and therefore require a disproportionate share of spending in order to have their rights realized. Child rights impact assessments should be part of each stage of the budget process and should complement other monitoring and evaluation efforts.[25]

The potential of CRIA to draw attention to children's rights in policy development, and to protect children from the negative impact of reforms is widely acknowledged. A recent report in 2019, for the Council of Europe (CoE) on protecting children from poverty noted that CRIA is 'regarded as vital to the development of a child rights-compliant approach to policy and budget-related decision-making'.[26] Earlier research in 2015, for the CoE Committee of the Regions on the role of regional and local authorities in safeguarding children from the impacts of austerity also identified CRIA as a key tool to support a child rights approach.[27] And a report from the UN High Commissioner for Human Rights to the Human Rights Council in 2014 noted:

> Children's rights, and those of future generations, must be a primary consideration in the planning and execution of all fiscal policies and budget decisions. ... Child rights impact assessments and evaluations must be conducted so that the likely impact of decisions on children's rights is understood and how far the best interests of the child has been taken into account during decision-making.[28]

Despite this, it is rare for children's interests to be addressed in economic policy or in processes to assess the impact of such policies.[29] The most commonly used tools for assessing the social consequences of economic reforms, for example social impact analysis or budget analysis, rarely pay attention to impacts on children.[30] Few government departments are aware of what resources are allocated to, or what impact government spending has on children's lives.[31] The Committee has therefore called on states to include information on whether governments carry out regular analysis to assess the impact of budgetary allocations on children when periodically reporting on progress toward implementation of the CRC.[32]

In many states implementation of children's rights is often the responsibility of subnational tiers of government.[33] Where resource allocation is carried out by devolved or decentralised government the Committee's General Comment on public budgeting requires that the realisation of children's rights should be prioritised in both national and subnational budgets.[34] In the context of fiscal decentralisation, the Committee has called on national governments to carry out CRIA on policies at sub-national level and to report on how funding allocations by internal levels of government are monitored in order to assess if such allocations are compliant with the state's obligations.[35] This is consistent with the general approach to decentralised governance adopted by UN mechanisms which maintain that national governments are primarily responsible for full compliance with human rights obligations.[36]

CRIA methodological considerations

While CRIA is suggested as a key policy tool for use by governments to help ensure they meet their children's rights obligations, the Committee has not provided a detailed methodological or procedural guide on the conduct of CRIA. While there is increasing interest in HRIA there is no universally agreed HRIA methodology, although a universal feature is the adoption of an explicit human rights normative framework as the standard against which any policy proposal is assessed.[37] The Committee has suggested that CRIA might involve a range of methods, and the *Guiding Principles* state that HRIA should employ a variety of qualitative and quantitative methods.[38] More particular guidance on HRIA has emerged from UN mechanisms[39] and along with the academic and practice literature this confirms a number of essential elements in any human rights focussed impact assessment. These are discussed next, drawing attention as relevant to their application to CRIA of economic policy.

Screening

In the context of economic reforms, the Committee and others such as UNICEF have emphasised that CRIA should be applied to macroeconomic policies as well as to a range of government measures affecting children, including proposals for legislation or policy and budgetary allocations.[40] The Committee has also underlined that legislation, policies or programmes cannot be implemented without sufficient resources and should therefore be accompanied by costs estimates.[41] Such a broad scope for CRIA means there is a risk of over-burdening of government resources, making a comprehensive assessment of all policies impracticable with the possibility that this will lead to a superficial 'tick-box' exercise.[42] Screening can help reduce the impact assessment burden by determining which economic or sectoral policies are most likely to have an impact on children and are therefore subject to CRIA.

Scoping and evidence gathering

Evidence gathering is key to effective CRIA. Without relevant data any assessment is likely to give undue weight to the preconceptions of those undertaking the procedure.[43] Effective assessment of economic policies will require child-specific, comprehensive and disaggregated data on the resources available to different groups of children.[44] States will need to make use of existing quantitative and qualitative data sources but should also seek to identify any data gaps and introduce new data gathering techniques where necessary to secure the evidence for rigorous CRIA taking into account the different environments in which children experience their rights (home, school, community, and so on) and particular factors affecting different groups of children.[45] Scoping or planning the impact assessment is an opportunity to identify populations of children likely to be affected by economic policy and the areas where evidence will be required in order to inform the analysis.[46]

Involving children

The *Guiding Principles* emphasise the importance of securing the 'meaningful participation' of those likely to be affected by economic policy in any HRIA.[47] Securing the participation of children is one of the most challenging aspects of the CRIA process.[48] The Committee has made it clear that CRIA should be informed by stakeholders including children, civil society organisations, experts, and academic institutions, and that children should be involved in decisions about economic policy.[49] The Committee has also emphasised that states have a responsibility to ensure children's participation in budgetary decisions that affect them and the need to give 'serious consideration' to the views of children as an aspect of public budgeting.[50] As a policy tool CRIA is an opportunity to introduce a child's perspective to policy analysis through a consultative and participative process as part of the procedure, making it more likely human rights issues that affect children in different situations will emerge (see below, CRIA in Bosnia–Herzegovina).[51]

Substantive analysis

As CRIA is based on the CRC any analysis should be carried out by persons with sufficient knowledge of children's rights. Given the breadth of issues likely to be dealt with in government legislation and policy there will be many instances where CRIA will be the responsibility of officials who are not experts in human rights, and who lack relevant knowledge and understanding of children's rights.[52] Effective analysis, including CRIA of budgets and budgetary allocations to support implementation of particular policies will require states to raise awareness and understanding of children's rights, and to develop capacity (amongst officials) to undertake the assessment.[53] Training or guidance on children's rights may be available to officials undertaking CRIA and may help meet any deficit in basic knowledge or awareness of rights, but if this is not sufficiently detailed there is a risk that CRIA will be superficial, meaning it will fail to identify relevant impacts or fully analyse mitigating measures or alternatives.[54] Where CRIA is applied to economic policy, training will need to ensure officials have sufficient knowledge of economic and social rights. Capacity building will help ensure duty-bearers are in the best position to use CRIA to help discharge their children's rights obligations.[55]

Reaching conclusions and publishing outcomes

In the context of public budgeting, the Committee has stated that CRIA should result in recommendations for amendments, alternatives and improvements to policy which should be publicly available.[56] It has also emphasised that states need to be accountable for meeting their budgetary obligations to realise the rights of children, including by disseminating information in the public domain.[57] Publication of CRIA in full (analysis and recommendations) promotes transparency and supports accountability by providing an 'audit trail' to enable outcomes to be scrutinised or challenged.[58] It will reveal how major spending decisions are likely to affect children and will demonstrate the extent to which the realisation of children's rights is supported by the allocation of resources.[59] Publication also contributes to informed public debate on policy alternatives and may help stimulate campaigns and policy advocacy.[60] However, publication can also introduce tension if officials undertaking CRIA are reluctant to reach strong conclusions where these contradict preferred policy options, especially if CRIA outcomes undermine a policy position advanced by ministers or government policy.[61]

Having established the core elements of CRIA procedure, the next section moves from methodological considerations to examine the experience in seven states where CRIA has been introduced at some level of government to inform policy decision-making.

CRIA in practice

While a UNICEF report in 2007 suggested that CRIA is amongst a range of mechanisms introduced as a result of widescale adoption of the CRC,[62] the literature on implementation of the CRC provides only a few examples of states where the procedure has been adopted by national or sub-national government, with even fewer detailed studies. Belgium, Bosnia–Herzegovina, Canada, Ireland, Sweden, New Zealand and the UK are all consistently mentioned in the literature as examples of states where CRIA features at some level of government.[63] This section therefore examines the experience of CRIA implementation in these states, drawing on published studies and commentaries, and Concluding Observations by the Committee following periodic review of the state concerned.

Belgium

The Flemish Community (Flanders) in Belgium has significant autonomy over policy on children and young people.[64] In 1997 the Flanders government introduced an *ex ante* 'child impact report' which was extended to a 'child and youth impact report' in 2008 (JoKER). JoKER is applied by officials to all draft decrees of the Flanders government with direct impact on children and young people under the age of 25.[65] A strength of JoKER may be seen as its underpinning by legislation which makes its application mandatory. However, in 2012 an evaluation of JoKER found that it had been applied to less than 20% of draft decrees between 2010 and 2011.[66] A possible reason for this low implementation rate is that JoKER is only mandatory for government draft decrees which directly impact on children. Other draft decrees and regulations, budgetary decrees and policy which might affect children are not included in the assessment. This has been described as a 'major weakness' of the procedure.[67] The possibility of extending the scope of JoKER to budgetary decrees was considered during the 2012 evaluation and was supported by civil society stakeholders. However, government officials expressed concern about capacity to undertake further impact assessment.[68] Partly in response to capacity issues, in 2005 JoKER was integrated into a Flemish government Regulatory Impact Assessment (RIA). While this led to children's rights being more fully mainstreamed into policy development, it was also found to have resulted in a tendency to further restrict the scope of JoKER to decrees included in RIA.[69] The 2012 evaluation highlighted a number of other weaknesses in the implementation of JoKER which included a complete lack of participation by children and young people, implementation too late in the law-making process to have any effect on draft decrees, a tendency to avoid analysis of negative impacts or alternatives to preferred government policy, and lack of expertise in children's rights amongst officials who were unable to develop their knowledge due to a lack of resources.[70]

When the Belgium government reported to the Committee in 2009 there was no indication that CRIA would be applied to federal government decision-making.[71] In response, in Concluding Observations in 2010 the Committee expressed concern at the state's failure to adopt CRIA, in particular to assess budgets and public expenditure.[72] However, rather than refer directly to CRIA in its recommendations the Committee instead called on the Belgium government to adopt a 'tracking system for the allocation of resources' to be 'used for impact assessments' of investment by sector.[73] When the state was next examined by the Committee in 2019 it recommended the introduction of a state-wide JoKER, but passed up the opportunity to expressly recommend the application of CRIA to state budgeting.[74]

Bosnia–Herzegovina

In 2006–2007, UNICEF and Save the Children UK developed a CRIA of economic reforms in Bosnia- Herzegovina. When this was implemented it was restricted to the assessment of a single policy, namely a proposal to increase the price of electricity in the country. In a report on the CRIA in 2008, Kreiger and others concluded that CRIA should focus on 'key reforms' likely to have the greatest impact on children as the procedure is not well-suited to the analysis of 'broad strategies' (such as strategies for national development or poverty reduction).[75] The Bosnia–Herzegovina CRIA took account of available quantitative data but also introduced a range of additional qualitative data gathering techniques, including consultation with children.[76] The 2008 report concluded that this helped identify a number of possible impacts in areas such as education and health care that might otherwise have been overlooked (e.g. the impact of increased electricity prices on schools and hospitals).[77]

Looking to the future, the 2008 report raises a concern at the lack of institutional capacity in Bosnia–Herzegovina for ongoing CRIA of economic policies.[78] This seems justified as when Bosnia–Herzegovina was next examined by the Committee in 2011 its report was silent on the continued application of CRIA to economic policies.[79] While the Committee urged the state to evaluate the distribution of resources in its Concluding Observations in 2012 it stopped short of expressly recommending CRIA.[80] In 2018, when the country last reported to the Committee there was no indication of how (if at all) the 2012 recommendation had been taken forward.[81] The Committee's Concluding Observations in 2019 repeated the recommendation that there should be an evaluation of resource allocation, but once again failed to specify CRIA.[82]

Canada

In 2009, UNICEF Canada recommended CRIA of all proposals for legislation, policies, budgets and programmes at federal and provincial levels.[83] Since then there have been a number of developments at provincial/local level. Notably, in 2013, the New Brunswick government introduced CRIA for all decisions having any impact on child well-being. This CRIA was developed by the New Brunswick Child and Youth Advocate which also published guidance setting out a number of methodological good practices.[84] These were: providing training for ministers in all government departments; implementing the procedure as early as possible in the decision-making process; using child-specific data; involving children and young people; and, devising policy alternatives.[85] However, while Canada's report to the Committee in 2018 referred to progress made in New Brunswick, there was no suggestion that CRIA would be adopted at state level.[86] (At the date of writing the Committee is yet to publish its Concluding Observations on Canada's 2018 State Party report.) The apparent failure to adopt CRIA at the federal level is despite a recommendation from the Committee in its Concluding Observations in 2012 that

Canada should introduce mechanisms to evaluate the distribution of resources allocated to CRC implementation.[87] This was followed by a report by UNICEF Canada in 2014 which identified the potential to move CRIA beyond the provinces to the national level. However, the UNICEF report also identified a number of challenges to its introduction at national level, which included: the possibility that adding CRIA to existing impact assessments would lead to assessment fatigue; limited resources; the lack of expertise on the part of those carrying out CRIA; and, the need to introduce structures to consult with children.[88]

Ireland

In 2005, the Irish government reported to the Committee that child impact statements would be central to implementation of the CRC in Ireland.[89] In 2006, the Children's Rights Alliance in Ireland, concerned at the negative impact on children of Ireland's immigration policy, developed a CRIA to be applied to deportation decisions involving children or their parents/carers.[90] A report to accompany the CRIA identified political commitment as key to its success, and recommended placing an obligation on the Children's Minister to support mainstreaming through the application of CRIA to all legislation, policy and administrative schemes.[91] The report also identified the need for CRIA to take account of the different environments where children experience their rights and any impact on particularly vulnerable children as 'basic principles' of CRIA.[92] In 2007, Corrigan observed that the Alliance's work had led to an increase in impact assessment on policy relating either directly or indirectly to the Irish government's Children's Strategy.[93] However, a study for UNICEF-UK in 2012 concluded that cutbacks in services affecting children resulting from the country's national debt and loan burden were having a serious impact on children's rights, noting that CRIA had not been applied to decisions to reduce expenditure on public services and concluding that little consideration had been given to the long-term impact on children.[94]

There is no reference to CRIA in Ireland's report to the Committee in 2013 but by the time the Children's Rights Alliance submitted its parallel report in 2015 the government had committed to carry out a social impact assessment (SIA) of major tax and welfare initiatives.[95] The Alliance took advantage of this commitment to call for disaggregation of the national budget to show expenditure on children.[96] At the same time the Irish Ombudsman for Children called for an expansion of SIA to include CRIA of budget decisions, while the Irish Human Rights and Equality Commission (IHREC) called for children to be made visible in the state's budgeting practices through a continuous CRIA process.[97] This strong call from the Ombudsman and IHREC seems to have been influential as the Committee's Concluding Observations in 2016 recommended the Irish government carry out CRIA in the framework of integrated SIA to ensure that fiscal and budgetary decisions are compliant with the country's CRC obligations.[98]

New Zealand

In 2002, the New Zealand government endorsed an Agenda for Children which included a proposal for child impact reporting which was widely supported by a coalition of non-governmental organisations and the New Zealand Law Commission, as well as in the political domain.[99] In 2006, however, Hanna and others, in an article on CRIA in the country, concluded that policy processes failed to take full account of the impact on children.[100] Renewed interest led to CRIA being piloted by local authorities in Auckland City (on inner-city development), and Manukau City (on waste management planning). A report by Mason and Hanna in 2009 on the city-based pilots identified an opportunity to integrate the city-based CRIA with other local authority impact assessments by broadening these to include children.[101] However, the report urged caution, recognising the risk that CRIA might be subsumed, leading to children becoming invisible in the impact assessment process.[102] The Manukau City CRIA did not proceed beyond the scoping stage. Mason and Hanna concluded that this was due to a loss of focus brought about by competing demands on resources and a failure to mandate the procedure as part of the authority's work programme.[103] The pilot in Auckland City was deemed more successful having made children's perspectives more visible in the project and raising awareness of children's issues.[104] Mason and Hanna attributed this to a range of factors which included: good quality information; adequate resourcing; early inception of the CRIA procedure; careful consideration of how to input the views of children; and, political commitment.[105]

In 2011, the Committee recommended New Zealand introduce a process to evaluate the impact of budgeting on children's rights, without expressly referring to CRIA.[106] When it next reported to the Committee in 2016 the country's Ministry of Social Development stated that CRIA options were being considered.[107] The New Zealand Human Rights Commissioner however informed the Committee that the government had failed to meet the 2011 recommendation.[108] The Committee's response was to recommend that the New Zealand government finalise its CRIA procedure and apply it to the allocation of public resources and budgeting.[109]

Sweden

In 1999, the Swedish parliament enacted legislation endorsing a national strategy for CRC implementation which included a requirement for CRIA of all government decisions affecting children.[110] A study of CRIA in Sweden by Sylwander in 2001 suggested that the CRC had been a driver for legal reform, but that this had not always led to recognition of children's rights.[111] Sylwander found that CRIA was being undermined by the failure to engage with children, and a lack of self-critical analysis with a tendency to ascribe only positive impacts to policy proposals.[112] A later report in 2006 by the Swedish Ombudsman for Children argued the importance of incorporating the views of children as the foundation for impact assessment.[113] Sylwander's report set out a number of factors likely to contribute to effective CRIA. These were: commitment of government to implement the CRC; a proper understanding of the purpose and meaning of children's rights; the provision of information and training to those responsible for giving effect to the CRC; information on the problems and challenges facing children; and, knowledge of the wider policy and administrative environment that affects children.[114]

In 2002, Sweden reported to the Committee on its adoption of a model CRIA put forward by the Ombudsman for Children and the potential to apply this to financial and budgetary decisions.[115] However, its next report to the Committee in 2008 is silent on the application of CRIA except to mention the application of the procedure by some municipalities as the level of government closest to the delivery of services to children.[116] In 2009 the Committee recommended the application of CRIA to government policy in a number of discrete areas which did not include economic policy or budgeting.[117] Following the most recent examination of Sweden in 2015, the Committee noted Sweden's failure to refer to CRIA in relation to state budgeting and recommended its application to future budgets.[118]

United Kingdom

An analysis carried out by Payne in 2019 found that between 2010 and 2017 five UK government Bills were assessed using CRIA (on average, 15–20 government Bills are enacted per year), all of which Payne concluded were 'narrations' rather than 'examinations', with minimal analysis from a child rights perspective or reference to children's views.[119] The devolved authorities in Northern Ireland, Scotland and Wales have significant responsibility for policy areas affecting children. In Northern Ireland there is an option to apply CRIA as part of a statutory Equality Impact Assessment, but this is rarely used.[120] In Scotland, the Scottish parliament has enacted legislation requiring the Scottish ministers to keep under consideration how devolved legislation and policy might give further effect to the CRC.[121] In 2015, the Scottish government introduced a non-mandatory Child Rights and Wellbeing Impact Assessment (CRWIA) which is applied to a range of government measures, including Bills, draft regulations, guidance and strategic documents.[122] Implementation of CRWIA is supported by a template and guidance, basic training for officials, and a policy lead to support those undertaking the assessment.[123] Responses to a Scottish government consultation on future incorporation of the CRC in Scotland show that the CRWIA is perceived as having introduced a 'preventative, proactive approach' to children's rights.[124] Responses to the consultation also showed support for CRWIA to be strengthened by making it mandatory for policy and legislation.[125]

In 2011, the National Assembly for Wales passed legislation requiring the Welsh ministers to have due regard to the CRC and its 1st and 2nd Optional Protocols when exercising any of their functions.[126] Ministers have published a children's scheme which includes a staged CRIA procedure utilising a template and guidance accompanied by training for officials and access to advice from the Welsh government Children's Branch.[127] Welsh government CRIA has a broad scope, covering policy, legislation, regulations, strategies, projects and programmes. A large number of CRIAs have been carried out: about 260 between 2012 and 2018.[128] An evaluation of the Welsh government CRIA in 2015 concluded that it had embedded the core objectives of HRIA into government decision-making.[129] However, the evaluation also found that implementation was often inconsistent and a departure from good practice because of a failure to consult with children, implementation late in the policy process, and limited knowledge of the CRC.[130] Significantly, the evaluation revealed that CRIA was not being applied to resource allocation as this was seen by officials as a matter relating to *ex post* implementation and therefore distinct from policy development.[131] A study of legal integration of the CRC in Wales in 2018 confirmed that CRIA had raised the profile of children's rights in policy development but also concluded that implementation remained patchy and inconsistent.[132] It noted that CRIA had not been applied to the Welsh government draft budget 2017–2018, which had been assessed using a Strategic Integrated Impact Assessment (SIIA).[133] SIIA was introduced by the Welsh government in order to reduce impact assessment complexity. While the SIIA template retains the core elements of CRIA, concerns have been raised that the interests of children will receive less attention.[134] These concerns seem justified as when SIIA was carried out on the Welsh government's draft budget 2020–2021 the CRIA element was not applied.[135]

The above examination of practice in seven states reveals a number of challenges that will need to be addressed generally if CRIA is to make an effective contribution to HRIA economic policy affecting children, and, in particular, budgets and resource allocation. These are discussed in the next section. What is immediately apparent however is that persuading states to adopt CRIA to assess economic policy is likely to be difficult. With the exception of Bosnia–Herzegovina, none of the CRIAs examined were in application to budgets or resource allocation, or indeed economic policy more broadly. This may be due to limitations on the scope of CRIA, capacity issues, or a result of integration with other impact assessments (next section). However, it may also be suggested that the Committee has failed to provide sufficient direction to individual states on the need to prioritise CRIA of budgets and resource allocation. Despite expressly referencing and prioritising CRIA of economic policy in several General Comments, in the majority of Concluding Observations examined for the purposes of this article the Committee failed to recommend the application of CRIA to resource allocation decisions or to refer to CRIA as the policy tool most appropriate to analysis of budgetary decisions. If CRIA is to be widely adopted to assess budgetary decisions the Committee needs to be clear in its recommendations to individual states that this is what is anticipated. In this respect, as the experience of Ireland demonstrates, a strong call from commissioners and civil society can influence the Committee to make direct reference to CRIA when making recommendations on state budgeting and resource allocation.

Challenges for CRIA of economic policy

The experience of CRIA in the seven states examined above suggests that persuading governments (at any level) to undertake CRIA on economic policy, budgets or resource allocation will be difficult. This is consistent with other research on children's rights more broadly which confirms the challenge of integrating children's rights into policy decision-making.[136] While political commitment may be a key step toward securing a children's rights approach, the examples of Flanders and Wales suggest that statutory underpinning for CRIA may be required if it is to be embedded as part of policy processes. However, even if CRIA is underpinned by statute, its scope may not extend to budgets or resource allocation. In Flanders, budgets are not included in the JoKER analysis framework, whereas in Wales the allocation of resources is seen as an *ex post* issue effectively excluding budgetary issues from consideration as part of policy development. The experience in these devolved nations is mirrored at national level in Sweden and Ireland which suggests that if budgets or decisions about resource allocation are to be included within the scope of CRIA this will need to be expressly required by underpinning legislation or in procedural guidance.

The discussion of methodological considerations earlier in this article drew attention to the need for CRIA to be undertaken by those with good knowledge of children's rights properly informed by evidence of how different groups of children experience their rights in different contexts. Limited knowledge of children's rights was identified as a factor undermining the quality of CRIA in Flanders and Wales, as well as New Brunswick. Both Scotland and Wales provide training through an online resource, while in Wales officials have access to a centralised source of expertise (something which was recommended following the Flanders JoKER evaluation). The introduction of adequate resources to support training for officials to undertake assessment of the impact of proposals for economic reforms, budgets or resource allocation is key to effective CRIA in this area. Training as an aspect of capacity building might also help overcome the problem of resistance to the introduction of CRIA of economic policy, which was noted as a recurrent issue in the discussion at the end of the last section.

The problem of capacity may also be eased if governments undertaking CRIA introduce effective screening measures to determine which proposals for economic policy should be subject to CRIA. But as the Flemish experience demonstrates, if this is too restrictive it can become a weakness and result in some policies with the potential to impact on children being excluded from assessment. Screening should therefore avoid formalities which exclude certain policies from assessment (as was the case for budgets in Flanders). Screening tools will need to be developed that are fully sensitive to the likely impact on children in a range of environments, and should expressly include budgetary policy, or resource allocation to support policy implementation. A proper screening procedure can help resolve the tension that exists between ensuring sufficient resources to undertake meaningful CRIA and ensuring all relevant policies are subject to assessment. Integrated impact assessment may also help relieve this tension by reducing the assessment burden on officials, while having the advantage of mainstreaming CRIA across a range of policy sectors.[137] However, the experience of Flanders and Wales suggests a cautionary approach as integration may reduce the number of policies subject to child-focussed analysis (Flanders), or the focus on children's rights (Wales). Where CRIA is integrated with other assessments which do not extend to budgetary considerations this may have the effect of removing assessment of resources from the scope of the assessment (Flanders and Wales). Despite this, the reality of policy development means it is likely to involve several impact assessments which will take place against a backdrop of limited capacity. Integrated assessment may be unavoidable to ensure adequate resources are available to undertake CRIA on the full range of legislation and policies likely to have an impact on children. The issue of limited capacity, which was found to be problematic in several of the examples discussed above, is likely to be more acute in the case of CRIA of budgets as the procedure will require specialist knowledge which may not be available to officials carrying out the procedure (Flanders, Canada and Bosnia–Herzegovina).

Where CRIA is introduced to policy development (integrated or otherwise), this should include procedures to identify the likely impact of the proposal on children or groups of children, including through the involvement of children. The above examination of practice suggests that securing the participation of children is likely to be one of the most challenging aspects of CRIA. The CRIA in Bosnia–Herzegovina confirmed the benefits of making special effort to engage with children through qualitative evidence-gathering techniques, but this CRIA was the exception amongst those examined. Flanders and Wales demonstrate how consultation can be overlooked even where CRIA is embedded and formalised within policy decision-making (something similar may be said of New Brunswick and Sweden). Sophisticated methodologies have been developed to engage children in policy development, and these should be used to provide a basis for engaging children in CRIA of economic policy and budgets.[138] Ensuring consultation and participation are meaningful however will often require special methods.[139] Children will need to be provided with age-appropriate information, including budget information such as pre-budget statements in accessible format, and suitable mechanisms may need to be introduced to create 'enabling environments' for children to participate.[140] Introducing innovative methods to support consultation and participation will often require funding to be provided by the state and may take time to implement, which may in turn introduce tension with other priorities such as the need for speedy CRIA outcomes, or minimising the cost or burden on officials.[141]

The examination of practice confirms that introducing CRIA at an early stage in the policy process in order to allow time for changes to be implemented, and providing 'space' for amendments or alternatives to be put forward, are key to effective CRIA. The studies carried out in Flanders and Wales found that introducing CRIA late in the policy process undermined its effectiveness to influence policy output, whereas in the Auckland City pilot early inception was seen as contributing to its success. Where CRIA is introduced late in the policy process the more likely it is that policy choices will have become entrenched. Relatedly, issues identified in Bosnia–Herzegovina, Flanders, Wales and Sweden included the failure to properly examine proposals for potential negative impacts and the closing off of policy alternatives. Late commencment of CRIA undermines its fundamental purpose to influence policy development. If the procedure is to be effective to influence economic policy, any legislation or guidance introducing CRIA should require early inception as well as full publication of outcomes to ensure accountability where government fails to act on changes recommended to remove or mitigate any predicted adverse impacts on children's rights.

Conclusion

This article has focussed on key procedural stages and challenges to be addressed in the application of CRIA to economic policy and budgetary decision-making. It is clear that while CRIA may be suggested as an appropriate procedure for prospective assessment of economic policy for its impact on children's rights, its potential should not be overstated.[142] There is much work to be done to persuade states, or indeed government at any level, to apply CRIA to economic policy, budgets and resource allocation. Even if more widespread adoption of CRIA can be achieved, governments will need to be supported to apply suitable methods to ensure that the procedure is both effective and meaningful. This should begin with the Committee which should support governments in undertaking CRIA on economic policy by issuing clear guidance on what this should involve.[143] Support for CRIA also needs to come from research. While there is a developed body of literature on CRIA methods, there is a dearth of research on how (or if) CRIA is influential on legislation or policy output, and on how (or if) this leads to better outcomes for children. This research is needed to support claims by the Committee and others (including in the *Guiding Principles*) that *ex ante* impact assessment helps ensure that human rights are properly respected.

The issues discussed above are relevant to HRIA of economic policy and reforms likely to effect children, as the most appropriate *ex ante* procedure to be applied in this scenario will be CRIA. As methods are comparable it is likely that the procedural challenges discussed above in relation to implementation of CRIA will arise when HRIA is applied to assess the impact of economic policy on vulnerable groups besides children. This suggests that governments and others will need to find ways to strengthen capacity and expertise, to engage rights-holders, and to ensure proper consideration of policy alternatives, if HRIA is to make a meaningful contribution to economic policy and reforms.

Notes

1. Human Rights Council, *Guiding Principles on Human Rights Impact Assessments of Economic Reforms*, A/HRC/40/57 (2019), *Summary*, Principle 17 and paras 18(4) and 18(5).
2. Ibid., Principle 18.
3. Article 1 CRC, defines a child as 'every human being below the age of eighteen years unless under the law applicable to the child, majority is attained earlier'.
4. UN Committee on the Rights of the Child, General Comment No. 5, *General Measures of Implementation of the Convention on the Rights of the Child*, CRC/GC/2003/5 (2003), para. 45. Although *ex post* impact assessment is often regarded as exclusively prospective and has been described as 'surveillance' or 'monitoring': J. Kemm, 'Perspectives on Health Impact Assessment', *Bulletin of the World Health Organization* 81, no. 6 (2003): 387. In particular, in policy fields where impact assessment is well established: G. MacNaughton, 'Human Rights Impact Assessment: A Method for Healthy Policymaking', *Health and Human Rights Journal* 17, no. 1, June 2015, https://www.hhrjournal.org/2015/04/human-rights-impact-assessment-a-method-for-healthy-policymaking/ (accessed 10 October 2020); S. Jay and others, 'Environmental Impact Assessment: Retrospect and Prospect', *Environmental Impact Assessment Review* 27, no. 4 (2007): 287–300. See also International Association for Impact Assessment, *What is Impact* Assessment, https://www.iaia.org/uploads/pdf/What_is_IA_web.pdf (accessed 17 April 2020).
5. UN Committee, General Comment No. 5, para. 34; UNICEF Canada, *Child Rights Impact Assessment, The Fundamentals* (Toronto: UNICEF Canada, 2014); Eurochild, *Applying the EU Charter of Fundamental Rights to Children's Rights in the EU* (Brussels: Eurochild, 2015), 17.
6. With the exception of the United States of America.
7. L. Payne, *Child Rights Impact Assessment (CRIA): A Review of Comparative Practice Across the UK* (London: UNICEF-UK, 2017); New Brunswick Child and Youth Advocate, *Child Rights Impact Assessment: A Primer for New Brunswick* (New Brunswick: Fredericton, 2016); UNICEF Canada, *Child Rights Impact Assessment, The Fundamentals* (Toronto: UNICEF Canada, 2014); L. Payne, 'A Children's Government in England and Child Impact Assessment', *Children and Society* 470 (2007): 21. K. L. Paton and G. Munro, *Child's Rights Impact Assessments: The SCCYP Model* (Edinburgh: SCCYP, 2006); C. Corrigan, 'Child Impact Statements: Protecting Children's Interest in Policy and Provision?', *Journal of Children's Services* 2, no. 4 (2007): 30–42.
8. L. Lundy and others, *The UN Convention on the Rights of the Child, A Study of Legal Implementation in 12 Countries* (London: UNICEF-UK, 2012), 24; U. Kilkelly, 'Operationalising Children's Rights: Lessons from Research', *Journal of Children's Services* 1, no. 4 (2006): 41.
9. UN Committee, General Comment No. 5, para. 45; L. Payne, *Child Impact Statements 1998/99: The Next Stage in Child-Proofing UK Parliamentary Bills* (London: National Children's Bureau, 2000), 11; Corrigan, 'Child Impact Statements', 38.

10. N. Mason and K. Hanna, *Undertaking Child Impact Assessments in Aotearoa New Zealand Local Authorities: Evidence, Practice, Ideas* (Auckland: IPP, AUT University, 2009), 4.
11. UN Committee, General Comment No. 5, paras 45 and 46; UN Committee on the Rights of the Child, General Comment No. 14, *On the Right of the Child to Have His or Her Best Interests Taken as a Primary Consideration*, CRC/GC/C/14 (2013), para. 99.
12. UN Committee, General Comment No. 5, para. 45; UN Committee on the Rights of the Child, General Comment No. 19, *On Public Budgeting for the Realization of Children's Rights*, CRC/C/GC19 (2016), paras 18 and 27.
13. Mason and Hanna, *Undertaking Child Impact Assessments*, 7; Centre for Economic and Social Rights, *Assessing Austerity, Monitoring the Human Rights Impacts of Fiscal Consolidation* (2018); B. Cantillon and others, *Children of Austerity, Impact of the Great Recession on Child Poverty in Rich Countries* (Oxford: Oxford University Press, 2017), https://www.cesr.org/sites/default/files/Austerity-Report-Online2018.FINAL_.pdf (accessed 17 April 2020).
14. G. Lansdown, *Promoting Children's Participation in Democratic Decision Making* (Florence: Innocenti Research Centre, 2001), 4; B. Byrne and L. Lundy, 'Reconciling Children's Policy and Children's Rights: Barriers to Effective Government Delivery', *Children and Society* 29, no. 4 (2015): 266–276; UN Committee, General Comment No. 16, *State Obligations Regarding the Impact of the Business Sector on Children's Rights*, CRC/C/GC/16 (2013), para. 4(b); A. Nolan, 'Economic and Social Rights, Budgets and the Convention on the Rights of the Child International Journal of Children's Rights', 21, no. 2 (2013): 248–277, 275.
15. Centre for Economic and Social Rights, *Assessing Austerity*, 17, https://www.cesr.org/sites/default/files/Austerity-Report-Online2018.FINAL_.pdf (accessed 17 April 2020).
16. Cantillon and others, *Children of Austerity*.
17. UN Committee, General Comment No. 5, para. 52.
18. Ibid.; and UN Committee on the Rights of the Child, *Report on the Twenty-Second Session, September/October 1999*, CRC/C/9 (1999), para. 291(m).
19. UN Committee, General Comment No. 19, para. 27.
20. Ibid., para. 45. See also, for example, UN Committee on the Rights of the Child, Day of General Discussion, *On Resources for the Rights of the Child, Responsibility of States*, 46th Session (2007), para. 16.
21. R. Hodgkin and P. Newell, *Implementation Handbook for the CRC* (UNICEF, 2007), 63.
22. UN Committee, General Comment No. 19, para. 31.
23. UN Committee, *Resources for the Rights of the Child*, paras 29–30.
24. Nolan, 'Economic and Social Rights', 276.
25. UN Committee, General Comment No. 19, para. 47. See also General Comment No. 5, para. 45; and General Comment No. 14, para. 99.
26. A. Nolan, *Protecting the Child from Poverty: The Role of Rights in the Council of Europe* (Strasbourg: Council of Europe, 2019).
27. S. Hoffman, *Championing Children's Rights in Times of Austerity: Local and Regional Authorities' Responsibilities* (Strasbourg: Council of Europe, Congress of Local and Regional Authorities, 2015).
28. Human Rights Council, *Toward Better Investment in the Rights of the Child: Report of the United Nations High Commissioner for Human Rights*, A/HRC/28/33 (2014), para. 16.
29. Hodgkin and Newell, *Implementation Handbook*, 6.
30. Y. P. Krieger and E. Ribar, *Child Rights Impact Assessment of Economic Policies: A Case Study from Bosnia and Herzegovina* (2008), 16, https://www.childimpact.unicef-irc.org/en/psia-cria/b-h-cria (accessed 17 April 2020).
31. Hodgkin and Newell, *Implementation Handbook*, 61.
32. UN Committee, *Report on 72nd-77th Session*, A/73/41, (2018), para. 35; UN Committee, General Comment No. 19.
33. S. Hoffman, 'The UN Convention on the Rights of the Child, Decentralisation and Legislative Integration: A Case Study from Wales', *International Journal of Human Rights* 23, no. 3 (2019).
34. UN Committee, General Comment No. 19, paras 12 and 13.

35. UN Committee, *Report on 72nd-77th Session*, para. 35.
36. UN Committee, General Comment No. 5, paras. 40 and 41. See also, Human Rights Committee, General Comment No. 31, *The Nature of the General Legal Obligation Imposed on States Parties to the Covenant*, para. 4.
37. S. Walker, *The Future of Human Rights Impact Assessments of Trade Agreements* (Utrecht: Intersentia, 2009), 30–34.
38. UN Committee, General Comment No. 19, para. 47; HRC, *Guiding Principles*, para. 17(4).
39. O. De Schutter, *Report of the Special Rapporteur on the Right to Food: Guiding Principles on Human Rights Impact Assessments of Trade and Investment Agreements*, UN Doc. No. A/HRC/19/59/Add.5 (2011), Part VI; J. Ruggie, *UN Special Representative of the Secretary-General on the Issue of Human Rights and Transnational Corporations and Other Business Enterprises, Human Rights Impact Assessment – Resolving Key Methodological Questions*, UN Doc. No. A/HRC/4/74 (2007).
40. UN Committee, General Comment No. 19, paras 71–72; UN Committee, *Report on the Twenty-Second Session*, para. 291 (m); and General Comment No. 5, para. 45; Hodgkin and Newell, *Implementation Handbook*.
41. UN Committee, General Comment No. 19, paras 11, 73 and 77.
42. Corrigan, 'Child Impact Statements', 33.
43. Harrison, 'Human Rights Measurement', 174.
44. UN Committee, General Comment No. 5, paras 48–50; and General Comment No. 19, paras 67 and 68.
45. UN Committee, General Comment No. 19, para. 67; K. Hanna, I. Hassall, and E. Davies, 'Child Impact Reporting', *Social Policy Journal of New Zealand* 29, no. 32–42 (2006): 35.
46. Harrison, 'Human Rights Measurement', 172–173.
47. HRC, *Guiding Principles*, para. 7(3); J. Harrison and A. Goller, 'Trade and Human Rights: What Does "Impact Assessment" Have to Offer?', *Human Rights Law Review* 8, no. 4 (2008): 587–615, 599.
48. A. Crowley, 'Is Anyone Listening? The Impact of Children's Participation in Public Policy', *International Journal of Children's Rights* 23, no. 3 (2015): 602–621.
49. UN Committee, General Comment No. 19, for example, paras 31 and 47.
50. UN Committee, General Comment No. 19, for paras 52, 53 and 68.
51. R. Croke and A. Crowley, 'Human Rights and Child Poverty in the UK: Time for Change', in *The Human Rights of Children: From Visions to Implementation*, ed. J. Williams and A. Invernizzi (Farnham: Ashgate, 2011).
52. Harrison and Stephenson, *Human Rights Impact Assessment*, 18–19.
53. UN Committee, General Comment No. 19, para. 17.
54. Harrison and Stephenson, *Human Rights Impact Assessment*, 18–19.
55. Walker, *The Future of Human Rights Impact Assessments*, 36–37; UN Development Group, *The Human Rights Based Approach to Development Cooperation: Towards a Common Understanding among UN Agencies* (New York: UNDP, 2003). Also vital is enhancing the capacity of children as rights-holders, and those who represent them, to take advantage of their rights.
56. UN Committee, General Comment No. 19, para. 47.
57. UN Committee, General Comment No. 19, for example, paras 21 and 83.
58. Harrison and Stephenson, *Human Rights Impact Assessment*, 55.
59. UN Committee, *Day of Discussion*, para. 32; OHCHR, *Human Rights and Poverty Reduction: A Conceptual Framework* (New York: United Nations, 2004), 16.
60. De Schutter, *Report of the Special Rapporteur*, para. 41.
61. Payne, *Child Rights Impact Assessment*, 22.
62. UNICEF, *Law Reform and the Implementation of the Convention on the Rights of the Child* (Florence: Innocenti Research Centre, 2007), 124.
63. While Finland and Denmark are also often mentioned as having introduced CRIA at some level, a literature search failed to find any study or commentaries on the experience of CRIA in these states.

64. Belgium is a federal state with three regions: the Flemish Community, the French Community and the German-language Community.
65. E. Desmett, H. Op de Beeck, and W. Vandenhole, 'Walking a Tightrope, Evaluating the Child and Youth Impact Report in Flanders', *International Journal of Children's Rights* 22 (2014): 79–81, fn 7 and 8.
66. Ibid., 96.
67. E. Desmett and H. Op de Beeck, 'Strategic Decisions in Setting Up Child Rights Impact Assessments', *Revue Générale de Droit* 44, no. 1 (2014): 150.
68. Desmett, de Beeck and Vandenhole, 'Walking a Tightrope'.
69. Ibid.
70. Ibid.
71. Belgium, *State Party Report*, CRC/C/BEL/3-4 (2009), paras 29–31 and 42.
72. Committee on the Rights of the Child, *Concluding Observations*, Belgium, CRC/C/BEL/CO/3-4 (2010), para. 19.
73. Ibid., para. 20.
74. Committee on the Rights of the Child, *Concluding Observations*, Belgium, CRC/C/BEL/CO/5-6 (2019), paras 7 and 10.
75. Krieger and Ribar, *Child Rights Impact Assessment*, 30–31.
76. Bosnia–Herzegovina: Child Rights Impact Assessment of Potential Electricity Price Increases (Innovation), https://www.unicef.org/innovations/index_48675.html.
77. Krieger and Ribar, *Child Rights Impact Assessment*, 2, 27–28 and 46.
78. Ibid., 29–46.
79. Bosnia and Herzegovina, *State Party Report*, CRC/C/BiH/2-4 (2011), para. 27.
80. Committee on the Rights of the Child, *Concluding Observations*, Bosnia and Herzegovina, CRC/C/BIH/CO/2-4 (2012), para. 16.
81. Bosnia and Herzegovina, *State Party Report*, CRC/C/BIH/5-6 (2018).
82. Committee on the Rights of the Child, *Concluding Observations*, Bosnia and Herzegovina, CRC/C/BIH/CO/5-6 (2019), paras 8–11.
83. Noted in Lundy et al., *Legal Integration*, 75.
84. New Brunswick Child and Youth Advocate (NBCYA), *Child Rights Impact Assessment: A Primer for New Brunswick* (Fredericton, New Brunswick: Office of the Child and Youth Advocate of New Brunswick, 2016), 3.
85. Ibid., 7–10.
86. Canada, *State Party Report*, CRC/C/CAN/5-6 (2018), para. 15. At the time of writing the Committee had not published its latest Concluding Observations on Canada.
87. Committee on the Rights of the Child, *Concluding Observations*, Canada, CRC/C/CAN/CO/3-4 (2012), paras 16–17.
88. UNICEF Canada, *Child Rights Impact Assessment, The Fundamentals* (Toronto: UNICEF Canada, 2014), 7–8.
89. Ireland, *State Party Report*, CRC/C/Irl/2 (2005), para. 201.
90. Corrigan, 'Child Impact Statements'.
91. Children's Rights Alliance, *Uniting Voices for Children, Are We There Yet?* (2015).
92. Ibid., 40–41.
93. Corrigan, 'Child Impact Statements', 30.
94. Lundy and others, *Legal Integration*, 56.
95. Ireland, *State Party Report*, CRC/C/IRL/3-4 (2013).
96. Children's Rights Alliance, *Uniting Voices for Children*, paras 33–34.
97. Ombudsman for Children, *Report of the Ombudsman for Children to the UN Committee on the Rights of the Child* (2015), para. 2(5.2); Irish Human Rights and Equality Commission, *Report to the UN Committee on the Rights of the Child* (2015), 14.
98. Committee on the Rights of the Child, *Concluding Observations*, Ireland, CRC/C/Irl/CO/3-4 (2016), para. 16(e).
99. Hanna et al., 'Child Impact Reporting', 33.
100. Ibid.

101. Mason and Hanna, K, *Undertaking Child Impact Assessments*, 7–8.
102. Ibid.
103. Ibid., 24.
104. Ibid., 21.
105. Ibid., 21–30.
106. Committee on the Rights of the Child, *Concluding Observations*, New Zealand, CRC/C/NZL/CO (2011).
107. New Zealand, *State Party Report*, CRC/C/NZL/5 (2016), para. 61.
108. Human Rights Commission, *Submission of the New Zealand Human Rights Commission to the Committee on the Rights of the Child's Pre Sessional Meeting* (2015), 14.
109. Committee on the Rights of the Child, *Concluding Observations*, New Zealand, CRC/C/NZL/CO/05 (2011), paras 7 and 9.
110. Noted by Lundy et al., *Legal Integration*, 97.
111. L. Sylwander, *Child Impact Assessments: Swedish experience of Child Impact Analyses as a Tool for Implementing the UN Convention on the Rights of the Child* (Stockholm: Ministry of Health and Social Affairs and Ministry of Foreign Affairs, 2001), 9.
112. Ibid., 5–16; Ombudsman for Children, 2006, 4.
113. Ombudsman for Children, *Child Impact Analysis* (Stockholm: Ombudsman for Children, 2006), 4.
114. Sylwander, *Child Impact Assessments*, 16–18.
115. Sweden, *State Party Report*, CRC/C/125/Add.1 (2002), paras 25, 29, 53 and 122.
116. Sweden, *State Party Report*, CRC/C/SWE/4 (2008), para.18. See also: Sweden, *State Party Report*, 2012, para. 73.
117. Committee on the Rights of the Child, *Concluding Observations*, Sweden, CRC/C/SWE/4 (2009), paras 24 and 30.
118. Committee on the Rights of the Child, *Concluding Observations*, Sweden, CRC/C/SWE/CO/5, (2015), paras 9 and 10.
119. Payne, *Child Rights Impact Assessment*, England, 411–412, 411.
120. Payne, *Child Rights Impact Assessment*, Northern Ireland, 412–413, 412, citing Byrne and Lundy, *Barriers to Effective Government Delivery*.
121. Section 1(1) of the Children and Young People (Scotland) Act 2014.
122. Scottish government website: https://www.gov.scot/policies/human-rights/childrens-rights/ (accessed 10 October 2020).
123. Ibid.
124. Scottish Government Consultation, UNCRC, Analysis Report, 14–15, https://www.gov.scot/publications/uncrc-consultation-analysis-report/ (accessed 17 April 2020).
125. Ibid., 48 and 95.
126. Rights of Children and Young Persons (Wales) Measure 2011, Section 1.
127. Ibid., Section 4; Welsh Government, *Children's Rights Scheme* (2014), https://www.assembly.wales/Laid%20Documents/GEN-LD9732%20-%20Children's%20Rights%20Scheme%202014-22042014-255569/gen-ld9732-e-English.pdf (accessed 17 April 2020).
128. S. Hoffman and S. O'Neill, *The Impact of Legal Integration of the UN Convention on the Rights of the Child in Wales* (Cardiff: Equality and Human Rights Commission, 2018), 24.
129. S. Hoffman and C. Morse, *Evaluation of the Welsh Government's Child Rights Impact Assessment Procedure under the Children's Rights Scheme Pursuant to the Rights of Children and Young Persons (Wales) Measure 2011* (Swansea: Wales Observatory on Human Rights of Children and Young People, 2015), 4.
130. Ibid., 4–5, and 18.
131. Ibid.
132. Hoffman and O'Neill, *The Impact of Legal Integration*.
133. Ibid.
134. C. Grace, *Reducing Complexity and Adding Value: A Strategic Approach to Impact Assessment in the Welsh Government* (Cardiff: Public Policy Institute for Wales, 2016); Payne, *Child Rights Impact Assessment*, Wales, 414–415, 415.

135. Welsh Government Draft Budget, 2020–2021, SIIS Annex C, https://gov.wales/sites/default/files/publications/2019-12/2020-2021-draft-budget-narrative.pdf.
136. Byrne and Lundy, 'Barriers to Effective Government Delivery', 10.
137. Harrison and Stephenson, *Human Rights Impact Assessment*, 76; P. Hunt and G. MacNaughton, *Impact Assessments, Poverty and Human Rights: A Case Study Using the Right to the Highest Attainable Standard of Health*, Health and Human Rights Working Paper Series No. 6 (Geneva: World Health Organization and UNESCO, 2006), 31.
138. Byrne and Lundy, 'Children's Rights and Policy-Making'.
139. HRC, *Guiding Principles*, paras 11(6), 19(1) and 10(3).
140. UN Committee, General Comment No. 19, para. 16, and for example paras 8(k) and 67(c). See also: B. Byrne and L. Lundy, 'Children's Rights and Policy-Making: A 6 P Framework', *International Journal of Children's Rights* 23, no. 3 (2019).
141. UN Committee, General Comment No. 19, para. 53; Hanna et al., *Child Impact Reporting*, 37.
142. Echoing Harrison, 'Human Rights Measurement', on HRIA, 183.
143. The European Network of Ombudsman for Children has commissioned research on a suitable CRIA model, https://enoc.eu/?p=3158 (accessed 17 April 2020). A recent report urged the Council of Europe's Ad Hoc Committee for the Rights of the Child to advance its activities toward development of a child impact assessment: Nolan, *Protecting the Child*, 13. Either of these initiatives may provide suitable guidance for government and others.

Disclosure statement

No potential conflict of interest was reported by the author(s).

Economic policy and women's human rights: a critical political economy perspective

Abby Kendrick

ABSTRACT

This article argues that in considering the effects of economic policy reform on women's human rights, we must also consider the political economy mechanisms through which these effects operate. Treating the distribution of policy costs and benefits as outcomes of a given state of the world is unsatisfactory because economic policy reforms both shape and are shaped by those costs and benefits. Using a political economy model of economic policymaking, the article shows how the choice of economic policy and its impacts on women's human rights are endogenous to various gendered political-economic forces, which have interest, institutional and ideational-based dynamics. It argues further that while the gender-related standards set out in the Guiding Principles on Foreign Debt and Human Rights are an ambitious step forward in addressing possible negative impacts on women's human rights, their relative salience in the shaping of economic policy will be mediated by these same political-economic forces.

Introduction

Economic policies do more than influence production, consumption and the distribution of income and wealth: they also empower interests and ideas, tilting the balance of political power in their wake. Economists have long assumed otherwise, leaving others to deal in the political consequences of economic policy.[1] Feminist scholars in their endeavours to identify the channels through which certain economic policy reforms affect women have often followed suit, bypassing political outcomes – more implicitly than explicitly – along the way.[2] This work has demonstrated that austerity measures, structural adjustment, fiscal consolidation and economic reform programmes more generally have affected the lives and human rights of women of all ages in different regions of the world in negative ways.[3] Indeed, it is worth noting upfront that the headway that researchers, civil society groups, and a growing number of women's organisations have made in illuminating the gendered costs of economic reform should not be underestimated. However, the question I would like to raise in response to this impressive body of scholarship is how can we be sure that we are asking the right questions and measuring the right things if there is a possibility that both economic policy and women's human rights outcomes are mediated by and through a third variable: 'politics'?

Consider the case where both economic policy and women's human rights outcomes are co-determined by politics. Here, politics is the real driver of any link between economic policy and outcomes: if politics is gendered, economic policy and outcomes will be gendered too. The link is inevitable. This contradicts the notion implicit in the empirical exercise where the selection of economic policy over possible alternatives is framed as an objective choice: austerity versus progressive spending, cuts to public budgets versus tax increases, prioritisation of the public versus the private, etc. – the (unpredictable) social and economic consequences of these choices then being the object of study.

In setting out hypotheses concerning the impacts of economic policy reform on women's human rights, this difference in starting points is important for two reasons. First, if we accept the possibility that political-economic forces have the potential to systematically influence both economic policy and outcomes, why should we expect *a priori* that variation in economic policy offers any causal explanation for variation in women's human rights outcomes? Second, even if we accept a more modest view, that choices over economic policy are only partly captured by politics, to what extent can empirical studies that exclude politics be relied upon as a valid test for falsifying or corroborating hypotheses? In the first instance it could indeed be the case that no causal relationship exists. In the second, it could be that empirical results return false positives. In either case, (unobserved) politics is doing most of the causal heavy lifting.

This possibility raises several further questions: Under what circumstances would we expect economic policy and its impacts to be independent? How might politics play into both economic policy choices and extant women's human rights outcomes? How relevant are these considerations for thinking about what can and should be done with respect to the making and implementation of economic policy to prevent and address the negative impacts on women's rights? Answers to these questions must be sensitive to the possible *endogeneity* of political-economic forces. Acemoglu and Robinson refer to these forces as coalescing in a 'political equilibrium', which can be broadly understood as 'the role of the balance of political power in society'.[4]

I argue in this paper that both economic policy and women's human rights outcomes are mediated by and through a political equilibrium. From this perspective, choices over economic policy alternatives are not free; instead, they are constrained by the prevailing political context in which they are made. Extant women's human rights outcomes are co-determined in this same power-related context also. I argue further that in considering the effects of economic policy reform on women's human rights, there may also be an over and above effect, depending on the nature of political power as a mediating force and the ways in which it interacts with economic policy.

Of course, I am not suggesting that policymakers' have zero agency in choosing over economic policy alternatives and efforts towards making economic policy more gender sensitive certainly remain urgent. But my argument implies that in addressing the revealed negative impacts on women, our advocacy efforts need to stretch even further than the material economic policy argument: they need also to tap into the more fundamental power issues at stake. This, admittedly, is a somewhat trickier endeavour.

In what follows, I develop a simple model that delineates the link between economic policy and the political equilibrium. I emphasise why, in the presence of political-economic forces, women's human rights impact assessments that overlook such a link can lead to spurious explanations and predictions. I then discuss three broad channels through which power operates in the political equilibrium, to which economic policy and women's human rights are endogenous. They are endogenous because the power processes by which they are determined and on which they have influence are one and the same. These channels involve the interactive and interdependent operations of structural, institutional and ideational power: so long as economic policy institutions are produced through gendered structural and ideational interactions, and all of these interactions are interconnected, then endogenous gendered economic policy effects on women's human rights will always be present.

Up to this point, the argument is principally theoretical. In the penultimate section, I aim to demonstrate how the issues given rise to in the theoretical framework feed into applied settings, where the links between economic policy and women's human rights are under investigation. I draw on the gender-related standards set out in the Guiding Principles on Foreign Debt and Human Rights by way of example. The standards are interpreted in view of political-economic considerations and the implications of adding a new power string to the advocacy bow is discussed. The paper closes with a call to action: if we are to better understand what we can do to address adverse outcomes on women's human rights, a more systematic empirical and theoretical analysis on the interactions between economic policy, women's human rights and political power is required.

A political economy model of economic policy

For simplicity, consider a policymaking process that has two periods and economic policy is chosen in both periods, call this x_1 and x_2, respectively. Let us assume, again for simplicity, that x_1 is chosen for efficiency and/or welfare maximising reasons only; for whatever reason policymaking is insulated from any political interests. However, in the second period, x_2 will be determined in a political equilibrium.

There are two ways in which the political equilibrium could shape x_2. First, politics might affect policy significantly but unsystematically. For example, some policymakers might simply be incompetent, leading (sometimes) to less than optimal policy in x_2. Or policy in x_2 might merely be a response to some random exogenous shock (e.g. climate, disease, crises). Here, political-economic forces in the political equilibrium have nothing to do with x_1; they are merely 'state of the world' forces. This scenario gives rise to three propositions: (i) x_2 is independent of x_1; (ii) the political equilibrium is independent of x_1; and (iii) x_2 is not independent of the political equilibrium but in determining x_2 the political equilibrium is exogenous. In this case, policy makers can choose economic policy in x_1 without regard for its political repercussions in the future: x_2 will simply be the most optimal response given the state of the world.

However, the assumption of independence between the two periods seems intuitively shaky. It would not be unreasonable to assume instead that economic policy made in x_1, while economically strengthening some groups over overs, will at the same time empower some political interests and disempower others, tilting the political equilibrium in one direction or another. In this case, x_2 is determined not only by state of the world forces but by political power forces also. In turn, the concentration of political power in the political equilibrium is determined in part by economic policies chosen in the first period, so that the political equilibrium is indeed a function of x_1. Hence, x_1 and x_2 are *not* independent, they are endogenous. It follows that the political equilibrium and x_2

are too. These relationships and their implications for theorising women's human rights impacts are set out graphically in Figure 1.[5]

In tracing the relationships in Figure 1, the forward and backward linkages that connect economic policy with women's human rights via the political equilibrium become clearer. Consider an empirical exercise that sets out to assess the impacts of x_1 on women's human rights *ex post* and findings reveal that the costs are disproportionally shouldered by women. With these results in hand, we might then wish to make policy recommendations with respect to x_2 that attempt to address these negative impacts: more attention to women's labour market constraints, greater space for gender-responsive social policies, the broadening of macroeconomic goals, for example. However, one question the model raises is how these policy recommendations fit alongside possible political effects that also result from changes in x_1. Since it is quite possible that the unevenly distributed economic policy costs simultaneously tilt the political equilibrium toward already favoured (male) groups in society, policy recommendations concerning women's human rights in x_2 need to take into account not only the economic costs and benefits but the political ones too: how useful is a recommendation to pay more attention to women's labour market constraints when the *meaning* of women's work is potentially shaped by gendered relations of power?

The framework is useful in the *ex ante* case also. Consider the research endeavour is predictive rather than explanatory: we would like to estimate what the likely impacts of x_2 on women's human rights will be. Given that x_2 is in part determined by the concentration of political power, and in turn the concentration of political power is in part determined by x_1, we would not only need to take into account the extant material realities of

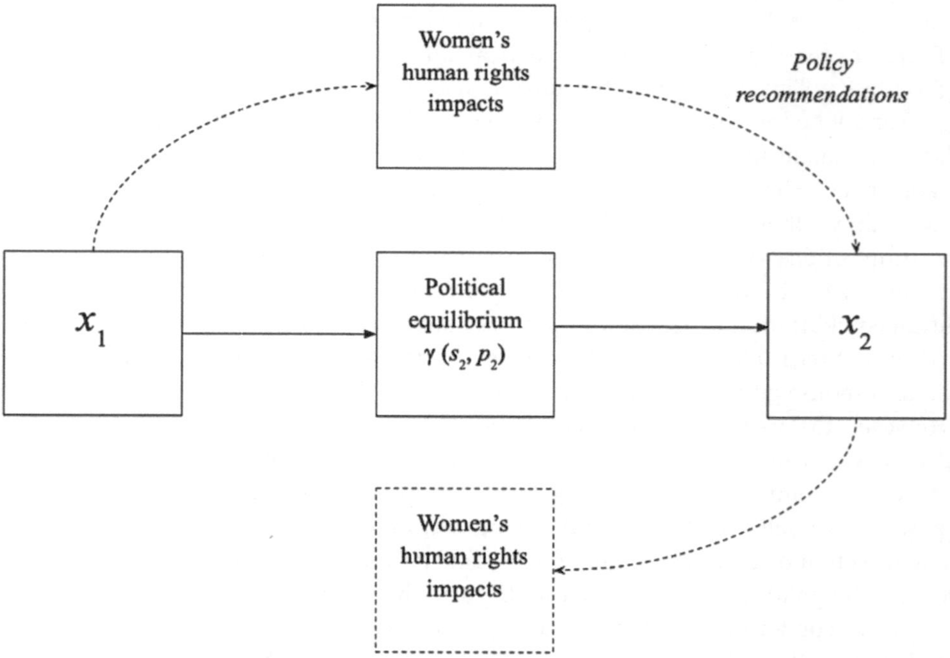

Figure 1. Endogenous economic policy and its impacts.

the post-x_1 policy environment but would need to understand how x_1 might have affected the concentration of political power, of which x_2 is a product. Policies in x_1 that lead to further inequalities are those that are most likely to have harmful political consequences for the already disadvantaged. That the already disadvantaged are most often women, not taking into account these consequences would dramatically underestimate the likely costs with which women will ultimately be burdened.

The model so far is a developed variation on Acemoglu and Robinson's theme, with room made for state of the world, as well as power-related political-economic forces in determining the political equilibrium. The model also speaks to but is conceptually distinct from the policy feedback literature, which in a broad sense refers to the idea that over time, existing policy can shape future political behaviour and policy choices.[6] It is distinct in the sense that the political economy model proposed provides a more formal mechanism for showing how: through the policy-augmented concentration of political power. Returning to the causality question posed earlier, the model suggests that variation in economic policy reform offers causal explanation for women's human rights outcomes to the extent that economic policy is shielded from political interests and/or increases or decreases the concentration of political power. Only in the case that the index of political power concentration is zero does the political equilibrium not matter.

There is, of course, a vast and divergent literature on what political power *is*. I will not devote any space to that discussion here for both practical and substantive reasons. Engaging in the ostensibly intractable disagreements over how power should be understood is too complex a task to be attempted presently. And, more crucially, whether we take power to mean power-over[7] or power-to,[8] whether we take power-to to be a derivative form of power-over or vice versa,[9] or whether we take power to be a potentiality and/or an actuality,[10] the general relationships between political power, economic policy and women elaborated below, hold.

Taking as the basic organising principle that underpinning power is the notion that *A* in some way affects *B* in some significant manner, one can then, for present purposes, remain agnostic as to what makes *A*'s affecting *B* significant. The key challenge here is to unravel what are the processes and practices through which power operates in connection to economic policy reform, and how those dynamics create space for a gendered tilting of the political equilibrium. To this task is where the next section turns.

Women and the channels of power

In providing an explanation of political action, Craig Parsons offers sound advice: 'To venture into explanation of action we need some broad sense of our explanatory options'. But he also points out that 'the basic field of alternatives is very difficult to construct'.[11] While recognising the legitimacy and irreconcilability of the deep theoretical issues at stake, fortunately, Parsons goes on to do some of this difficult work for us. I take his typology of political action and its logical distinctions to be particularly useful in setting out what are the options when it comes to unravelling possible mechanisms for political action as it relates to gendered power.

Parsons offers a convincing account of why explanations of political action can be bound within four logics: structural, institutional, ideational, and psychological, and why these logics can be distinguished along positional versus interpretive lines. On the one hand, he argues that structural and institutional explanations are entailed by a logic-of-position: how someone acts will depend on where they are *positioned* relative to a given material structure or an iteratively arrived at set of institutionalised rules. In this sense we can see power as operating through the constitution of people's capacities in direct structural relation to one another or through the legitimacy of formal and informal institutions that mediate between *A* and *B*.[12] On the other hand, ideational and psychological explanations are entailed by a logic-of-interpretation: how someone acts will depend on an *interpretation* of the world (conscious or unconscious) that orders their thinking. It 'explains by showing that someone arrives at an action only through one interpretation of what is possible and/or desirable'.[13] The distinction between ideational and psychological explanations is that interpretations are based on historically constructed beliefs and perceptions in the former, and are arrived at through 'hard-wired instincts, affective commitments, and/or cognitive shortcuts' in the latter.[14] Respectively, power operates through shaping cultural assumptions that carry meanings about the world[15] or through pulling or pushing people to action through cognitive responses to socio-political forces.[16]

While each of the explanatory logics can be presented as analytically distinct, there is of course clear scope for interaction: there are likely to be many instances where one power channel facilitates or limits the explanatory force of another. Indeed, much has been written about the interaction of interests, institutions and ideas,[17] which Parsons argues equate roughly to the first three of his logical types – where people's interests would be given by their relative structural positions. Regarding the gender-policy nexus, Tasleem Padamsee goes a step further and suggests that thinking about these dynamics not only as interactions but as *interdependencies* improves our understanding of the various processes through which gendered power operates in a number of important ways.[18]

Padamsee's arguments are based on Saussure's understanding of 'meaning'[19] where our interpretations regarding people, groups and things do not spring out of a state of nature from which meanings emerge. Instead, 'meaning is fundamentally relational, associative, and derived through contrasts between linguistic terms'.[20] It is created by each individual interpreter and while individuals may share meanings about the world, they do so only through reliance on 'local conventions'[21] and interpretations held by a given language community to which they hold membership. This view of meaning then creates space for the role of power: given meanings being entailed by unequal social relationships.[22]

Gender signifies one such relation of power and through this lens gender is seen not merely as representative of naturally given difference but as a construction that is constitutive of our social practices and relationships. Gendered ideational elements provide us with meanings about the categories to which people and groups are identified. They shape how we individually and as part of a group identify with and relate to others. They enable and limit the types of actions we are able and willing to take.[23]

On this account, a person's interests are surely not wholly determined based on their position – structural or institutional. Instead, a person's understanding of their interests as well the actions they take based upon them are likely to be mediated by the ideational structures available to them: some actions that could advance our potential interests will never be taken, even thought of, because of the limits set by embedded meanings about what is possible and/or desirable. The ideational elements that inform these perceptions are constructions of our own identity in structural relation to others:[24] our perceived self-interests, and political actions based upon them, as wives, mothers and citizens being malleable to the extent that different meanings of the family and the state affect the very contexts in which these interests are structured. Likewise, gender scholars have long stressed the importance of cultural assumptions about gender difference in the organisation of institutions, such as the welfare state,[25] where inequalities are reproduced by the very ways in which these assumptions become institutionalised. While differentiated institutional structures need not be seen as a singular set of gender expectations on women,[26] as Padamsee points out, these meanings 'help constitute the larger institutional structures through which individual decisions are patterned'.[27]

Of course, ideational elements are likely to be mediated by structural and institutional factors also, setting the parameters of and limits to our interpretations. Selection of *a* meaning of the family, the state, etc., amongst possible alternatives will be furthered by the degree to which it resonates with institutionalised rules of the game, as well as the extent to which it resonates with structurally entrenched power relations between women and men.

Exploring ideational dynamics points us towards the conclusion that economic, political and social outcomes between women and men are closely related to gendered identities and categorical inequalities, which are constitutive of gendered power relations. While I do not wish to imply that ideas account for everything, treating ideational, structural and institutional forces as mutually constitutive does seem to represent the multicausal pathways of power that pass through the political equilibrium more honestly, albeit less parsimoniously.

Plugging these considerations into the model shows how gendered ideational power sets limits to economic policy alternatives, either by rendering some perspectives on given issues irrelevant – if they can even be conceived of in the first place – or by barring others from the policymaking table altogether.[28] Disproportionate costs to women's human rights in gendered ideational contexts are then inevitable, where costs are seen in this light not as the results of a rationalistic and technocratic process but as a reproduction of gendered categorical inequalities that have become institutionalised. If at the same time those disproportionate costs tilt the concentration of power further, then the ideational vocabulary available to policymakers and other political actors in the future will be limited still. In order to find a way out of this vicious cycle, asking when and how gendered ideas are appealed to in the processes of economic policymaking must then be the focus.

Economic policy impacts on women's human rights: including power in the causal pathway

Study after study has corroborated evidence on the ways in which economic policy reforms have disproportionately affected the human rights of women in negative ways. In consideration of how we might address these negative impacts from occurring, most analyses start with international and national law.

The Committee on the Elimination of Discrimination against Women (CEDAW Committee) has explicitly addressed economic policy reforms a number of times and their link to the women's enjoyment of these social and economic rights in particular. It has underlined that 'even in times of fiscal constraints and economic crisis, special efforts must be made to respect women's human rights, sustain and expand social investment and social protection and employ a gender-sensitive approach, giving priority to women in vulnerable situations'.[29] It has called on states to ensure that any response to financial crises incorporates a gender perspective; and that sufficient funds are allocated to address or mitigate severe negative impacts of austerity measures on women's life. More recently, the new UN *Guiding Principles on Human Rights Impact Assessments of Economic Reforms* warn that:

> economic reforms which encourage, among other things, labour market flexibilization, reductions in the coverage of social protection benefits and services, cuts to public sector jobs and the privatization of services tend to have a negative impact on women's enjoyment of human rights. Economic reform should aim to prevent gender discrimination and transform existing inequalities, instead of creating such situations.[30]

The *Guiding Principles* are a bold step forward in making more visible the connections between human rights and economic policy. They also prompt consideration of how the potential costs of reform might be shared across different social groups, including gender. They move the conversation on from one consisting of treaty body recommendations, which highlight key human rights principles and standards against which economic policies should be reviewed, to one that sets out how human rights impact assessments might be designed and implemented in practice. While the Principles respect the difficult economic choices that often need to be made in response to urgent fiscal constraints, they provide normative guidance for policymakers on how to make these difficult choices in a way that upholds the state's human rights commitments.

With respect to the arguments presented throughout this paper, Principle 8.3 is particularly pertinent:

> Human rights impact assessments, incorporating a clear gender focus and women's central participation in the assessment process, can support the realization of women's human rights in practice through contextualized analysis aimed at identifying and preventing direct and indirect discrimination; addressing structural socioeconomic and sociocultural barriers; redressing current and historical disadvantage; countering stigma, prejudice, stereotyping and violence; transforming social and institutional structures; and facilitating women's political participation and social inclusion.[31]

Interpreting the principles through an ideational power lens means stepping outside of the known ideational context, or what Jane Jenson refers to as the '*universe of political discourse*, a space in which socially-constructed identities emerge in discursive struggle'.[32] With a view to truly *transforming* social and institutional structures, the politics-policy context should not be taken as given and in our advocacy efforts we must interpret the gender-related standards and principles in a way that not only considers the anticipated or revealed material impacts on women's lives from say privatisation or labour flexibilization but in a way that also considers more fundamentally if, how and why these policies and their potential impacts are ideational products, which are themselves the consequence of earlier contingent actions.

There are various channels through which gendered ideas feed into the policymaking process – channels, which have long been the preoccupation of policy scholars.[33] Taking Jal Mehta's typology as a guide, these can be generally summarised as problem definitions, policy solutions and public philosophies or zeitgeist.[34] First, for problems to even be defined as such, there must be some underlying ideational elements that construct a particular circumstance as a problem.[35] With the help of existing institutional settings, relationships among categorical inequalities and relationships of power give the circumstance meaning as a problem. This meaning then sets the parameters for policy actors' ability to make sense of the circumstance as a problem, as well as some sense of how it became to be, offering a guide to possible solutions.

In assessing the impact of economic policy on women's human rights we must then ask prior questions related to the gendered nature of the problem(s) the proposed policy is supposed to solve. The social construction of economic problems as problems is just one example. To quote Diane Elson, (1993) 'an "economically active person" is one who earns or seeks to earn money for their work ... the work that is particularly "women's work" is defined as "non-economic"'.[36] Since most if not all countries, as well at the World Bank and International Monetary Fund, (IMF) define economic activity in this way,[37] difficult circumstances that affect women but that fall outside of this definition might then not be seen as *economic* problems, or even problems at all.

There is, of course, an impressive body of work that catalogues the hidden contribution of missing women in 'non-economic' reproductive work.[38] Indeed, time use surveys reveal the significant share that unpaid care work represents in terms of a country's GDP: the figures are 14% in South Africa and Canada, 23% in Argentina, France and New Zealand, and 33% in China, for example.[39] However, the ideational approach to measuring impacts on women's human rights needs to go further than identifying and counting the costs of these miscalculations. It also needs to trace instances where ideational symbols that legitimise them – implicitly *and* explicitly – are appealed to more broadly.

Second, even if we take problems as given, to say that solutions to problems are chosen purely on functional grounds again seems rather naïve. Daniel Béland discusses Campbell's concept of 'bricolage',[40] and suggests that new policy solutions are instead advanced through an 'instrumental recombination of institutional elements ... and by drawing on existing symbols and values to increase [their] apparent cultural legitimacy'.[41] Indeed, some of the most influential work on the gender-policy nexus concerns the deeply embedded cultural assumptions that influence the design and selection of specific policy alternatives.[42]

From a feminist perspective, this means that for an idea (in the form of a policy solution) to succeed, it must naturalise particular accounts of the social and economic world in a way that sustains specific gendered social conditions and practices. Many feminist scholars have argued that austerity policies, owing to the fundamentally gendered spheres of finance, production and reproduction, have done just that.[43] Here, if gender issues are considered at all in the discussion of policy alternatives, they must fit neatly alongside other economic policies that are the order of the day. These tend to be of the supply-side kind, focussing on women's perceived deficiencies, such as mentoring or increasing women's skills. Policy alternatives are less likely to consider the demand-side failures linked to structural inequalities.[44] This may also go some way to explain recent evidence that IMF programmes continue to be pro-cyclical and oblige borrowers to implement austerity,[45] despite Christine Largarde and Kristalina Georgieva's (the Fund's two most recent chiefs) public claims concerning the importance of a gender sensitive approach to economic policy reform.[46]

Again, an ideational power-oriented impact assessment must chart the prevailing ideational political winds and assess the degree to which they have helped shape perceptions of which alternatives are legitimate and/or offer a potentially effective solution to the economic policy 'problem' at stake.

While linking backwards to problem definitions, the policy solution stream also links forwards to the third of Mehta's ideation-policy streams: zeitgeist. Zeitgeist can be thought of a set of meta-ideas that offer fast and frugal heuristics for defining problems related to policy issues that might enter a policy agenda. These meta-ideas can determine to a significant extent who ends up in positions of policy decision making power, thus setting the parameters for which policy solutions are ever considered. They can also be appealed to in making some issues or perspectives seem more legitimate than others; political actors can draw on these meta-ideational elements to influence the way other actors see their interests and identify with shared policy goals. Concerning gendered economic policymaking, zeitgeist encapsulates meta-ideas such as *the market is more efficient than the government*, *liberalisation is the key to development*, or *workfare* (as a counter to) *welfare*. All of these meta-ideas can be found in the World Bank's most recent World Development Report. (World Bank, 2020).[47]

Moreover, the idea of 'gender ideology' has given new energy to socially conservative agenda all around the world.[48] The concept 'serves as both a political and epistemological counterclaim to emancipatory conceptions of gender, sex, and sexuality'[49] and has become a key rhetorical tool in the construction of a new consensus about what is normal and legitimate in society. Indeed, by relying on and reimagining ideational elements that symbolise it – whether strategically or unconsciously – problems such as 'fiscal spending' and policies such as 'privatisation of care' have particular resonance with what Padamsee would call the 'cultural repertoire' of society.[50]

Framing analysis of the gendered costs of economic policy reform in a broader ideational context brings to light the notion that outcomes of economic policy reform are not apolitical. They are fundamentally influenced by what we take for granted about women and men. I would argue that this notion, to a significant extent, provides causal explanation for the tangible negative impacts that economic policy reforms have had on the realisation of women's human rights – news that is perhaps not so new to many feminist scholars. I would also argue that it explains why economic policy is resistant to women's human rights concerns, ideational or otherwise: the meanings to which feminist assessments must appeal simply make no sense in the universe of political discourse that prevails. But the political economy approach suggests there could still more of a story to be told. That these negative impacts might have tilted the political equilibrium in the favour of men even further, in our efforts to identify and evidence violations of women's human rights, it could be that we are proverbially missing the wood for the trees.

There are many feminisms and I do not have the space to do justice their differences here. However, in a broad sense, what can be said is that there are certainly many disagreements about whether the inclusion of feminist discourse in mainstream culture and institutions indeed facilitates an equality agenda. Notwithstanding some claims that the oppositional, political practice of feminism remains an ongoing concern is outdated,[51] for some feminist scholars, the inclusion of feminist ideas into key institutions has instead facilitated and promoted a version of feminism that is more moderate and as a consequence is more amenable to conserving, rather than challenging, prevailing norms.[52]

Through detailed content analysis, Sally Budgeon draws conclusions about the nature of feminist discourse circulating during the period of austerity in the UK.[53] The findings from news reports speak similarly to the evidence cited here: austerity unfairly impacts women. References are made to denunciations of the coalition's austerity policy and their failure to be more proactive in advancing gender equality and evidences how these narratives were out there, amidst the prevailing universe of political discourse. However, concerning the expressions of feminism that underwrote these sentiments, the conclusions are threefold:

> Firstly, the aim of feminism is to pursue equal treatment of men and women within social institutions placing emphasis on fairness and equality of opportunity. Secondly, gender is understood as an attribute of individuals and not of institutions. This leads to the proposition that equality can be achieved by the inclusion and integration of women into existing systems rather than requiring a radical overhaul of deep-seated social structures. Thirdly, 'women' and 'men' represent stable and coherent categories situated in a binary relation.[54]

On assessing the impact of austerity policy and other economic reform policies, these findings pose interesting questions for reflection. If in our assessments we focus on how these reforms have materially impacted on women's rights to work, social security and health, are we also privileging an equality discourse that treats power as a resource that needs to be redistributed more equally? By defending equality in economic terms are we transmuting 'feminist ideals such as self-empowerment and choice ... into an instrumental language that favours empowerment as autonomy in the market.[55] By relying upon an essentialist positioning of men and women, are we reflecting a belief that women share pre-determined interests? It seems that if answers to these questions are in the affirmative, these patterns do indeed reflect 'the materialization of a moderate, liberal feminist discourse'.[56]

While offering rigorous evidence that gives substance to these questions is beyond the scope of this paper, it should perhaps be no surprise if the feminism we encounter most in policy analysis and debate is of a more moderate kind. Returning to what Padamsee refers to as 'the multiplicity of cultures, ideas, and discourses',[57] different discourses compete, coexist, accommodate and reinforce, and within the 'multiverse' of circulating discourses, some are relatively empowered, and others are relatively disempowered. Those that coalesce in the prevailing universe of political discourse are winners of competitive games where different players are endowed with varying levels of power and persuasiveness.[58] Disproportionate economic policy impacts only serve to exacerbate these endowment inequities. Seldom do policy problems and articulated policy alternatives draw on cultural material lying outside of the universe of empowered discourses – it is not that this material does not exist, it merely falls outside the parameters of how political decision makers perceive the world.

In this sense, moderate liberal feminism can be more easily reconciled with the empowered norms associated with our prevailing capitalist economic system but in so doing marginalises more radical feminist discourses that would be required to challenge it.[59] In the political economy model, this has implications for both the concentration of political power and the context in which we make recommendations about economic policy reform with respect to women's human rights. While it might seem that gender norms are being contested, bent and relaxed, they are not being broken fully and changed. At worst, they might even serve to give greater credence to 'the legitimacy of political and economic structures of neoliberal capitalism'.[60] This in essence is the materialisation of the political equilibrium's over and above effect.

It is not difficult to spot the challenges involved in augmenting women's human rights impact assessments in the way I have argued is necessary. Guided by the Principles, women's human rights impact assessments that challenge the prevailing universe of political discourse will make policy actors feel uncomfortable. Indeed, as Martha Finnemore and Kathryn Sikkink argue, 'to challenge existing logics of appropriateness, activists may need to be explicitly "inappropriate"'.[61] Those with power will resist. They may also seek to shut down inappropriate action through all appropriate means. So, if indeed we are all ideationally conditioned to perceive our interests in structural relation to one another, and we structure our institutions accordingly, might challenging the prevailing universe of political discourse be too great an ask of anyone? From the bottom-up, how can we challenge problem definitions and consider alternatives when the meanings we have available make them non-envisageable? From the top-down, why would any policymaker listen to alternatives if they fall way outside of their own interpretations of the world?[62] From this understanding, as Finnemore and Sikkink point out, 'conformance driven by a logic of appropriateness starts to look deterministic'.[63] But while it might seem that resisting the turning force of the political equilibrium requires some kind of ideational supernova, I would still like to offer reason for optimism: nothing lasts forever.[64]

Discourses are not permanently empowered or disempowered. When an existing discursive context is faced with problems it cannot make sense of or when we lose confidence in those articulating problems using certain ideational frames, there is a moment of opportunity for ideational transition. This is where power-oriented advocacy on women's human rights is particularly important. As Illan Rua Wall, regarding the radical potential of human rights in general, so aptly puts it:

> human rights do not only lead to the establishment of some pacified neutered analysis of the global order ... They also mark a dissensus, rupturing and tearing through the pacifying tedium of everyday relations, with the demand that things should and could be otherwise.[65]

Applying Wall's analysis to women's human rights in particular, identifying moments of gendered discourse in the relationship between rights and economic policy becomes a strategy for social and economic change in a 'capillary fashion', and in so doing holds within itself the possibility of its 'generalisation and radicalisation'.[66]

While the feedback from women's human rights impact assessments on the political equilibrium might for a long time be rather muted, in order to realise the potentiality of ideational transformation, the foot cannot be taken off the gas, so to speak. Instead, one way to see women's human rights impact assessments and advocacy efforts more generally is not so much as in providing black letter recommendations that will be transformative in and of themselves, but as part of a broader and more complex discursive struggle, which agitates an assessment of the norms and assumptions that are called upon to justify why and for whom a specific economic policy or practice is positive or good.[67] As Charlotte Bunch explains, reflecting on her classic 1990 *Human Rights Quarterly* article, women's human rights and transnational feminist activism are 'both difficult, because of the complex political dynamics that must be negotiated to advance human rights causes of all kinds, and absolutely necessary, given the forces aligned against them'.[68]

Of course, whether a more radical feminist discourse will gain 'epistemic privilege'[69] out of a moment of flux is no forgone conclusion. But continued advocacy efforts that challenge prevailing norms and the power structures that underpin them could help build a 'compelling truth', which while emphasising gender neutrality as the basis of discursive categories, rather than gender difference, redefines our understanding of our interests and the institutions that regulate them.[70]

I hesitate to offer any sort of sketch of what a more radical feminist approach to assessing the politically induced impacts of economic reform on women's human rights would look like. But it would at least need to have at its centre the gendered construction of economic policy reform policies and the constitutive power of those constructions in structuring our social relations. It would be an approach that sees power not as a resource to be distributed equally,[71] but as relational and reflective of the broader structural, institutional and ideational contexts that shape it.[72] It would likely involve unravelling deeply normative challenges concerning the individuality of human rights and their liberal foundations, as well as the potentiality of changing or expanding the universe of political discourse. Not easy tasks. Nevertheless, I hope these insights provoke reflection when institutionalised feminist discourse is interpreted as a means to promote the realisation of women's human rights, such as the gender-related recommendations set out in the *Guiding Principles*.

Conclusions

The paper set out with an ambition to give greater nuance to our understanding of the causal channels through which economic policy reforms impact women's human rights than has been offered before. Along the way, a simple model that delineates the link between economic policy and what has been termed the political equilibrium has been developed. The model shows in principle how the link matters for predicting, explaining and making recommendations about impacts on women's human rights. The main results of the basic model are twofold: first, economic policy made today will politically empower some and disempower others, tilting the political equilibrium in one direction or another; and second, the new political equilibrium will at least in part determine the economic policy choices made in the future, as well as the distributional consequences that flow from them.

The paper has also gone some way to opening the political equilibrium black box. It has been argued that the political-economic forces that mediate between economic policy reform and women's human rights are entailed by the interactions and interdependencies of structural, institutional and ideational forces that reproduce categorical inequalities. These forces at once determine negative women's human rights outcomes in the first place and have the potential to create further negative impacts in the future through the ever greater concentration of this political power mix. The degree of this shift will depend in large part on how the multiplicity of discourses compete; the relative empowerment and disempowerment of these discourses will be key to our understanding of whether, how and why economic policy might be subject to reform.

This, however, poses nontrivial empirical questions. The interactions and interdependencies that run between interests, institutions and ideas are contingent and are likely to be shaped in non-functional ways: pulling a lever on one explanation may or may not result in predictable changes in another. But such scientific messiness is true of the real political and economic policy process and I see no reason why future research endeavours, feminist or otherwise, could not take on this challenge.

Notes

1. Exceptions include the many works of Daron Acemoglu and James A. Robinson. Exceptions can also be found in the economic literature on endogenous trade policy. See, e.g. Stephen P. Magee, William A. Brock and Leslie Young, *Black Hole Tariffs and Endogenous Policy Theory: Political Economy in General Equilibrium* (Cambridge: Cambridge University Press, 1989); Giovanni Maggi and Andres Rodríguez-Clare, (2007); Stephen P. Magee, William A. Brock and Leslie Young, 'A Political-Economy Theory of Trade Agreements', *The American Economic Review* 97, no. 4 (2007): 1374–406.
2. Hannah Bargawi, Giovanni Cozzi and Susan Himmelweit, *Economics and Austerity in Europe: Gendered Impacts and Sustainable Alternatives* (Abingdon: Routledge, 2017); Maria Karamessini and Jill Rubery, *Women and Austerity: The Economic Crisis and the Future of Gender Equality* (Abingdon: Routledge, 2013); Hélène Périvier, 'Recession, Austerity and Gender: A Comparison of Eight European Labour Markets', *International Labour Review* 157, no. 1 (2016): 1–37; Mary-Ann Stephenson, 'Feminist Challenges to Austerity', *Globalizations* 13, no. 6 (2016): 915–8; UN Women, *Progress of the World's Women 2015–2016: Transforming Economies, Realizing Rights* (New York: UN Women, 2015).
3. International Labour Organization, *Fiscal Space for Social Protection and the SDGs: Options to Expand Social Investments in 187 Countries* (Geneva: ESS Working Paper No. 48, 2017).
4. Daron Acemoglu and James A. Robinson, 'Economics Versus Politics: Pitfalls of Policy Advice', *Journal of Economic Perspectives* 27, no. 2 (2013): 174, 176.
5. Where γ represents the political economy parameter in a general sense, which is a function of state of the world political-economic forces (denoted by s) and political power forces (denoted by p).
6. Daniel Béland, 'Reconsidering Policy Feedback: How Policies Affect Politics', *Administration & Society* 42, no. 5 (2010): 568–90; Daniel Béland, *How Ideas and Institutions Shape the Politics of Public Policy* (Cambridge: Cambridge University Press, 2019); Andrea Louise Campbell, 'Policy Makes Mass Politics', *Annual Review of Political Science* 15 (2012): 333–51; Theodore J. Lowi, 'American Business, Public Policy, Case Studies and Political Theory', *World Politics* 16, no. 4 (1964): 677–715; Suzanne Mettler and Mallory SoRelle, 'Policy Feedback Theory', in *Theories of the Policy Process*, ed. Christopher M. Weible and Paul A. Sabatier (Boulder, CO: Westview, 2014), 151–81; Paul Pierson, 'Review: When Effect Becomes Cause: Policy Feedback and Political Change *World Politics* 45, no. 4 (1993): 595–628.
7. Robert A. Dahl, 'The Concept of Power', *Behavioural Science* 2, no. 3 (1957): 201–15; Steven Lukes, *Power: A Radical View* (New York: New York University Press, 1974).
8. Peter Morriss, *Power: A Philosophical Analysis* (Manchester: Manchester University Press, 2002).
9. Pamela Pansardi, 'Power To and Power Over: Two Distinct Concepts of Power?', *Journal of Political Power* 5, no. 1 (2012): 73–89.
10. Peter Bachrach and Morton S. Braratz, 'Two Faces of Power', *American Political Science Review* 56, no. 4 (1962): 947–52; Robert A. Dahl, *Who Governs?: Democracy and Power in an American City* (New Haven: Yale University Press, 1961); Richard M. Emerson, 'Power-Dependence Relations', *American Sociological Review* 27, no. 1 (1962): 31–41; Dennis H. Wrong, 'Some Problems in Defining Social Power', *American Journal of Sociology* 73, no. 6 (1968): 673–81.
11. Craig Parsons, *How to Map Arguments in Political Science* (Oxford: Oxford University Press, 2007), 6.
12. Michael Barnett and Raymond Duvall, 'Power in International Politics', *International Organization* 59, no. 1 (2005): 39–75.
13. Parsons, *How to Map Arguments in Political Science*, 13.
14. Ibid.
15. Pierre Bourdieu, *Outline of a Theory of Practice* (Cambridge: Cambridge University Press, 1977); Clifford Geertz, *The Interpretation of Cultures* (New York: Basic Books, 1973).
16. Jon Elster, *The Cement of Society*. (Cambridge: Cambridge University Press, 1989).

17. Daniel Béland, 'Ideas, Institutions, and Policy Change', *Journal of European Public Policy* 16, no. 5 (2009):701–18; Daniel Béland and Alex Waddan, 'Breaking Down Ideas and Institutions: The Politics of Tax Policy in the US and the UK', *Policy Studies* 36, no. 2 (2015): 176–95; John L. Campbell, *Institutional Change and Globalization* (NJ: Princeton University Press, 2004); Robert C. Lieberman, 'Ideas, Institutions, and Political Order: Explaining Political Change', *American Political Science Review* 96, no. 4 (2002): 697–712; Vivien A. Schmidt, 'Reconciling Ideas and Institutions Through Discursive Institutionalism', in *Ideas and Politics in Social Science Research*, ed. Daniel Béland and Robert H. Cox (Oxford: Oxford University Press, 2010), 47–64.
18. Tasleem Padamsee, 'Culture in Connection: Re-Contextualising Ideational Processes in the Analysis of Policy Development', *Social Politics* 16, no. 4 (2009): 413–45.
19. Ferdinand de Saussure, Charles Bally and Albert Sechehaye, *Course in General Linguistics* (New York: McGraw-Hill, 1966).
20. Padamsee, 'Culture in Connection', 421.
21. Kenneth J. Gergen, *An Invitation to Social Construction* (London: Sage, 1999).
22. Michel Foucault, *Power/Knowledge: Selected Interviews and Other Writings, 1972–1977* (New York: Pantheon Books, 1980); Nancy Fraser, *Unruly Practices: Power, Discourse and Gender in Contemporary Social Theory* (Minneapolis: University of Minnesota Press, 1989); Susan J. Hekman, *Feminist Interpretations of Michel Foucault* (University Park, PA: The Pennsylvania State University Press, 1996); Johanna Oksala, *Foucault On Freedom* (Cambridge: Cambridge University Press, 2005); Johanna Oksala, *Feminist Experiences: Foucauldian and Phenomenological Investigations* (Evanston, IL: Northwestern University Press, 2016).
23. Ann S. Orloff, 'Motherhood, Work, and Welfare in the United States, Britain, Canada, and Australia', in *State/Culture: State-Formation After the Cultural Turn*, ed. George Steinmet (Ithaca: Cornell University Press, 1999), 291–320; Padamsee, 'Culture in Connection'.
24. Julia Adams and Tasleem Padamsee, 'Signs and Regimes: Rereading Feminist Work on Welfare States', *Social Politics* 8, no. 1 (2001): 1–23; John L. Campbell, 'Ideas, Politics and Public Policy', *Annual Review of Sociology* 28, no. 1 (2002): 21–38.
25. Jane Lewis, 'Gender and Welfare Regimes: Further Thoughts', *Social Politics* 4, no. 2 (1997): 160–77; Ann S. Orloff, 'Gendering the Comparative Analysis of Welfare States: An Unfinished Agenda', *Sociological Theory* 27, no. 3 (2009): 317–43.
26. Lynne Haney, 'Homeboys, Babies, Men in Suits: The State and the Reproduction of Male Dominance', *American Sociological Review* 61, no. 5 (1996): 759–78.
27. Padamsee, 'Culture in Connection', 427.
28. Peter A. Hall, 'Policy Paradigms, Social Learning and the State: The Case of Economic Policy-making in Britain', *Comparative Politics* 25, no. 3 (1993): 275–96.
29. UN General Assembly, *Convention on the Elimination of All Forms of Discrimination against Women*, 18 December 1979, A/RES/34/180.
30. UN Human Rights Council, *Guiding principles on human rights impact assessments of economic reforms – Report of the Independent Expert on the effects of foreign debt and other related international financial obligations of States on the full enjoyment of human rights, particularly economic, social and cultural rights*, 19 December 2018, A/HRC/40/57, Principle 8(2).
31. Ibid., Principle 8(3).
32. Jane Jenson, 'Paradigms and Political Discourse: Protective Legislation in France and the United States Before 1914', *Canadian Journal of Political Science* 22, no. 2 (1989): 238.
33. Campbell, *Institutional Change and Globalization*; John W. Kingdon, *Agendas, Alternatives, and Public Policies* (Boston: Little Brown, 1984); Jal Mehta, 'The Varied Roles of Ideas in Politics: From "Whether" to "How" in *Ideas and Politics in Social Science Research* (see note 17), 23–46; Deborah A. Stone, *Policy Paradox: The Art of Political Decision Making* (New York: W.W. Norton, 2012).
34. Mehta, 'The Varied Roles of Ideas in Politics'.
35. Michel Foucault, 'Polemics, Politics and Problematizations: An Interview with Michel Foucault', in *Ethics: Subjectivity and Truth*, ed. Michel Foucault (London: Allen Lane, 1997), 111–

9; Deborah A. Stone, 'Causal Stories and the Formation of Policy Agendas', *Political Science Quarterly* 104, no. 2 (1989): 281–300.

36. Diane Elson, 'Gender Relations and Economic Issues', *Focus on Gender* 1, no. 3 (1993): 4.
37. International Monetary Fund, *World Economic Outlook: The Great Lockdown* (Washington, DC: International Monetary Fund, 2020).
38. Susan Himmelweit, 'Making Visible the Hidden Economy: The Case for Gender-Impact Analysis of Economic Policy', *Feminist Economics* 8, no. 1 (2002): 49–70; Gaëlle Ferrant, Luca Maria Pesando and Keiko Nowacka, *Unpaid Care Work: The Missing Link in the Analysis of Gender Gaps in Labour Outcomes* (Paris: OECD Development Centre Policy Brief, 2014); Nancy Folbre, Developing Care: Recent Research on the Care Economy and Economic Development (Ottawa: International Development Research Centre Canada, 2018); Plan International UK *Real Choices, Real Lives: Girls' Burden of Unpaid Care* (London: Plan International UK, 2017); Francesca Francavilla and Gianna Claudia Giannelli 'Dressing a Ghost: Size and Value of Unpaid Family Care', *Applied Economics* 51, no. 28 (2019): 3015–30.
39. Gaelle Ferrant and Annelise Thim *Measuring Women's Economic Empowerment: Time Use Data and Gender Inequality* (Paris: OECD Development Policy Papers no. 16, 2019)
40. Béland's discussion relates to bricolage as originally theorised by Campbell, *Institutional Change and Globalization.*
41. Béland, *How Ideas and Institutions Shape the Politics of Public Policy*, 40.
42. Jenson, 'Paradigms and Political Discourse'.
43. Bargawi, Cozzi and Himmelweit, *Economics and Austerity in Europe*; Bob Jessop 'Narratives of Crisis and Crisis Response: Perspectives from North and South', in *Global Crisis and Transformation*, ed. Peter Utting, Sharah Razari and Rebecca Varghese Buchholz (Basingstoke: Palgrave, 2012), 23–41; Karamessini and Rubery, *Women and Austerity*; Julie MacLeavy, 'A New Politics of Austerity, Workfare and Gender? The UK Coalition Government's Welfare Reform Proposals', *Cambridge Journal of Regions, Economy and Society* 4, no. 3 (2011): 355–67; Ruth Pearson and Diane Elson, 'Transcending the Impact of the Financial Crisis in the United Kingdom: Towards Plan F – A Feminist Economic Strategy', *Feminist Review* 109, no. 1 (2015): 8–30.
44. Diane Perrons, 'Gender and Inequality: Austerity and Alternatives', *Intereconomics* 52, no. 1 (2017): 28–33.
45. Gino Brunswijck, *Unhealthy Conditions: IMF Loan Conditionality and its Impact on Health Financing* (Brussels: Eurodad, 2018).
46. Christine Lagarde, 'Empowerment – the Amartya Sen Lecture' (lecture, London School of Economics and Political Science, London, 6 June 2014); Kristalina Georgieva, 'IMF-World Bank Annual Meetings' (talk, World Bank, Washington, DC, 2 November 2019).
47. World Bank, *World Development Report 2020: Trading for Development in the Age of Global Value Chains* (Washington, DC: World Bank, 2020). See Figure 7.13 on p. 187 for a particularly enlightening overview.
48. Agnieszka Graff, Ratna Kapur and Suzanna Danuta Walters 'Gender and the Rise of the Global Right', *Signs: Journal of Women in Culture and Society* 44, no. 3 (2019): 541–60.
49. Elizabeth S. Corredor, 'Unpacking "Gender Ideology" and the Global Right's Antigender Countermovement', *Signs: Journal of Women in Culture and Society* 44, no. 3 (2019): 617.
50. Padamsee, 'Culture in Connection', 420.
51. Angela McRobbie, *The Aftermath of Feminism: Gender, Culture and Social Change* (London: Sage, 2009).
52. Carol Bacchi and Joan Eveline, 'Mainstreaming and Neoliberalism: A Contested Relationship', *Policy and Society* 22, no. 2 (2003): 98–118; Penny Griffin, 'Crisis, Austerity, and Gendered Governance: A Feminist Perspective', *Feminist Review* 109, no. 1 (2015): 49–72.
53. Sally Budgeon, 'The Resonance of Moderate Feminism and the Gendered Relations of Austerity', *Gender, Work & Organization*, 26, no. 8 (2019): 1138–55.
54. Ibid., 1147–8.
55. Ibid., 1140.
56. Ibid., 1147.

57. Padamsee, 'Culture in Connection', 428–32.
58. Hall, 'Policy Paradigms, Social Learning and the State'.
59. Linda M.G. Zerilli, *Feminism and the Abyss of Freedom* (Chicago: University of Chicago Press, 2005).
60. Budgeon, 'The Resonance of Moderate Feminism', 1149.
61. Martha Finnemore and Kathryn Sikkink, 'Norm Dynamics and Political Change', *International Organization*, 54, no. 4 (1998): 897.
62. This latter point has particular relevance for explaining what I expect will be a relatively lacklustre response to the Principles in practice and provides reason why I am – albeit heavy heartedly – pessimistic about the likelihood that states and international financial institutions will undertake or be responsive to women's human rights impacts assessments of a power-augmented type, at least in the short term. See Human Rights Council resolution 40/L.13, which called on UN agencies and IFIs to consider taking into account the Guiding Principles in the formulation and implementation of their economic reforms and measures.
63. Finnemore and Sikkink, 'Norm Dynamics and Political Change', 913.
64. Lieberman, 'Ideas, Institutions, and Political Order'.
65. Illan Rua Wall, 'On a Radical Politics for Human Rights', in *The Meanings of Rights: The Philosophy and Social Theory of Human Rights*, ed. Conor Gearty and Costas Douzinas (Cambridge: Cambridge University Press, 2014): 109.
66. Ibid., 118. Here, Wall is engaging with Lefebvre's suggestion of the 'right to autogestion' as operating as both 'the site and stake of struggle' as a means to illustrate his more fundamental argument regarding the disruptive potential of human rights in the critical tradition to 'radically open a particular situation to being-otherwise'. Another take on this argument is discussed in Sumi Madhok, 'Developmentalism, Gender and Rights: From a Politics of Origins to a Politics of Meanings', in *Human Rights: India and the West*, ed. Jay Drydyk and Ashwani Peetush (Delhi: Oxford University Press, 2015).
67. These sentiments are also implicit throughout, Radhika Balakrishnan, James Heintz and Diane Elson, *Rethinking Economic Policy for Social Justice: The Radical Potential of Human Rights* (Abingdon: Routledge, 2016). Although the authors do not theorise the radicalness of human rights *per se*.
68. Charlotte Bunch and Niamh Reilly 'Women's Rights as Human Rights: Twenty-Five Years On', in *International Human Rights of Women*, ed. Niamh Reilly (Singapore: Springer, 2019); Charlotte Bunch 'Women's Rights as Human Rights: Toward a Re-Vision of Human Rights', *Human Rights Quarterly*, 12, no. 4 (1990): 486–98.
69. For a persuasive critical account of the various feminisms that have been relied upon in contemporary political discourse, see, Clare Hemmings, Why Stories Matter: The Political Grammar of Feminist Theory (Durham, NC: Duke University Press, 2011).
70. I give thanks to the Editors of this Special Edition for prompting me to reflect on this potentiality.
71. John Stuart Mill, *The Subjection of Women* (Cambridge: MIT Press, 1970); Susan Moller Okin, *Justice, Gender and the Family* (New York: Basic Books, 1989).
72. Iris Marion Young, *Justice and the Politics of Difference* (New Jersey: Princeton University Press, 1990).

Disclosure statement

No potential conflict of interest was reported by the author(s).

Re-righting the international tax rules: operationalising human rights in the struggle to tax multinational companies

Olivier De Schutter, Nicholas J. Lusiani and Sergio Chaparro

ABSTRACT
Who finances government, and *how*, is foundational to realising human rights for all, without discrimination. This is especially pertinent during the COVID-19 pandemic, which is only exacerbating health and economic disparities. This article reviews what a national human rights-aligned tax policy would look like, and then dissects how the international tax rules currently impede individual States, and particularly low- and middle- income countries, to bring their national tax policies in line with human rights. The authors then discuss how international human rights law, including the *UN Guiding Principles on Human Rights Impact Assessments of Economic Reforms*, can provide a stronger normative foundation to curb harmful tax competition and help resolve disputes over the right to tax multinational companies. Given the paucity of practical tools to embed human rights norms into the process and substance of reforming international tax policies, the authors then develop a set of assessment questions to help operationalise human rights norms into current efforts to re-write the international tax rules.

I. Introduction

The COVID-19 shock has brought our global economy to its knees, with millions left without decent work. Governments have tried to respond with massive economic recovery plans, including subsidies to companies, temporary unemployment benefits and cash transfer schemes to cushion the shock. Considerable resources have been mobilised to this effect, leading to a sharp increase in the sovereign debts of States. Yet at the same time, COVID-19 has placed severe stress on many of the traditional ways in which governments raise the revenue sufficient to finance needed public services. In this context, it is more imperative than ever that national fiscal reforms be guided by a human rights framework – that they are progressive rather than regressive, and that they have as an express guiding mission to reduce deepening poverty and the entrenchment of inequalities.

Yet, achieving such a national human rights-aligned tax policy requires an international policy environment that enables individual States, and particularly low- and middle-income countries, to opt for and implement a human rights-aligned tax environment internationally.[1] Such an enabling international environment is one in which polities would regain the capacity to make their own collective fiscal choices about the size of the budget and the level of domestic redistribution – two key components of global tax justice. In this article, we explore how international human rights law, including the UN *Guiding Principles on Human Rights Impact Assessments of Economic Reforms* ('*GPs*'),[2] can contribute to build a more solid conception of global tax justice that might serve as a normative foundation to curb harmful tax competition and help resolve disputes over the right to tax cross-border economic activity. This is especially relevant as tax avoidance by multinational companies continues to deprive countries from the revenues they need even more now with the tremendous financing needs to rebuild better after COVID-19.

To that end, we first consider the parameters of a human rights-aligned approach to domestic tax policy (Part II). This framework takes its departure point in the International Covenant on Economic, Social and Cultural Rights, the main international human rights treaty in the area of economic and social rights, in its interpretation by the Committee on Economic, Social and Cultural Rights, as well as the *GPs*. In Part III, we note that economic globalisation, as it has proceeded over the past forty years, has significantly reduced the ability of States to make collective fiscal choices about the size of its budget and the level of domestic redistribution. This is not just a singular problem of poorer countries, but ultimately reduces the ability of all countries to mobilise domestic resources through taxation. To break this vicious cycle, new forms of international cooperation are required. Part IV therefore examines whether general international law, and human rights law in particular, imposes such a duty of international cooperation. Part V presents the current normative approaches to justify the use of the State power to tax multinational companies in an inter-connected, global economy. We introduce some of the pitfalls of these different approaches, and then discuss how invoking the norms and principles embedded in human rights law, including those reflected in the UN *Guiding Principles on Human Rights Impact Assessments of Economic Reforms*, could help resolve some of these normative gaps. Part VI wraps a framework of questions that policy makers and advocates can use for assessing current efforts to rewrite the international tax rules.

II. A national human rights-based tax policy

COVID-19 has put immense pressure on government budgets worldwide. The realisation of human rights – civil, political, economic, social or cultural – depends on various factors, but especially the material means available to fund the policies and programmes to give human rights life. The International Covenant on Economic, Social and Cultural Rights requires that States parties should move 'as expeditiously and effectively as possible towards [the] goal [of the full realization of economic, social and cultural rights]'.[3] This has a number of consequences for the budgetary policies of the States parties. First, the introduction of retrogressive measures is *prima facie* suspect: the Committee considers that such measures, 'would require the most careful consideration and would need to be fully justified by reference to the totality of the rights provided for in the Covenant and in the context of the full use of the maximum available resources'.[4] Any budgetary measure that would lower the level of provision of certain public services, such as in the areas of education, or of water or electricity provision, or that would diminish the right to social security, including the right to an old age pension, are also suspect, since such budgetary choices may have especially severe impacts on women who – in the current division of gender roles that is still dominant in most regions of the world – have traditionally been assuming the burden of caring for infants, children and older persons, as well as stepping in for non-existent or crumbling energy, water or health infrastructure by, for example, fetching firewood or caring for ill family members to meet the household needs.[5] Secondly, when facing resource constraints, the State should demonstrate that it has given priority to the 'satisfaction of, at the very least, minimum essential levels of each of the rights' of the Covenant, which correspond to the core obligations of States under this instrument: the Committee expresses the view that:

> a State party in which any significant number of individuals is deprived of essential foodstuffs, of essential primary health care, of basic shelter and housing, or of the most basic forms of education is, prima facie, failing to discharge its obligations under the Covenant.[6]

Thirdly, in accordance with the principle of non-discrimination in the enjoyment of Covenant rights[7], priority should be given to improving the situation of groups who have traditionally been disadvantaged.[8] Fourth and finally, although the Covenant on Economic, Social and Cultural Rights itself is silent about such a requirement, the principle of participation is relevant to assessing whether the budgetary choices made by States comply with its prescriptions. For instance, where retrogressive measures are adopted in the area of social security, the Committee considers it relevant to ask whether such measures were taken with the 'genuine participation of affected groups in examining the proposed measures and alternatives',[9] and where a State cannot ensure a minimum level of protection against all risks and contingencies of life, it is recommended that it 'select a core group of social risks and contingencies', based on 'a wide process of consultation'.[10]

These broad principles have immediate and precise consequences for the design and implementation of taxation policies. First, and especially in the COVID-19 recovery, most countries need to expand the tax base in order to ensure that taxation, combined with other sources of public revenue, can fund public policies that support the realisation of economic, social and cultural rights – including access to healthcare, to education and to housing, and to social security. Even low-income countries now have the capacity to mobilise domestic resources to support at least the minimum essential level of all social rights.[11] It has been calculated in 2014 that, if developing countries were to raise even 15 percent of their national income in tax (a rather modest figure, compared to the average of 37 percent in OECD countries), the additional revenue collected ($198 billion per year) would represent more than all foreign development assistance combined.[12] Yet in many developing countries, the tax base remains very low, and does not allow the States concerned to effectively fulfil the rights of the Covenant.[13] Favourable fiscal treatment granted to foreign investors in order to attract capital (despite the weak evidence that such a strategy actually works[14]) further reduces the ability of States to mobilise enough domestic resources to finance economic and social rights.

Secondly, in order to support substantive equality, there is a need to ensure that the tax structure is sufficiently progressive, in order to accelerate the progress towards the eradication of poverty.[15] Whenever tax policy is either insufficient or discriminatory in nature, the CESCR is increasingly presuming non-compliance with the 'maximum available resources' (MAR) clause,.[16] Redistributive fiscal policies and social spending, particularly on social security, have had a major role to play to reduce the levels of inequality that would result from market incomes for different groups of the population. In OECD countries, public cash transfers, together with income taxes and social security contributions, were estimated to reduce inequality among the working-age population (measured by the Gini coefficient) by an average of about one-quarter across OECD countries during the period from the mid-1980s to the late 2000s.[17] A progressive tax system has a key role to play in this regard, since it can both reduce the weight of pre-tax income inequalities and increase the capacity of the State to provide public services to the population. This explains why the Committee on Economic, Social and Cultural Rights has regularly expressed its concern at reforms of the taxation system that would make it less progressive – for instance, by shifting the burden from corporations to the families, or by increasing VAT rates on essential items.[18]

Assessing whether a fiscal system is progressive enough requires looking beyond simply how taxes are raised. It should also examine how the money raised is to be spent. A progressive tax system's impact on the reduction of inequalities is heightened if the revenue from the taxes collected is redistributed through social and economic policies that benefit the poor, rather than being spent on investments that shall only allow the rich to become richer. Unfortunately, many of the initial COVID-19 economic relief packages have done just that.[19] For the effective realisation of economic, social and cultural rights, it is the *combination* of revenue mobilisation and of spending choices that matters,[20] and neither of these two elements alone shall in itself suffice to assess whether the efforts of the State are sufficient: just like one can easily imagine a State with generous social policies addressed at tackling poverty, but in which such policies are essentially financed by the poor themselves,[21] it is possible to have a State tax the rich but not use the revenues collected in ways that have a significant impact on the reduction of inequalities.

Moreover, the ability for even a progressive tax system to reduce inequalities depends not only on the contribution of the richest part of the population to public revenue in *percentage* terms, but also on the *absolute* levels of such contributions: if, for example, the richest decile of the population pays 90 per cent of the total income taxes collected in the country, the taxation system may be said to be progressive according to the most common measure of tax progressivity known as the Kakwani index. But if those richest 10 per cent are taxed at very low rates, the redistributive capacity of the taxation remains very limited: such a redistributive capacity is captured by another index, known as the Reynolds-Smolensky index, which measures the difference in income distribution before and after the tax is imposed.[22] One important consequence of this distinction is that a tax reform that may at first appear as regressive because the proportion of the total tax revenue paid by the richest part of the population will decrease (leading, in other terms, to the effort being spread across a larger part of the population), nevertheless may have progressive consequences if the overall tax rates and thus the revenue the State may mobilise are increased and social spending is progressive enough to offset the effect of the higher tax burden across the population, providing domestic resources to invest in human rights.

Of course, the introduction of a progressive taxation scheme could have counter-productive impacts if it resulted in choking the economy and significantly slowing down economic activity, thus, in the medium- to long-term, destroying the very revenue base the State may be able to count on in order to finance human rights-aligned social and economic policies. This however is an argument in favour of, not against, progressive taxation schemes combined with strong redistributive policies. Based on the 'Kuznets curve' showing a positive correlation between the rise of inequality and GDP growth in countries going through a fast industrialisation process, it has sometimes been alleged that the growth of inequality is an inevitable price to pay for economic growth, so that the introduction of policies to combat inequalities, if it occurs too early, might damage the prospects for development.[23] However, quite apart from the fact that the original reasoning of Simon Kuznets, which applied to fast-growing nations going through rapid processes of industrialisation and urbanisation, could not be transposed to advanced industrial economies in which these processes are further along, the ideological uses made of his work does not correspond to the actual findings of Kuznets. Whereas there may have been, historically, a correlation between the structural transformation linked to industrialisation and the increase of inequality, it does not follow that such increase should be treated as a condition for industrialisation. Indeed, one may suspect that industrialisation would have been far less damaging to social cohesion, and thus far more sustainable, if it had included robust redistributive schemes compensating the losers by transferring resources from the gainers. In fact, there is now a consensus that high levels of taxation, allowing the State to adopt robust redistributive policies and provide high-quality public services, far from being an obstacle to economic growth, are an indispensable ingredient thereof: even researchers from the International Monetary Fund (IMF) now refer to the inverse relationship that exists between the income share accruing to the richest part of society and economic growth.[24] Indeed, inequality reduction plays a more important role than growth itself in poverty alleviation: the World Bank notes that a reduction of the Gini index by 1 percent per year would have a larger impact on global poverty than increasing annual growth one percentage point above current forecasts.[25] The importance of fiscal redistribution for the anti-poverty, as well as for the development agenda more broadly, motivated the adoption of the Redistributive Impact of Fiscal Policy indicator by the United Nations Statistical Commission to monitor progress on SDG 10.[26]

Empirically, therefore, there does not seem to be a trade-off between the understandable desire of low-income countries to grow their economy, and the reduction of inequality within these countries by progressive taxation and redistribution schemes: the two are in fact mutually supportive, and should be seen that way.[27] Bold reforms to invest in programmes that realise human rights and curb inequalities, therefore, should be seen as a boon to sustainable and dynamic economic progress.[28]

The adoption of strongly progressive tax and spending programmes should therefore be seen as a condition for the realisation of economic, social and cultural rights especially under COVID-19, and thus as a duty for the States parties to the Covenant on Economic, Social and Cultural Rights.[29] Yet, for many governments, progressive taxation with powerful inequality-reducing impacts may be difficult to achieve. Indirect taxes (such as VAT) are easier to collect, and therefore, despite their regressive impacts (since poor households spend a higher proportion of their incomes on buying consumer goods[30]), they may be the path of least resistance for governments with a weak administrative capacity to collect revenue. Moreover, because capital is more mobile than labour and households, it is tempting to reduce the levels of taxation of capital, particularly by lowering the corporate tax and the person income tax for the highest income earners,[31] and to compensate this by increasing the taxation of wage-earners and households. Finally, fiscal competition between countries is perpetuated by the myth according to which investors can be attracted by lowering the corporate tax base – as if the comparative advantage of countries should consist in restricting their chances to educate a highly-qualified workforce, to maintain well-functioning public services, and to improve the quality of life for those working under their jurisdiction.

Instead of shifting more of the tax burden on to the wealthiest corporations and the richest individuals as both economic common sense and human rights would require, the result of such pressures is that we have fiscal policies which end up taxing wage earners and consumers through VAT and imposing user fees in sectors such as health or education – adversely affecting the accessibility and affordability of key socio-economic rights According to the World Bank, the average total tax rate payable by businesses on their commercial profits decreased from 53.5% to 40.8% between 2005 and 2015.[32] Some countries moved in the opposite direction: Argentina and Chile are examples in Latin America; Malaysia and Niger provide illustrations in Asia and in Africa. In general, however, the trend downwards is massive: for many countries, the reduction of corporate taxes is measured in double digits, and the phenomenon is especially spectacular in the countries classified by the UN as least-developed, where the rate went down on average from 75.4% to 44.7%; if we consider heavily indebted poor countries alone, the decrease is from 81.2% to 52.7%.

In sum, the broad outlines of a human rights-aligned approach to domestic tax policy are apparent, with the task of more effectively taxing multinational companies a priority. Yet, challenges remain, in particular in light of the global constraints to taxing cross-border economic activity and putting an end to corporate tax abuse.

III. Economic globalisation and the policy space for progressive taxation

Whereas we can identify the broad outlines of a human rights-compliant approach to taxation domestically, whether countries are in fact realistically in a position individually to move in this direction remains questionable. The lowering of obstacles to trade and investment across borders, facilitated both by technological advances and by regulatory and policy changes, in addition to the diffusion of consumption styles modelled on those that have colonised the advanced Western economies, had led to the emergence of 'competitive States', whose chief concern is to maintain their competitive advantage in the global economy, in particular by shaping 'business friendly' environments.[33] Economic globalisation has thus narrowed down the policy space States have, a situation this has been further worsened by the failure of the international community to take decisive measures against tax avoidance strategies by transnational corporations – our particular focus in this chapter.[34] This Part examines these different obstacles, in order to identify what forms of international cooperation in the field of taxation would be required to overcome them.

A first obstacle to the adoption of human rights-aligned domestic taxation schemes relate to the provisions protecting foreign investors' rights in bilateral or multilateral trade or investment agreements.[35] Because such investment treaties (or provisions on investors' rights in trade agreements) protect investors from the adoption of regulations that amount to indirect expropriation, situations may arise in which the rights of investors are pitted against those of the individuals or communities whose rights are negatively affected by the investment. Most recently, law firms specialising in the use of investment treaties to sue governments have developed the groundwork to bring arbitration against governments for taking emergency measures to halt the spread of COVID-19 and save lives, with the argument being that these actions constitute indirect expropriation under relevant treaties by impinging on corporate earnings.[36] This is why the Guiding Principles on Business and Human Rights – a particularly authoritative text since they were unanimously welcomed by the Human Rights Council[37] – insist that 'States should maintain adequate domestic policy space to meet their human rights obligations when pursuing business-related policy objectives with other States or business enterprises, for instance through investment treaties or contracts'.[38] In order to avoid the risk that investment treaties result in obstacles to human rights, for instance by chilling a State from adopting certain measures that an investor may seek to challenge as discriminatory or as imposing a disproportionate cost, investment treaties (or investment chapters in free trade agreements) may have to include specific references to the human rights obligations of the host State. Where investment agreements are insufficiently explicit about the right of the State to regulate foreign investors in order to ensure full compliance with the State's human rights obligations, as such obligations may evolve from time to time in the name of progressive realisation, there is a need to ensure that these human rights obligations are fully taken into account in investor-State dispute settlement proceedings.[39] The *GPs* further clarify that:

> host States should enact foreign investment laws in such a way that includes an obligation on investors to undertake human rights impact assessments [...] to enhance[e] the sustainability and development impact of investments in such a way that is beneficial to all stakeholders.[40]

Tax evasion and corporate tax avoidance presents a second layer of obstacles to the adoption of progressive taxation policies which mobilise sufficient resources for human rights. In Latin America for instance, on average 50 per cent of personal and corporate income taxes are either evaded or avoided, with Guatemala topping the league with an evasion rate of 70 per cent.[41] Such practices by corporations and high-net worth individuals represent a huge loss to countries, and they are of particular consequence (as a percentage of their public budgets) in low- and middle-income countries.[42] It has been noted, for instance, that the total financial flows for 1970–2008 represents a sum far in excess of the external debt of all African countries[43]: in other terms, taking into account the broader concept of illicit financial flows, Africa is a net creditor to the world.[44]

World leaders have come to some agreement – on paper at least – that tax abuse is a global priority. The Sustainable Development Goal 16, target 4 call for a significant reduction in illicit financial flows, arguably including corporate tax avoidance.[45] In the Addis Ababa Action Agenda – a major international agreement on financing sustainable development – the Heads of State and Government and High Representatives 'recognize [d] that significant additional domestic public resources, supplemented by international assistance as appropriate, will be critical to realising sustainable development and achieving the sustainable development goals'. They committed to 'enhancing revenue administration through modernized, progressive tax systems, improved tax policy and more efficient tax collection',[46] and to broaden the tax base.[47] Governments agreed further 'to assess the impact of their policies on sustainable development,' at least implicitly expressing support for investigating how their national tax systems spill over to undermine the ability of other countries to raise revenue.[48] While not legally binding, these political commitments make clear global concern with tax abuse and recognition of the need to remedy it [or something].

Although the main responsibility in tackling corporate tax avoidance lies with governments, the private sector – banks and other financial institutions – also have a role to play in this regard. The due diligence obligations of corporations in terms of the Guiding Principles on Business and Human Rights[49] – insisting that they put in place 'a human rights due-diligence process to identify, prevent, mitigate and account for how they address their impacts on human rights'[50] – compel companies that they take measures to ensure that their clients do not evade their duties to pay taxes in the jurisdictions in which they reside. This interpretation is confirmed by Principle 17 of the Guiding Principles on Business and Human Rights, which provides that human rights due diligence should cover 'adverse human rights impacts that the business enterprise may cause or contribute to through its own activities, or which may be directly linked to its operations, products or services by its business relationships'.[51] In sum, where and how much multinational companies pay in tax is intimately connected to governments' ability to protect and fulfil human rights, as well as companies' responsibilities to respect human rights.

IV. The role of international cooperation in combating corporate tax avoidance

Domestic efforts to address tax avoidance will only be fully effective if supported by international cooperation. States' extraterritorial human rights obligations, also reflected in the *GPs*, provide a useful framework to better delineate respective duties between countries over cross-border economic activity.[52] Though classic forms of international cooperation have a role to play in this regard, such as 'aid for tax' strategies in which donor governments support tax administrations to strengthen tax collection,[53] these will remain insufficient unless complemented by reforms in the countries which facilitate corporate tax avoidance. This concerns in particular the countries under whose jurisdiction tax havens are currently left unaddressed, or whose financial secrecy or lax corporate tax regulations facilitate tax avoidance. The Committee on Economic, Social and Cultural Rights encouraged in this regard States parties to 'combat abusive tax practices by transnational corporations', in particular by 'combat[ing] transfer pricing practices and deepen[ing] international tax cooperation, and explor[ing] the possibility to tax multinational groups of companies as single firms, with developed countries imposing a minimum corporate income tax rate during a period of transition'.[54]

The duty of international cooperation, as part of the human rights duties of States, may also play a role. Under international human rights law, State Parties have the obligation to cooperate internationally to realise human rights.[55] This means they must not cause harm beyond their borders, or prevent other States from meeting their human rights obligations.[56] The duty of international cooperation and the extraterritorial obligations have implications on tax issues.[57] This is evident from the work of various UN treaty bodies. For instance, the Committee on Economic, Social and Cultural Rights noted in concluding observations related to the United Kingdom that:

> financial secrecy legislation [allowing its Overseas Territories and Crown Dependencies to prosper as tax havens] and permissive rules on corporate tax are affecting the ability of the State party, as well other States, to meet their obligation to mobilize the maximum available resources for the implementation of economic, social and cultural rights,

and it recommended that it 'intensify its efforts, in coordination with its Overseas Territories and Crown Dependencies, to address global tax abuse'.[58] The Committee on the Elimination of Discrimination against Women also recommended that Switzerland:

> undertake independent, participatory and periodic impact assessments of the extraterritorial effects of its financial secrecy and corporate tax policies on women's rights and substantive equality, and ensure that such assessments are conducted in an impartial manner with public disclosure of the methodology and finding.[59]

There are signs that governments are finally taking these issues more seriously. As mentioned above, the Addis Ababa Action Agenda explicitly acknowledges the need for enhanced international tax cooperation on these issues.[60]

Yet in the absence of meaningful international cooperation, transnational corporations shall continue to rely on various techniques to reduce their tax liability, depriving States from the revenues they need to finance public services. One favoured technique is profit-shifting, when corporations declare profits in low-tax jurisdictions where they may have no staff or productive activities or only minimal activities, rather than declaring such profits (and paying the corresponding taxes) where their activities take place.[61] Transfer-pricing between different companies of a multinational group allows to achieve such profit-shifting, in ways which are difficult for a judge at domestic level to find illegal. And it plays an increasingly important role in the global economy: intra-group trade is currently estimated to represent 30 per cent of global trade.[62] This is why instruments such as the United Nations Model Double Taxation Convention between Developed and Developing Countries[63] or the OECD Model Tax Convention on Income and on Capital (most recently revised in 2017)[64] encourage countries to adopt the 'arm's length standard', according to which they should prohibit mispricing between different parts of the multinational group, which is deemed to occur where such relations between related enterprises 'differ from those which would be made between independent enterprises'.[65] The Convention on Mutual Administrative Assistance in Tax Matters[66] also provides for various forms of administrative cooperation between States in the assessment and collection of taxes, facilitating the exchange of information and the recovery of foreign tax claims with a view to supporting States' efforts to combat tax avoidance and evasion. Furthermore, on 1 July 2018, the Multilateral Convention to Implement Tax Treaty Related Measures to Prevent Base Erosion and Profit Shifting (MLI) entered into force, with various anti-abuse provisions and amending a large number of bilateral tax treaties concluded to eliminate double taxation between the parties. These efforts are ongoing: the G20 has identified base erosion and profit shifting (BEPS) as a major concern for tax justice worldwide, and the OECD adopted a 15-point action plan in 2013 in order to address this, to be progressively implemented in the next few years ('OECD/G20 BEPS package').[67] We turn now to these efforts to improve how States can tax multinational corporate activity.

V. What are the current normative justifications grounding States' rights to tax cross-border business activity – and what is missing?[68]

We have argued above how the adoption of strongly progressive taxation schemes is a precondition for the realisation of human rights, especially economic, social and cultural rights. Yet, at the same time the current international tax system denies the capacity of countries to implement these sorts of human rights-consistent tax policies, especially when it comes to raising sufficient revenue from the activity of multinational enterprises. This raises a number of key questions. Namely, how can the international community make progress towards enabling individual countries to implement such polices? Article 23 of the International Covenant on Economic, Social and Cultural Rights refers to 'the conclusion of conventions' among the measures that States should take in order to comply with the duties of international assistance and cooperation under the Covenant. And general international law recognises a duty to negotiate in good faith where it is only through negotiation that States can discharge their international obligations and solve situations of conflict.[69] It may therefore be argued that in order to strengthen international cooperation in this area, States have a duty, minimally, to enter into negotiations and to pursue them in good faith – an obligation of means, to be distinguished from the obligation of result to achieve agreement. According to the CESCR, for example,

> the extraterritorial obligation to respect requires States parties to refrain from interfering directly or indirectly with the enjoyment of the Covenant rights by persons outside their territories. As part of that obligation, States parties must ensure that they do not obstruct another State from complying with its obligations under the Covenant. This duty is particularly relevant to the negotiation and conclusion of trade and investment agreements or of financial and tax treaties, as well as to judicial cooperation.[70]

What human rights considerations should individual countries take into account, however, in order to comply with their duty to negotiate in good faith for building such an environment in the ongoing multilateral negotiation processes on international tax matters?

This section attempts to answer these questions by focusing on the problem of how to allocate the right to tax multinational companies between States where multinational companies operate. We focus here on the negotiation process within the OECD's Inclusive Framework on BEPS for reaching a solution on this issue (as well as on other challenges in the field of corporate international taxation arising from the digitalisation of the economy). These deliberations would arguably have more democratic legitimacy if carried out between member states within the UN, where the principle of sovereign equality and one-member, one-vote can be more adequately protected.[71] Yet, we focus on this OECD-led process because it is currently the main locus of negotiation between States to re-shape what is a thoroughly outdated and broken set of international tax rules. We first present the current normative approaches to justify the use of the State power to tax multinational companies in an inter-connected, global economy. We then discuss some of the pitfalls of these different approaches. Finally, we explore how invoking the norms embedded in human rights law, including those captured in the *GPs*, could help resolve some of these normative gaps.

A. Economic nexus and its discontents

Taxation is the act of preserving a portion of economic resources for the use of a polity instead of an individual person or business. Scholars, philosophers and governments justify taxation as necessary to pay for public goods and services, correct market failures, or to distribute economic gains more fairly. Cross-border economic activity – especially carried out by multi-national companies – creates a set of competitive claims between States on the right to tax. While each State is understood to enjoy sovereignty over its power to tax, an individual State's sovereignty is inevitably wrapped up in the sovereignty other States when each attempts to tax the profits and/or value generated by the same company. This is especially so when States seek to avoid double-taxation. So, who has the right to tax a company operating in a variety of countries?

According to Christians,[72] States generally lay their claim for a jurisdiction to tax multinational taxpayers on three different rationales. The first is *national sovereignty*. Under this rationale, States – either as the representative of the 'will of the people' or the ultimate provider of the people – are entitled to absolute authority to rule in tax matters, with the only constraint being other States' sovereignty.[73] Competing claims between sovereign States over the right to tax certain individuals or entities are generally resolved with reference to the 'nationality' of that taxpayer, who is seen as an object of the State rather than an active agent. That is, the nexus between the State and the taxpayer is defined by a *political*, not necessarily the economic, connection.[74] This principle of national sovereignty lends itself to the primary goal of producing public revenue and economic growth for the national government and/or its people, even if that comes at the expense of other governments and other people.

The second justification for taxing cross-border activity relies on *economic nexus*, according to Christians.[75] This rationale for the jurisdiction to tax multinational activity rests not on the basis of a taxpayer's nationality, especially difficult to define in the era of globalisation in which multinational companies operate to great scale and great depth across jurisdictions. Instead of national allegiance, jurisdiction is defined here by the early work of the League of Nations as the taxpayer's 'economic allegiance' with, and within, the state.[76] In making the case for basing tax jurisdictional claims on economic ties instead of political adherence, this rationale argues that economic nexus should be assessed primarily with respect to two factors: the jurisdiction of physical residence by the subject of the tax ('residence'), and the 'origin' of the activity to be taxed ('source').[77] This remains the principal way governments today justify their right to tax international economic flows. This rationale is at the heart of much of current international tax law (e.g. permanent establishment rules) guiding the allocation of taxing rights over multinational companies. While the traditional focus on revenue potential is surely an important consideration, the principle of economic nexus lends itself more seamlessly than the national sovereignty view toward a vision that the primary goal of international taxation to advance worldwide economic efficiency.

A third normative explanation for the jurisdiction to tax multinational companies, according to Christians, is the *membership*, or benefit principle.[78] Tax subjects, according to this justification, are identified neither by their nationality nor by their specific economic relationships, but instead by the degree to which they benefit from the tax and public spending decisions of all country in question. Certain tax-derived benefits – be they infrastructure, an educated and healthy workforce, protection of private property, a stable climate, etc. – are essential economic foundations without which a particular company would not succeed. By implicitly choosing to benefit from these public services, according to this principle, businesses voluntary express their membership in the political community, and accordingly accept their reciprocal tax obligations. While taxing in reference to benefits received might contribute to increased economic equity between States, this approach is not principally guided by a concern for distributive justice: it aims, rather, to ensure better reciprocity between taxpayers and the governments which provide the good and services they need to operate.[79]

Most of modern international tax law (expressed for example in over 3,000 bilateral tax treaties, a multilateral instrument, and some elements of customary international tax law[80]) is normatively based on the economic nexus rationale as a normative foundation for allocating taxing rights between countries. This very much flows from the post-war global political agreement on the superiority of free trade and the belief that commercial barriers between countries should be abolished. More recently, the OECD Base Erosion and Profit Shifting (BEPS) project – which now brings together over 130 countries to adapt the international tax rules to more effectively tax today's multinational companies – rests on the fundamental principle of economic nexus. Much of the heat in these debates rests on how to define economic nexus (for instance, in order to adapt the concept of a permanent establishment to a digital economy), how to allocate between States the taxable economic value companies produce (Pillar I of the BEPS 2.0 debate), and how to ensure companies pay at least a minimum level of tax wherever they operate (Pillar II of the BEPS 2.0 debate).[81] In theory, all States and even most civil society organisations involved in this seminal process agree that companies should be taxed where they produce economic value.[82] Parties engage in intense debates on *how* to define and allocate that value (i.e. arms-length pricing vs. formulary apportionment methods); however, in our reading, next to no one argues for taxing multinationals based on their nationality alone, or in reference to the tax-derived benefits they receive from different governments alone.

From a human rights perspective however, there are at least two factors that urge caution when taking the economic nexus principle as the sole normative foundation undergirding international tax law in the twenty-first century. First, there are serious practical considerations which limit the ability to implement this principle in the real world. In practice, national sovereignty very often prevails,[83] especially where transactions are more complex and subjective. That is, the *de facto* and disproportionate power of some nations to better administer, regulate and enforce their tax prerogatives leads in practice to a disconnect between the *de jure* jurisdiction to tax defined in economic terms on the one hand, and – on the other hand – the actual behaviour adopted by States as a result of their effective power as manifest in superior administrative capacity, economic positioning or geo-political weight. The US role in the OECD negotiations is paramount, for example, even if on the surface they have the same voting rights in the process as other states.

Further widening the gap between law and practice, the largest multinational companies have achieved such effective power that they are able to effectively chose where, when and sometimes whether to pay tax at all.[84] These companies, and their tax advisors, actively seek to take advantage of national differences in tax law, administrative/ enforcement capacity, political will and information in order to boost their own short-term returns.[85] While the nationality principle may have little cogence in international tax law, global companies based in the US or Europe, for example, respond very differently to their home states' strong tax administrations than to those of less powerful countries.[86]

In sum, practical coherence over the implementation of the three principles discussed above is tempered strongly by asymmetries of effective power between States, which have resulted in a set of global tax arrangements biased against the weakest countries. The current international tax regime could be said to be un-governed in many practical respects, embodying in practice the principle of 'might is right'.

Advocates have advanced various proposals to remedy these power imbalances in ways which would ensure multinational companies pay more in tax, and to the right countries.[87] These include efforts to reduce information asymmetries (e.g. public country-by-country reporting requirements),[88] to strengthen the administrative and enforcement capacities of LMICs (e.g. Tax Inspectors Beyond Borders),[89] and to more fairly allocate the right to tax (e.g. by replacing the subjective arms-length principle with a formulary apportionment model).[90] Unfortunately, even if these were all implemented equitably across countries, we would still be faced with a fundamental dilemma at the heart of the basing the right to tax on economic value creation: it inevitably locks low-*income* countries into being low-*tax* countries. How is that?

Today's global economy rests on a stark division of labour between richer on the one hand, and poorer countries on the other. High-income countries on the whole capture the highest value-added portions of a company's value chain (such as research, intellectual property, design, branding, marketing, sales and service) while poorer countries contribute lower value-added parts of the value chain (including the provision of raw materials and low-wage manufacturing).[91] Without enhancing the value of the economic activities these countries are involved in, simply assigning these countries' taxation rights as a function of how much value they add to the economic chain will put them in a consistently inferior position with regard to the revenue they can mobilise. Investigating one particular case study of the UK-based global telecom giant Vodafone, researchers have found that using a more objective formula to apportion taxable profits between countries ('formulary apportionment') based on sales, assets and payroll – all oft-used indicators of economic value – are valuable, but not necessarily transformative in providing more material benefit to lower-income countries.[92]

B. Elaborating on the membership principle, and remaining gaps in the normative justifications governing States' rights to tax

If economic nexus then is a flawed normative principle, what can come in its place? Though increasingly hinted at by nationalist politicians, reverting back to a company's supposed nationality to justify the right to tax fundamentally global companies arguably poses more problems than solutions—especially when most of the most profitable global companies are based in already-wealthy places like the US and the European Union. So, how might the membership principle work in practice to define which countries can tax multinational companies?

The membership principle – complemented by efforts to constrain harmful real tax competition – provides an useful alternative which could harmonise relevant national tax policies, and without having to transfer core tax decisions from national States to the global level. According to Dietsch and Rixen, along with the generalisation of the membership principle, a constraint on fiscal policy – enforced by a possible International Tax Organization – that rules out fiscal arrangements which can be shown to be based on strategic intent, can help to restore States' capacity to tax multinationals according to polities' will without fears that their tax base will be eroded by other States' policies.[93] This would require assessing whether the country would have pursued the same corporate tax policy in the absence of the resulting capital inflows.[94] This would go a long way towards avoiding the collectively sub-optimal outcomes that might otherwise result from undermining effective control that other States have over their main fiscal decisions – thus reducing the aggregate extent of fiscal self-determination.

However, establishing a social and international order in which States can enjoy *de facto* sovereignty to achieve the aims of their people is not sufficient to establish the needed enabling environment for the realisation of human rights. The jurisdictional proposals outlined above must be complemented by more substantive principles if this is to be achieved. As Dietsch and Rixen recognised:

> A world in which the two principles are respected is not yet a just world. It is merely a world that guarantees international background justice in one important way: national polities would regain the capacity to make collective fiscal choices about the size of the budget and the level of domestic redistribution. In other words, the principles ensure that the costs of fiscal choices fall on those who make them, at least to the extent that this can be achieved under conditions of fiscal interdependence. However, the two principles will have to be complemented by substantive principles of global tax justice.[95]

So, what are these more substantive principles of global tax justice? To the extent that countries respect both their own constitutional principles and their international human rights obligations analysed in part II, there are multiple valid conceptions on what an ideal tax system should be. In each country, different actors advance their visions of tax justice within an institutional framework to settle a collective agreement on the issue. There are places, such as Sweden, that provide more social services to citizens, but in turn also 'charge' more in terms of taxes. There are others, like the United Kingdom, where voters seem to prefer a leaner set of services and hence pay less. As long as democratic choice is constrained at the national level, different fiscal settlements, with different levels of required tax revenue, will differ by country. Democracies have this right to decide, as long as these decisions are in line with the obligation to international cooperation, including the duty to respect other countries' right to take different approaches.

Thus, a normative proposal on the right to tax based on substantive grounds cannot simply assume – or worse impose – a universal recipe for a just form of public finance. International rules must respect the plurality of national collective fiscal settlements as they emerge over time. How can international regimes define legitimate limits to state tax prerogatives based on substantive principles, while at the same time respecting both self-determination and pluralism?

We argue that justifying a State's right to tax can benefit from broadly accepted and universal meta-agreements on particular political values. International human rights law is the closest version of such a meta-agreement for building a sort of conditionality on justice grounds to self-determination and pluralism. These rules of justice do not prescribe a specific new rationale for a State's right to tax. Yet, as shown in the next section, these substantive and procedural principles provide complementary criteria to assess how better to empower States and their people to make global companies pay their 'fair share'.

VI. Human rights norms and questions to assess the adequacy and impact of international tax rules

As argued elsewhere,[96] relevant international human rights norms – as usefully distilled in the UN *Guiding Principles on Human Rights Impact Assessments of Economic Reforms*[97] and the Maastricht Principles on the Extraterritorial Obligations of States in the Area of Economic, Social and Cultural Rights – are a potentially powerful foundation upon which to ground international taxation. As shown above with regard to the United Kingdom and Switzerland, various human rights treaty bodies, including the UN Committee on Economic, Social and Cultural Rights, are currently using these principles to hold States parties accountable for the overseas impact of their tax policies, including in how these affect human rights outside their own borders. Human rights norms compel States to conduct assessments to evaluate and address any foreseeable effects of their tax policies.[98] Injecting human rights principles into the analysis will not address all the existing gaps in terms of normative failures of the current international tax architecture. Yet, using widely-accepted human rights norms can help arrive at the right questions to ask when developing proposals to allocate tax rights between jurisdictions or tackle tax avoidance,questions that might form the basis of a human rights impact assessment of proposals to re-write the international tax rules.[99]

For our purposes, international human rights law can be defined as socio-political claims founded on the inherent dignity of people, and the resulting foundational obligations of government to uphold human dignity. These claims have increasingly been codified in national, regional and international law through an extensive process of negotiation and interpretation within and between countries. Over time, a significant body of law and jurisprudence as emerged which provides a coherent set of principles. In this sense, a first added value of embedding human rights into the normative debates on the right to tax cross-border economic activity is that it provides a strong set of binding norms protecting important human freedoms as substantive values. This collective set of global agreements can thus help to define the legitimate limits to State's tax prerogatives based on substantive principles, while also respecting States' self-determination and pluralism. International human rights law is a sort of meta-agreement between States that can provide a basis for important substantive and procedural principles of global tax justice, described below.

Second, international human rights law disrupts the traditional understanding that international law and international relations be based on inter-state relationships, in which the primary tension is between States, and that any resulting duties and obligations be owed from one State to another. Under this 'billiard-ball' conception of international relations, it was unthinkable that international law should concern itself with protecting the interests of an individual or a community against its own government.[100] Yet, what was once inconceivable has started to change as human rights treaties – which expressly protect inherent dignity of people as their primary objective – have gained widespread adoption.[101] Human rights law, in other words, has arguably re-framed the concept of legitimate State sovereignty to strengthen the self-determination of 'peoples' as enjoying equal moral, if not yet equal legal, value.[102] A State's legitimacy to enact public policies, including tax policies, depends upon its realisation of the human rights of individuals and communities.[103] In this sense, human rights norms are valuable to the global tax debate in that they are flexible enough to both include global requirements of justice that take seriously the moral value of each person as a rights-holder regardless of the polity he/she pertains, while also respecting the internationalist approach concerned with protecting the right to self-determination of particular polities to define their own fiscal future within the boundaries of respecting human dignity.

The non-exhaustive table below sketches out some of the implications of substantive and procedural principles of human rights for assessing efforts to rewrite the rules around international corporate taxation. For each, a human rights framework poses questions which might be fruitfully used to assess the impacts of the current debate on creating fairer rules to tax cross-border economic activity.

Relevant human rights norm/ obligation	Implications on international matters on corporate taxation	Questions to assess adequacy and impacts of international tax rules
Obligation to *respect* human rights beyond borders	Requires countries to avoid conduct that has foreseeable risks of impairing the enjoyment of human rights by persons beyond their borders.[104]	Are reforms to current rules effective for making real progress in the fight against tax avoidance?
	Governments must collaborate with – and not undermine – other governments' efforts to mobilise the maximum of available resources for human rights and sustainable development.[105] By corollary, government laws and policies which have the effect of enabling corporate tax avoidance clearly work against the achievement of human rights goals.	Are reforms effective to curb harmful tax competition?
	Consideration of the spill-over effects[106] of such laws and policies must therefore be central to determining whether states, international institutions and large business actors are meeting their human rights and sustainable development responsibilities	Do reforms effectively prevent the negative spillover effects of some countries upon others, especially lower income countries?
Obligation to *protect* against third-party abuses of human rights overseas	'States Parties should encourage business actors whose conduct they are in a position to influence to ensure that they do not undermine the efforts of the States in which they operate to fully realise the Covenant rights, for instance by resorting to tax evasion or tax avoidance strategies in the countries concerned.'[107]	Are reforms to current rules effective in preventing revenue losses stemming from corporate tax avoidance, particularly in low- and middle-income countries?
	'To combat abusive tax practices by transnational corporations, States should combat transfer pricing practices and deepen international tax cooperation, and explore the possibility to tax multinational groups of companies as single firms, with developed countries imposing a minimum corporate income tax rate during a period of transition'.[108]	Are reforms effective for making real progress on combatting base erosion and profit-shifting and eliminating loopholes that allow multi-national not paying their fair share?
	'Lowering the rates of corporate taxes with a sole view to attracting investors encourages a race to the bottom that ultimately undermines the ability of all States to mobilize resources	

(Continued)

Continued.

Relevant human rights norm/ obligation	Implications on international matters on corporate taxation	Questions to assess adequacy and impacts of international tax rules
	domestically to realize Covenant rights. As such, this practice is inconsistent with the duties of the States Parties to the Covenant.'[109] 'Providing excessive protection to bank secrecy and permissive rules on corporate tax may affect the ability of States where economic activities are taking place to meet their obligation to mobilize the maximum available resources for the implementation of economic, social and cultural rights'[110]	
Obligation to support the universal *fulfilment* of economic and social rights	States are also obligated under the Covenant to cooperate internationally to mobilise the maximum available resources to fulfil economic, social, and cultural rights[111]—including in matters of taxation so critical to the creation of an enabling environment for the realisation of these rights.[112]	Are States complying with their duty to negotiate in good faith in the relevant multilateral fora on tax matters for creating an international environment that enables the universal fulfilment of human rights?
Substantive human rights obligations: - Minimum core - Non-discrimination - Progressive realisation using the maximum available resources (MAR)	Duty of each State acting, commensurate with its capacities, resources and influence, in accordance with the principle of common but differentiated responsibilities and respective capabilities, to improve the system of international taxation, according priority to countries which are struggling to meet the minimum essential levels of economic and social rights.[113]	Do the economic and revenue impacts of international tax rules exacerbate economic, gender, or other inequalities within a given country?
	'States must not only use existing resources to fulfil this obligation [of mobilising the maximum available resources for the progressive enjoyment of rights] but also generate potential resources in a sustainable way when the former are not sufficient to ensure the realisation of rights. This requires, for example, seeking international assistance and cooperation, mobilising domestic resources in ways compatible with environmental sustainability and with the rights of people affected by extractive industries, as well as regulating the financial sector.'[114]	Do international tax rules exacerbate inequalities between countries, for example in their respective abilities to raise corporate tax revenue? Do proposals foster substantive equality between countries in their rights and capacity to tax multinationals?
	'States' obligation to mobilise resources includes: tackling tax evasion and avoidance; ensuring a progressive tax system, including by widening the tax base with regard to multinational corporations and the richest; avoiding international tax competition; improving the efficiency of tax collection; and reprioritizing expenditures to ensure, among other things, adequate funding of public services.'[115]	Do reforms to international tax rules empower countries to strengthen equitable tax collection for progressive realisation of human rights and to prevent austerity measures? Is tax administration capacity a priority?
Procedural principles: transparency, participation, accountability (TAP Principles), and self-determination	States 'must observe international human rights standards, including the right to self-determination and the right to participate in decision-making, as well	Are LMICs empowered to using their voice and collective leverage in international tax forums to be able to capture more of their right to tax?

(*Continued*)

Continued.

Relevant human rights norm/ obligation	Implications on international matters on corporate taxation	Questions to assess adequacy and impacts of international tax rules
	as the principles of non-discrimination and equality, including gender equality, transparency, and accountability'.[116] Human rights law protects the right to self-determination of peoples as a core element of most treaties and instruments. Therefore, the interest to protect and circumscribe the fiscal prerogatives of the state in order to allow national polities regain the capacity to make collective fiscal choices about the size of the budget and the level of domestic redistribution is perfectly compatible, and even required, by the right to self-determination. 'Genuine participation can only be possible if Governments provide timely, comprehensive and accessible information on all aspects of public finance, including budgets and macroeconomic performance. Governments should also provide adequate justifications of policy choices to the population in general, and specifically to those most likely to be affected by the reform'.[117]	Do LMICs have the ability and capacity to participate on equal footing in the spaces where negotiations on international tax matters are taking place? Are all issues on the agenda for discussion, especially topics particularly critical for LMICs (e.g. revising the nexus rules to capture digital companies with very little sales but huge numbers of users in certain, unitary taxation vs arm-length principle, or the duty of HICs to assist developing countries in improving tax administration). Is participation of all countries involved must genuine and meaningful as members with the same rights of voice and vote? Do all stakeholders have all the information they need to make informed decisions?

This table shows that the *GPs*, and the international human rights framework more broadly, offers important content to a background conception of global tax justice. A just global tax system is not only one in which polities regain the capacity to make collective fiscal choices about the size of the budget and the level of domestic redistribution, whatever they may be. It is also one that enables individual States to fulfil their human rights obligations. To that end, it is critical that any global tax cooperation effort must be transparent, participatory and accountable, especially to those most affected. Importantly, one must consider both the position of LMICs, as well as those people most affected by lower tax revenues, to participate in the elaboration and implementation of the rules.

These requirements of a human-rights based conception of global tax justice are particularly important in the context the COVID-19 pandemic. A massive investment of resources are needed to tackle the impacts of the crisis, particularly within the LMICs that are already under-resourced and may well suffer the worst consequences.[118] Tax policy is an essential tool for aiding governments in dealing with the COVID-19 crisis. Yet this requires adapting tax rules to ensure sufficient policy space.[119] Some have begun to talk about the need for a 'new deal' on international taxation.[120] What should this 'new deal' look like if it took human rights obligations seriously?

A new deal for tax would need to focus on issues relevant to LMICs such as bringing back to the table the G24 proposal to tax on a formulary basis according to 'Significant Economic Presence',[121] expansion and protection of source taxation, adoption of anti-abuse provisions that effectively prevent the shifting of profits from these countries,[122] improving tax collection from resource extraction,[123] enhancing capacities of revenue authorities, strengthening tax and financial transparency to effectively respond to the challenges raised by illicit financial flows, internalising costs associated with social and environmental risks within profit allocation rules,[124] among others.[125] In order to respond to the pandemic in a way which ensures shared sacrifices and prevents certain companies from expanding their market power during a pandemic, the proposal of a COVID-19 Excess Profits Tax is also a promising option to not only raise revenue but also to level the playing field, curb corporate consolidation and restore a sense of public trust in institutions.[126]

Finally, the determination of whether a State complies or not with normative criteria of tax justice when adopting policies that can harm others States' fiscal prerogatives, eroding their capacities to fulfil human rights, requires a dual plank. First, empirical assessments are indeed essential, since it has to be based on technical tools that allow to demonstrate that the State are causing a restriction on fiscal sovereignty. Yet, a normative assessment is also necessary to help weigh trade-offs based upon a common set of standards and principles. A process of public reasoning should then develop between State parties and a monitoring body on tax issues. The experience of the implementation of the *GPs*, as well as the work of the Committee on Economic, Social and Cultural Rights and other monitoring bodies combining normative standards about the content of the duties of States in the area of economic, social and cultural rights and technical information and methodologies that help evaluate the compliance those standards could work as a model.

VII. Concluding remarks

This article demonstrated the need to rewrite the currently outdated and broken rules on how countries tax multinational companies as a condition for creating an enabling environment for implementing human rights-based tax policies at domestic level, particularly in LMICs. In order to understand on what grounds those reforms can be considered just, we argued for expanding the understanding of global tax justice as a situation in which polities regain the capacity to make collective fiscal choices about the size of the budget and the level of domestic redistribution to one in which States also operate in an enabling environment to fulfil their human rights obligations.

T.S. Adams, the key figure in fashioning U.S. international tax law and the League of Nations Model Treaty in the period from 1918 to 1928, once said:

> [M]odern taxation or tax making in its most characteristic aspect is a group contest in which powerful interests vigorously endeavor to rid themselves of present or proposed tax burdens. It is, first of all, a hard game in which he who trusts wholly to economics, reason and justice will in the end retire beaten and disillusioned. Class politics is the essence of taxation.[127]

While it is essential to get the normative foundations right, politics and influence of elite tax professionals trump normative considerations in most interactions.[128] Ultimately there is a need for champions in governments and key international institutions on tax governance – where the influence of human rights norms remains very limited. This article has suggested that if human rights are to have a say in the shaping of global tax rules, then there is an urgent need to bring the value-added of human rights norms, and the types of impact assessments the *GPs* push for, into the spaces where global tax governance is played out and to embed a defence of a rights-based order into the hard game of international political economy.

Notes

1. In the past few years, the Committee on Economic, Social and Cultural Rights (CESCR) has consistently recommended State Parties to take the measures needed to ensure that its tax policy is socially just. See CESCR, Concluding observations: Paraguay, 20 March 2015, E/C.12/PRY/CO/4, para. 10; CESCR, Concluding observations: Spain, 25 April 2018, E/C.12/ESP/CO/6, para. 16.b; CESCR, Concluding observations: Burundi, 15 Oct 2015, E/C.12/BDI/CO/1, para. 1(4).
2. Juan Pablo Bohoslavsky, *Guiding Principles on Human Rights Impact Assessments of Economic Reforms: Report of the Independent Expert on the Effects of Foreign Debt and Other Related International Financial Obligations on the Full Enjoyment of Human Rights, Particularly Economic, Social and Cultural Rights*, Report to the Human Rights Council. UN. Doc. A/HRC/40/57 (19 December 2018).
3. General Comment No. 3 (1990): The nature of States parties' obligations (E/1991/3), Annex III, UN ESCOR, Supp. (No. 3) (1991), at 83, para. 9.
4. Id. See also General Comment No. 19 (2007): The right to social security (art. 9) (E/C.12/GC/19), para. 42; and the Letter dated 16 May 2012 addressed by the Chairperson of the Committee on Economic, Social and Cultural Rights to States parties to the International Covenant on Economic, Social and Cultural Rights (noting that, in order to comply with the Covenant, austerity measures or adjustment programmes, as have been adopted by a number of States to face the financial and economic crisis after 2009, must be 'necessary and proportionate, in the sense that the adoption of any other policy, or a failure to act, would be more detrimental to economic, social and cultural rights').
5. See Report of the Special Rapporteur on extreme poverty and human rights, Magdalena Sepulveda Carmona, presented at the sixty-eighth session of the General Assembly, A/68/293 (9 August 2013).
6. General Comment No. 3 (1990): The nature of States parties' obligations (E/1991/3), para. 10.
7. See art. 2(2) of the International Covenant on Economic, Social and Cultural Rights and Committee on Economic, Social and Cultural Rights, General Comment No. 20: Non-Discrimination in Economic, Social and Cultural Rights (art. 2, para. 2) (E/C.12/GC/20) (2009).
8. General Comment No. 20: Non-Discrimination in Economic, Social and Cultural Rights (art. 2, para. 2), cited above note 7, para. 8. In his Letter of 16 May 2012 to the States parties to the Covenant on austerity measures, the Chairperson of the Committee emphasized that fiscal consolidation policies 'must not be discriminatory and must comprise all possible measures, including tax measures, to support social transfers to mitigate inequalities that can grow in times of crisis and to ensure that the rights of the disadvantaged and marginalized individuals and groups are not disproportionately affected'.
9. General Comment No. 19 (2007): The right to social security (E/C.12/GC/19), para. 42.
10. Id., para. 59.
11. This results from the significant growth that almost all developing countries, including low-income countries, have witnessed during the past decade. Comp. Martin Ravallion, 'Do Poorer Countries have less Capacity for Redistribution?', Policy Research Working Paper 5046 (Washington DC: World Bank, 2009) with Chris Hoy and Andy Sumner, 'Gasoline, Guns and Giveaways: Is there New Capacity for Redistribution to End Three Quarters of Global Poverty?', CGD Working Paper 433 (Washington, DC: Center for Global Development, 2016).
12. Report of the Special Rapporteur on extreme poverty and human rights, Magdalena Sepulveda Carmona, presented at the 26th session of the Human Rights Council (A/HRC/26/28) (22 May 2014), para. 56 (citing ActionAid, *Accounting for Poverty: How international tax rules keep people poor*, 2009), 5).

13. See for instance Report of the Special Rapporteur on the right to food to the thirteenth session of the Human Rights Council, Addendum: Mission to Guatemala (3-5 September 2009), A/13/33/Add.4, para. 87. In Latin American countries for instance, the personal income tax generates only 1.4 percent of GDP, in comparison to 8.4 percent of GDP in developed countries (Ana Corbacho, Vicente Frebes Cibils and Eduardo Lora, eds, *More than Revenue: Taxation as a Development Tool* (Inter-American Development Bank and Palgrave Macmillan, 2013), at 115. This discrepancy, as a measure of the degree of progressivity of the tax system (i.e., of its ability to reduce inequalities) is hardly attenuated by taking into account the proportion the personal income tax represented in the total tax burden: in OECD countries, the total tax burden represents 34.8 per cent of the GDP, and it is 23.4 per cent in Latin America. Therefore, the personal income tax represents about one quarter of the tax burden in OECD countries, but only 5.98 per cent of the tax burden in Latin American countries.
14. For a more systematic treatment, see Olivier De Schutter, Johan F. Swinnen and Jan Wouters, 'Introduction: Foreign Direct Investment and Human Development', in *Foreign Direct Investment and Human Development. The Law and Economics of International Investment Agreements*, ed. O. De Schutter et al. (Routledge: London and New York, 2012), 1–24. See also Ana Teresa Tavares-Lehmann et al., eds., *Rethinking Investment Incentives: Trends and Policy Options* (New York: CUP, 2016); Maria R. Andersen, Benjamin R. Kett and Erik von Uexkull, 'Corporate tax incentives and FDI in developing countries' in World Bank, Global Investment Competitiveness Report 2017/2018: Foreign Investor Perspectives and Policy Implications (Washington DC: World Bank, 2018); Hania Kronfol and Victor Steenbergen, 'Evaluating the costs and benefits of corporate tax incentives: Methodological approaches and policy considerations', FCI In Focus, World Bank, 2020; World Bank, *Results of Investor Motivation Survey Conducted in the EAC (East African Community)*, presentation made to the Tax Compact in Lusaka, Zambia (Global Tax Simplification Team, 2013), cited in OECD, *Development Co-Operation Report 2014. Mobilising Resources for Sustainable Development* (Paris: OECD Publishing, 2014), at 151 (according to which 'A large majority of investors covered by investor motivation surveys of the World Bank's Investment Climate Advisory claim that in the majority of cases (for instance over 90% in Rwanda, Tanzania and Uganda) they would have invested even if incentives were not provided').
15. Report of the Special Rapporteur on extreme poverty and human rights, Magdalena Sepulveda Carmona, presented at the 26th session of the Human Rights Council (A/HRC/26/28) (22 May 2014), para. 16; Report of the Special Rapporteur on extreme poverty and human rights, Philip Alston, to the 29th session of the Human Rights Council (A/HRC/29/31) (26 May 2015), para. 53.
16. For this and other unfavorable presumptions on States' actions regarding the MAR clause that are part of the 'emerging doctrine' of the CESCR, see Rodrigo Uprimny, Sergio Chaparro Hernández, and Andrés Castro Araújo, 'Bridging the Gap: The Evolving Doctrine on ESCR and "Maximum Available Resources"', in *The Future of Economic and Social Rights*, ed. K. Young (Cambridge Univ. Press, 2019), 624–53.
17. Organisation for Economic Co-operation and Development, *Divided we Stand: Why Inequality Keeps Rising* (Paris: OECD, 2011).
18. See, e.g., Committee on Economic, Social and Cultural Rights, Concluding Observations: The United Kingdom of Great Britain and Northern Ireland, E/C.12/GBR/CO/6 (14 July 2016), para. 16.
19. Jack Kelly, 'Loans Intended For Small Businesses To Retain Workers Were Hijacked By Large Corporations And The Rich', Forbes (July 7, 2020), https://www.forbes.com/sites/jackkelly/2020/07/07/loans-intended-for-small-businesses-to-retain-workers-were-hijacked-by-large-corporations-and-the-rich/#3f15d9dc316d
20. See, e.g., Committee on the Rights of the Child, General comment No. 19 (2016) on public budgeting for the realization of children's rights, CRC/C/GC/19, 20 July 2016; Olivier De Schutter, *The Rights-Based Welfare State: Public Budgets and Economic and Social Rights* (Geneva: Friedrich-Ebert-Stiftung Geneva Office, November 2018).

21. See, e.g., Report of the Special Rapporteur on the right to food, Olivier De Schutter, to the thirteenth session of the Human Rights Council, Addendum: Mission to Brazil (12-18 October 2009) (A/HRC/13/33/Add.6), para. 36: 'The tax structure in Brazil remains highly regressive. Tax rates are high for goods and services and low for income and property, bringing about very inequitable outcomes. [...] [W]hile the social programmes developed under the 'Zero Hunger' strategy are impressive in scope, they are essentially funded by the very persons whom they seek to benefit, as the regressive system of taxation seriously limits the redistributive impact of the programmes. Only by introducing a tax reform that would reverse the current situation could Brazil claim to be seeking to realize the right to adequate food by taking steps to the maximum of its available resources'.
22. The Kakwani and the Reynolds-Smolensky indexes appeared simultaneously in the economic literature : see Nanak C. Kakwani, 'Measurement of Tax Progressivity: An International Comparison', *The Economic Journal* 87, no. 345 (1977): 71–80; and Morgan O. Reynolds and Eugene Smolensky, *Public Expenditures, Taxes and the Distribution of Income: The United States, 1950, 1961, 1970* (New York: Academic Press, 1977). For a general presentation, see Jonathan Haughton and Shahidur Khandker, *Handbook on Inequality and Poverty* (Washington, DC: World Bank, 2009) (chap. 15: 'The Effects of Taxation and Spending on Inequality and Poverty'). The reliance on these measures has been criticized on the ground that they fail to take into account the changes in revenue that may result from the introduction of tax reforms: see Santiago Díaz de Sarralde, Carlos Garcimartín and Jesús Ruiz-Huerta, 'The paradox of progressivity in low-tax countries: income tax in Guatemala', *CEPAL Review* no. 102 (Dec. 2010): 85–99.
23. See Simon Kuznets, 'Economic Growth and Income Inequality', *American Economic Review* 45 (March 1955): 1–28.
24. See IMF Staff Discussion Note, *Causes and Consequences of Income Inequality: A Global Perspective* (Era Dabla-Norris, Kalpana Kochhar, Nujin Suphaphiphat, Frantisek Ricka, Evridiki Tsounta), June 2015, 7; and see also Jonathan D. Ostry, Andrew Berg and Charalambos G. Tsangarides, 'Redistribution, Inequality and Growth', IMF Staff Discussion Note, February 2014 (Washington, DC: International Monetary Fund, 2014).
25. Christoph Lakner, et al., 'How Much Does Reducing Inequality Matter for Global Poverty', World Bank Working Paper 8869 (2019), 14.
26. Nora Lustig, Chiara Mariotti, Carolina Sánchez-Páramo, 'The redistributive impact of fiscal policy indicator: A new global standard for assessing government effectiveness in tackling inequality within the SDG framework', World Bank Blogs (June 11, 2020), https://blogs.worldbank.org/opendata/redistributive-impact-fiscal-policy-indicator-new-global-standard-assessing-government
27. In today's economic debate, the value of economic growth in and of itself is being challenged by several approaches, including de-growth, steady-state and circular economy theories. However, it is worth noting that champions of this approach as Jason Hickel talk about de-growth as a planned downscaling of excess energy and resource use in high-income nations to bring the economy back into balance with the living world, in a way that delivers justice, equality, democracy and human flourishing (Jason Hickel, *Less is More: How Degrowth Will Save the World* (London: Penguin Random House, August 2020)). See also, on how poverty reduction and the fight against inequalities can gain from the transformation towards a low-carbon economy that sees redistribution rather than economic growth as its priority, 'The "just transition" in the economic recovery', Report of the Special Rapporteur on extreme poverty and human rights, Olivier De Schutter, to the seventy-fifth session of the General Assembly (A/75/181) (20 July 2020).
28. On the normative, conceptual and empirical links between economic inequality and human rights, see Rodrigo Uprimny Yepes and Sergio Chaparro Hernández, 'Inequality, Human Rights, and Social Rights: Tensions and Complementarities', *Humanity: An International Journal of Human Rights, Humanitarianism, and Development* 10, no. 3 (2019): 376–94.

29. Center for Economic and Social Rights (CESR),. 'Progressive Tax Measures to Realize Rights', Recovering Rights Series, No, 2 (2020), https://www.cesr.org/sites/default/files/Brief%203%20Progressive%20Tax_.pdf
30. Diane Elson, Radhika Balakrishnan and James Heintz, 'Public Finance, Maximum Available Resources and Human Rights', in *Human Rights and Public Finance: Budgets and the Promotion of Economic and Social Rights*, ed. Aoife Nolan, R. O'Connell and Colin Harvey (Oxford: Hart Publishing, 2013), 13–39, at 28; and in the same volume, Ignacio Saiz, 'Resourcing Rights: Combating Tax Injustice from a Human Rights Perspective', 77–104, at 84. It is important to note, however, that although VAT taxes are regressive when calculations are made on income (the poorest households contribute more as a proportion of their income), this regressivity either disappears or is significantly attenuated when calculated on the basis of consumption (that is, the higher levels of consumption of the rich and the high VAT rates on luxury items that are only affordable to the rich, leads to a situation in which the rich contribute more to the revenues collected through VAT than the poor). See Corbacho et al., *More than Revenue: Taxation as a development tool*, cited above (note 13), at 167–168.
31. International Monetary Fund Policy Paper, *Fiscal Policy and Income Inequality*, Jan. 2014, 37 (estimating that top personal income taxes were lowered by about 30% on average since 1980).
32. This is a non-weighted average: small economies count as much as large ones in the calculation of the average. The total tax rate, for the purpose of this calculation, is the 'amount of taxes and mandatory contributions payable by businesses after accounting for allowable deductions and exemptions as a share of commercial profits'. For more details, see http://data.worldbank.org/indicator/IC.TAX.TOTL.CP.ZS?end=2015&start=2005&view=chart (last consulted on September 9th, 2016). Some countries have lowered corporate taxes faster than others: during this ten-year period, Albania lowered corporate taxes from 58.2% to 36.5%, Belarus from 137.3% to 51.8%, and Uzbekistan from 96.7% to 41.1%; Canada went from 47.5% to 21.1%, and Paraguay from 54.5% to 35.0%. Turkey moved from 52.8% to 40.9%.
33. On this notion, see Joachim Hirsch, *Der nationale Wettbewerbsstaat: Staat, Demokratie und Politik im globalen Kapitalismus (The Competitive National State: State, Democracy and Politics in Global Capitalism)* (Berlin and Amsterdam: Edition ID-Archiv, 1995).
34. On how failures in international tax cooperation exacerbate the challenges of Latin American States to build sufficient and more progressive tax systems to meet their needs, see Juan Pablo Jiménez, Jose Antonio Ocampo, Andrea Podestá y Maria Fernanda Valdés 'Explorando sinergias entre la cooperación tributaria internacional y los desafíos tributarios latinoamericanos', Friedrich Ebert Stiftung (February 2020), Bogotá, Colombia, http://library.fes.de/pdf-files/bueros/kolumbien/16021.pdf
35. See, for instance, Ryan Suda, 'The Effect of Bilateral Investment Treaties on Human Rights Enforcement and Realization', in *Transnational Corporations and Human Rights*, ed. O. De Schutter (Oxford and Portland, Oregon: Hart Publ., 2006), 73–160. For an empirical review collecting evidence from 113 developing countries from 1981 to 2009, concluding that investors' rights routinely may impede measures related to the realization of human rights in the host country, see Cristina Bodea and Fangjin Ye, 'Investor Rights versus Human Rights: Do Bilateral Investment Treaties Tilt the Scale?', *British Journal of Political Science* 50, no. 3 (2020): 955–77.
36. See for example, Corporate Europe Observatory, 'Cashing in on the pandemic: how lawyers are preparing to sue states over COVID-19 response measures', May 2020, https://corporateeurope.org/en/2020/05/cashing-pandemic-how-lawyers-are-preparing-sue-states-over-covid-19-response-measures
37. HRC Res. 17/4 (16 June 2011). For an assessment of the influence of the Guiding Principles on Business and Human Rights, see Michael K. Addo, 'The Reality of the United Nations Guiding Principles on Business and Human Rights', *Human Rights Law Review* 14, no. 1 (March 2014): 133–47.

38. A/HRC/17/31, Principle 9.
39. See Committee on Economic, Social and Cultural Rights, General Comment No. 24 (2017) on State Obligations under the International Covenant on Economic, Social and Cultural Rights in the context of business activities (E/C.12/GC/24), para. 13 (encouraging States parties to 'insert a provision explicitly referring to their human rights obligations in future [trade or investment agreements], and to ensure that mechanisms for the settlement of investor-State disputes take human rights into account in the interpretation of investment treaties or of investment chapters in trade agreements').
40. Para. 14(4).
41. Ana Corbacho, et al., eds., *More than Revenue: Taxation as a development tool*, cited above (note 13), at 121 (fig. 7.4.). These estimates are based on data from the period 2003-2010, with different years for the different countries (for Guatemala for instance, the reference year in 2006). They should therefore be treated with caution as a source of cross-country comparisons. They do provide, however, an idea of the magnitude of the problem.
42. For a useful assessment, see OECD, *Development Co-Operation Report 2014. Mobilising Resources for Sustainable Development*, cited above (note 14), chapter II.13.
43. Dev Kar and Devon Cartwright-Smith, *Illicit Financial Flows from Africa: Hidden Resource for Development* (Washington DC: Global Financial Integrity, 2010).
44. This was also the conclusion reached by Ndikumana, Léonce and James K. Boyce, *New Estimates of Capital Flight from Sub-Saharan African Countries: Linkages with External Borrowing and Policy Options* (University of Massachusetts, Amherst, April 2008).
45. See e.g. Alex Cobham, 'The significance and subversion of SDG 16.4Multinational tax avoidance as IFF', Tax Justice Network, 2017, https://www.un.org/esa/ffd/ffdforum/wp-content/uploads/sites/3/2017/05/ED1-Cobham.pdf
46. Outcome document adopted at the Third International Conference on Financing for Development (Addis Ababa, Ethiopia, 13–16 July 2015) and endorsed by the General Assembly in its resolution 69/313 of 27 July 2015, para. 22.
47. Id.
48. Id., para. 103. For more detail on these tax spillover assessments, see N. Lusiani and M. Cosgrove, 'A Strange Alchemy: Embedding human rights into tax policy spillover assessments', in *Tax, Inequality and Human Rights*, ed. P. Alston and N. Reisch (Oxford University Press, 2019).
49. A/HRC/17/4 (and, for the text of the Guiding Principles on Business and Human Rights, A/HRC/17/31). On the due diligence component of the responsibility to respect human rights, see Olivier De Schutter, Anita Ramasastry, Mark Taylor and Robert Thompson, *Human Rights Due Diligence: The Role of States* (International Corporate Accountability Roundtable, European Coalition for Corporate Justice and Canadian Network on Corporate Accountability, 2012). See also, Office of the High Commisioner for Human Rights, 'Corporate human rights due diligence – identifying and leveraging emerging practice', https://www.ohchr.org/EN/Issues/Business/Pages/CorporateHRDueDiligence.aspx
50. See, for a more detailed description of what this entails, Principle 17 of the Guiding Principles on Business and Human Rights.
51. See, for a more detailed description, Principle 13 of the Guiding Principles on Business and Human Rights. See also Inter-American Commission on Human Rights (IACHR), 'Business and Human Rights: Inter-American Standards' (Spanish version only). OEA/Ser.L/V/II. CIDH/REDESCA/INF.1/19, para. 254-267.
52. The Maastricht Principles on Extraterritorial Obligations of States in the Area of Economic, Social and Cultural Rights seek to bring together the rather disparate contributions from judicial and non-judicial bodies to this fast-developing area of human rights law, http://www.icj.org/wp-content/uploads/2012/12/HRQMaastricht-Maastricht-Principles-on-ETO.pdf. They were endorsed on 28 September 2011 by a range of non-governmental organisations and human rights experts, including mandate-holders within the Special Procedures established by the Human Rights Council. See Olivier De Schutter, et al., 'Commentary to

the Maastricht Principles on Extraterritorial Obligations of States in the area of Economic, Social and Cultural Rights', *Human Rights Quarterly* 34 (2012): 1084–171.

53. See in this regard OECD, *Tax and Development: Aid Modalities for Strengthening Tax Systems* (Paris: OECD Publishing, 2013).
54. CESCR, General Comment No. 24 (2017) on State obligations under the International Covenant on Economic, Social and Cultural Rights in the context of business activities (E/C.12/GC/24, 10 August 2017), para. 37.
55. Universal Declaration of Human Rights (1948), G.A. res. 217A (III), U.N. Doc A/810 at 71 (1948), arts, 22 and 28; Charter of the United Nations, June 26, 1945, 59 Stat. 1031, T.S. 993, 3 Bevans 1153, entered into force Oct. 24, 1945; International Covenant on Civil and Political Rights, UN Doc. A/6316 (1966) (999 UNTS 171), article 2(1); International Covenant on Economic, Social and Cultural Rights, UN Doc. A/6316 (1966) (993 UNTS 3), article 2(1).
56. Maastricht Principles on Extraterritorial Obligations of States in the Area of Economic, Social and Cultural Rights, cited above (note 51).
57. See CESR., 'Governments' Obligation to Cooperate Internationally to Realize Human Rights'. Recovering Rights Series, No, 3 (2020), https://www.cesr.org/sites/default/files/Issue%20Brief%202__.pdf
58. Committee on Economic, Social and Cultural Rights, Concluding Observations on the sixth periodic report of the United Kingdom of Great Britain and Northern Ireland (E/C.12/GBR/CO/6, 14 July 2016), paras 16-17.
59. Committee on the Elimination of Discrimination against Women, Concluding Observations on the combined fourth and fifth reports of Switzerland (CEDAW/C/CHE/CO/4-5) (18 November 2016), para. 41. See also recommendations in Juan Pablo Bohoslavsky, 'Report of the Independent Expert on the effects of foreign debt and other related international financial obligations of States on the full enjoyment of all human rights, particularly economic, social and cultural rights, on his visit to Switzerland, UN Doc. A/HRC/37/54/Add.3, para. 92 (March, 2018), https://www.un.org/en/ga/search/view_doc.asp?symbol=A/HRC/37/54/Add.3
60. Outcome document, cited above (note 45), para. 27.
61. Final study on illicit financial flows, human rights and the 2030 Agenda for Sustainable Development of the Independent Expert on the effects of foreign debt and other related international financial obligations of States on the full enjoyment of all human rights, particularly economic, social and cultural rights, Juan Pablo Bohoslavsky (A/HRC/31/61) (15 January 2016), para. 18.
62. *United Nations Practical Manual on Transfer Pricing for Developing Countries*, UN Department of Economic and Social Affairs (ST/ESA/347) (New York: United Nations, 2013), para. 1.1.3. Estimates of the volume of intra-group trade (trade between different enterprises related to a same multinational group) are however notoriously difficult to arrive at: see Rainer Lanz and Sébastien Miroudot, 'Intra-Firm Trade: Patterns, Determinants and Policy Implications', *OECD Trade Policy Papers* No. 114 (Paris: OECD Publishing, 2011).
63. The United Nations Model Double Taxation Convention between Developed and Developing Countries was initially adopted in 1980, and revised subsequently in 1999 and in 2011.
64. See http://www.oecd.org/ctp/model-tax-convention-on-income-and-on-capital-full-version-9a5b369e-en.htm (last consuleted on 20 July 2020).
65. Id., article 7 ('Business profits').
66. Initially the result of a joint effort of the OECD and the Council of Europe in 1988, the convention was amended in order to allow for the participation of developing countries. The new text was opened for signature on 1 June 2011 and now covers 109 jurisdictions (including 15 jurisdictions covered by extension).
67. OECD, *Development Co-Operation Report 2014. Mobilising Resources for Sustainable Development*, cited above (note 14), at 167-176.
68. Section V is partially based, and further developed, in an article pending publication by the Center for Economic and Social Rights.

69. International Court of Justice, *Fisheries Jurisdiction Case*, 1974 I.C.J., p. 31 (negotiations are required between Iceland and Great Britain who both have legitimate fishing rights in certain maritime areas); International Court of Justice, *Case concerning the Obligation to Negotiate Access to the Pacific Ocean (Bolivia v. Chile)*, judgment of 1 October 2018, paras 86-87. See also M.A. Rogoff, 'The Obligation to Negotiate in International Law: Rules and Realities', *Michigan Journal of International Law* 16 (1994): 141–85; and Olivier De Schutter, 'A Duty to Negotiate in Good Faith as Part of the Duty to Cooperate to Establish "An International Legal Order in which Human Rights can be Fully Realized": the New Frontier of the Right to Development', *Cridho Working papers series* 2018/5.
70. CESCR, General Comment No. 24 (2017) on State obligations under the International Covenant on Economic, Social and Cultural Rights in the context of business activities (E/C.12/GC/24, 10 August 2017), para. 29.
71. Independent Commission on the Reform of International Corporate Taxation (ICRICT), 'BEPS 2.0. What the OECD BEPS has achieved and what real reform should look like', 14–15 (Jan. 2019), https://www.icrict.com/press-release/2019/1/17/icrict-is-launching-a-new-paper-the-fight-against-tax-avoidance-beps-20-what-the-oecd-beps-has-achieved-and-what-real-reform-should-look-like
72. Allison Christians. 'Human rights at the borders of tax sovereignty.' Available at SSRN 2924925 (2017).
73. Allison Christians. 'Human rights at the borders of tax sovereignty.', p. 3-11.
74. Ibid., 3–11.
75. Ibid., 11–16.
76. See Gijsbert W. J. Bruins, Luigi Einaudi, Edwin R. A. Seligman, and Sir Josiah Stamp, 'Report on double taxation' (5 April 1923).
77. Id., at 22-26.
78. Allison Christians. 'Human rights at the borders of tax sovereignty.', pp.16-19.
79. Allison Christians. 'Human rights at the borders of tax sovereignty.', p. 16-19; See also P. Dietsch and T. Rixen, 'Tax competition and global background justice', *Journal of Political Philosophy* 22, no. 2 (2014): 150–77.
80. See R.S. Avi-Yonah, *International Tax as International Law: An Analysis of the International Tax Regime* (Cambridge Univ. Press, 2009).
81. See ICRICT, 'Submission to OECD's 'Unified Approach' under Pillar 1 proposal', (Nov. 2019), https://www.icrict.com/icrict-documents-submission-to-oecds-unified-approach-under-pillar-1-proposal; ICRICT, 'ICRICT response to the OECD Consultation on Global Anti-Base Erosion Proposal ('GloBE') - Pillar Two', (December 2019), https://www.icrict.com/icrict-documents-icrict-response-to-the-oecd-consultation-on-global-anti-base-erosion-proposal; Oxfam, 'Policy Note: In support of a comprehensive tax reform to stop corporate tax dodging and limit tax competition', https://www.oxfamnovib.nl/Redactie/Downloads/Rapporten/Oxfam%20Policy%20Note%20BEPS%202.0.pdf
82. See the full list of submissions to the first round of public consultations, at https://www.oecd.org/tax/beps/public-comments-received-on-the-possible-solutions-to-the-tax-challenges-of-digitalisation.htm
83. As just one example, the basic ability to merely identify those companies subject to tax in any given jurisdiction is very unevenly distributed between States given the practical obstacles many poorer governments face when seeking to understand the taxable presence of companies in their jurisdiction, leading many advocates to call for a public registry of country-by-country tax and financial information of large multinationals. For various other examples, see A. Christians, Human Rights at the Borders of Tax Sovereignty
84. Kimberly Clausing, Emmanuel Saez and Gabriel Zucman., 'Ending Corporate Tax Avoidance and Tax Competition: A Plan to Collect the Tax Deficit of Multinationals' (2020), http://gabriel-zucman.eu/files/CSZ2020.pdf.
85. See e.g. Rasmus Christensen, (2020) Elite Professionals in Transnational Tax Governance, *Global Networks*. DOI: 10.1111/glob.12269; (2019) The New Politics of Global Tax

Governance: Taking Stock a Decade After the Financial Crisis (with Martin Hearson), *Review of International Political Economy* 26, no. (5). DOI: 10.1080/09692290.2019.1625802

86. Salvador Barrios, Huizinga Harry, Laeven Luc, and Nicodeme Gaetan, *International taxation and multinational firm location decisions* (European Commission: Directorate-General for Economic and Financial Affairs, 2008).
87. See, for example, the summary made by the UN High Level Panel on International Financial Accountability, Transparency and Integrity for Achieving the 2030 Agenda (FACTI Panel). 'Overview of existing frameworks and understanding priorities' (2020), https://assets.website-files.com/5e0bd9edab846816e263d633/5e8df72aec8ff1144d3773f3_FACTI%20BP%201%20Overview%20of%20frameworks.pdf
88. Andres Knobel, 'ABCs of tax transparency', Tax Justice Network (Dec. 2018), https://www.taxjustice.net/tag/abc-of-tax-transparency/
89. Tax Inspectors Without Borders (TIWB) is a joint initiative of the Organisation for Economic Co-operation and Development (OECD) and the United Nations Development Programme (UNDP) supporting countries in building tax audit capacity. For more, see http://www.tiwb.org/
90. ICRICT, 'BEPS 2.0. What the OECD BEPS has achieved and what real reform should look like', 14–15 (Jan. 2019), https://www.icrict.com/press-release/2019/1/17/icrict-is-launching-a-new-paper-the-fight-against-tax-avoidance-beps-20-what-the-oecd-beps-has-achieved-and-what-real-reform-should-look-like
91. Christians, 'Taxing According to Value Creation', 90 *Tax Notes International* 1379–1383 (June 18, 2018), 6
92. Tommaso Fitzgerald & Valpy Faccio, 'Sharing the Corporate Tax Base: Equitable Taxing of Multinationals and the Choice of Formulary Apportionment', *Transnat. Corporations* 25, no. 2 (2018): 67–90.
93. P. Dietsch and T. Rixen, 'Tax competition and global background justice', *Journal of Political Philosophy* 22, no. 2 (2014): 150–77.
94. Id., 36.
95. Id.
96. CESR, ACIJ, Dejusticia, CELS, Fundar, INESC, RJFALC. 'Commentaries to the OECD call for public input on the tax challenges of digitalisation, and possible solutions', March 6, 2019, https://www.cesr.org/sites/default/files/OECD%20March%202019%20-%20EN.pdf, see also Int'l Bar Ass'n, *Tax Abuses, Poverty and Human Rights* (Oct. 2013), http://www.ibanet.org/Tax_Abuses_Poverty_and_Human_Rights_Report.aspx
97. Juan Pablo Bohoslavsky, *Guiding Principles.*
98. Juan Pablo Bohoslavsky, *Guiding Principles*, Principle 3.
99. For more on how human rights norms can be leveraged to carry out impact assessments of the international spillovers of domestic corporate tax reforms, see Lusiani, Nicholas and Cosgrove, Mary, 'A Strange Alchemy: Embedding Human Rights in Tax Policy Spillover Assessments' (July 23, 2017), https://doi.org/10.2139/ssrn.3218597
100. See Arnold Wolfers, *Discord and Collaboration: Essays on International Politics* (1962), 19-2, as discussed in Anne-Marie Slaughter, 'International Law in a World of Liberal States', *European Journal of International Law* 6 no. 3 (1995): 503–38, https://doi.org/10.1093/oxfordjournals.ejil.a035934
101. Damrosch, Henkin, Pugh, Schachter, Smit, eds., *International Law: Cases and Materials*, 4th edition, Chapt. 8.
102. Cosmopolitan human rights theories have explored the prospects of this idea. See for example, W. Moka-Mubelo, 'A Cosmopolitan Human Rights Regime', in: *Reconciling Law and Morality in Human Rights Discourse. Philosophy and Politics. Critical Explorations*, vol 3. Springer (2017). For an understanding of indigenous peoples' right to self-determination as opposed to State-centered visions of sovereignty, see José Martinez Cobo, Study of the Problem against Indigenous Populations, vol. v, Conclusions, Proposals and Recommendations, UN Doc E/CN 4/ Sub 2 1986/7, Add 4, para. 379–381.

103. The conception of human rights as one of the overarching aims around which other States' actions should be aligned with is stated in article 103 the UN Charter 'In the event of a conflict between the obligations of the Members of the United Nations under the present Charter and their obligations under any other international agreement [including human rights obligations], their obligations under the present Charter shall prevail'. United Nations, Charter of the United Nations, 24 October 1945, 1 UNTS XVI, https://www.refworld.org/docid/3ae6b3930.html (accessed July 23, 2020)
104. See *GPs*, Principles 13 and 14; see also Guiding Principles on Extreme Poverty and Human Rights, Human Rights Council resolution 21/11 (2012) para. 92.
105. See *GPs*, Principle 9; see also Maastricht Principles on the Extraterritorial Obligations of States in the Area of Economic, Social and Cultural Rights, cited above (note 51), Principle 29.
106. The IMF, OECD, UN and World Bank have already recommended that 'spillover analyses' of tax policies should be conducted by developed countries. See IMF, OECD, UN and World Bank, 'Supporting the development of more effective tax systems, Report to the G20 Development Working Group', 2011, http://www.imf.org/external/np/g20/pdf/110311.pdf. An IMF paper is forthcoming on the subject, but is limited to economic spillovers, not human rights impacts.
107. Concluding Observations on the sixth periodic report of the United Kingdom of Great Britain and Northern Ireland (E/C.12/GBR/CO/6, 14 July 2016), paras 16-17; CEDAW Concluding Observations on the combined fourth and fifth reports of Switzerland (CEDAW/C/CHE/CO/4-5) (18 November 2016), para. 41.
108. See Committee on Economic, Social and Cultural Rights, General Comment No. 24 (2017), cited above (note 69), para. 37.
109. Ibid.
110. Ibid.
111. *See* Maastricht Principles on Extraterritorial Obligations of States in the Area of Economic, Social and Cultural Rights, cited above (note 51), Principle 29.
112. *See* Special Rapporteur on Extreme Poverty and Human Rights, *Report of the Special Rapporteur on extreme poverty and human rights,* U.N. Doc. A/HRC/26/28, ¶¶ 29–32 (May 22, 2014) (by Magdalena Sepúlveda Carmona) (discussing why 'providing an avenue for high-net-worth individuals and transnational corporations to evade tax liabilities (such as through the establishment of tax havens) could be contrary to obligations of international assistance and cooperation' under the ICESCR and other international human rights treaties); *see also* Independent Expert on the effects of foreign debt and other related international financial obligations of States on the full enjoyment of all human rights, particularly economic, social and cultural rights, *Advance Edited Version: Final Study on Illicit Financial Flows, Human Rights and the 2030 Agenda for Sustainable Development,* ¶ 43, U.N. Doc. No. A/HRC/31/61 (2016) (by Juan Pablo Bohoslavsky).
113. The principle of common but differentiated responsibilities first enshrined in the 1992 Rio Declaration helps to underscore both the universality of the tax cooperation agenda for achieving the SDGs, as well as the need for differentiation of responsibilities for its realization. Universality is not legitimate or effective without clear differentiation of responsibilities based on varying and diverse degrees of national capacity, resources, levels of development and effective influence. Based on this differentiation, developed countries have far greater responsibility on tax cooperation matters. Human rights legal obligations of an extraterritorial nature help to delineate common but differentiated obligations across sustainable development in all of its dimensions, including tax cooperation. See CESR and Third World Network. 'Universal Rights, differentiated responsibilities. Safeguarding human rights beyond borders to achieve the Sustainable Development Goals'. Human Rights Policy Briefing, 2015. For the importation of the principle of common but differentiated responsibilities and respective capabilities to international human rights law, see O. De Schutter, *The international dimensions of the right to development: a fresh start towards improving accountability. Report prepared at the request of the United Nations Working Group on the Right to Development* (UN doc. A/HRC/WG.2/19/CRP.1) (2018), paras 47–52.

114. Juan Pablo Bohoslavsky, *Guiding Principles*, para. 9(4).
115. Juan Pablo Bohoslavsky, *Guiding Principles*, para. 9(5).
116. Maastricht Principles on Extraterritorial Obligations of States in the Area of Economic, Social and Cultural Rights, cited above (note 51), Principle 32.
117. Juan Pablo Bohoslavsky, *Guiding Principles*, para. 19.
118. See Initiative for Human Rights Principles and Guidelines in Fiscal Policy, 'A Comprehensive Response to COVID-19 Demands Redistributive Fiscal Policies', April 23th, 2020, https://derechosypoliticafiscal.org/en/news/13-a-comprehensive-response-to-covid-19-demands-redistributive-fiscal-policies
119. OECD 'Tax and Fiscal Policy in Response to the Coronavirus Crisis: Strengthening Confidence and Resilience', May 2020, https://read.oecd-ilibrary.org/view/?ref=128_128575-o6raktc0aa&title=Tax-and-Fiscal-Policy-in-Response-to-the-Coronavirus-Crisis. See also, IMF, 'Tax Issues: An Overview', Fiscal Affairs Department. Special Series on Fiscal Policies to Respond to COVID-19, May 2020, https://drive.google.com/file/d/1b2z_HSJXCX7bqsFQz8Av6e7ufYUaoTp5/view
120. International Centre for Tax and Development, 'What should a "new deal" on international tax look like for developing countries?', May 2020, https://www.ictd.ac/blog/what-should-new-deal-international-tax-look-like-developing-countries/
121. G-24 Working Group on tax policy and international tax cooperation, 'Proposal for Addressing Tax Challenges Arising from Digitalisation', January 17, 2019, https://www.g24.org/wp-content/uploads/2019/03/G-24_proposal_for_Taxation_of_Digital_Economy_Jan17_Special_Session_2.pdf
122. Brian J. Arnold, 'Protecting the tax base of developing countries: the taxation of income from services', UNDESA. Papers on Selected Topics in Protecting the Tax Base of Developing Countries. Draft Paper No. 2, 2013, https://www.un.org/esa/ffd/wp-content/uploads/2014/10/20140604_Paper2_Arnold.pdf
123. Michael C. Durst, 'Improving the Performance of Natural Resource Taxation in Developing Countries', ICTD Working Paper 60, November, 2016, https://opendocs.ids.ac.uk/opendocs/bitstream/handle/20.500.12413/12797/ICTD_WP60.pdf
124. Allison Christians, 'Aligning Taxation and Development Goals', presentation at the XVII International CIFA forum (New York, 6–7 May 2019) (available at: https://www.youtube.com/watch?v=1e4EYVF1xiU).
125. For an agenda of reform from lower income countries' interests standpoint see ICRICT. 'International Corporate Tax Reform. Towards a fair and comprehensive solution', 2019, https://static1.squarespace.com/static/5a0c602bf43b5594845abb81/t/5d979e6dc5f7cb7b66842c49/1570217588721/ICRICT-INTERNATIONAL+CORPORATE+TAX+REFORM.pdf
126. See Nicholas Lusiani, 'Pandemic Profits Exposed: A COVID-19 Pandemic Profits Tax as one essential tool to reverse inequalities and rebuild better post-pandemic', Oxfam America (July 22, 2020), https://assets.oxfamamerica.org/media/documents/Pandemic_Profits_Exposed.pdf; Reuven Avi-Yonah, 'It's Time to Revive the Excess Profits Tax', *American Prospect*, March 27, 2020, https://prospect.org/coronavirus/its-time-to-revive-the-excess-profits-tax/; Allison Christians and Tarcisio Diniz Magalhes, 'It's Time for Pillar 3: A Global Excess Profits Tax for COVID-19 and Beyond', *Tax Notes*, May 1, 2020, https://www.taxnotes.com/featured-analysis/its-time-pillar-3-global-excess-profits-tax-covid-19-and-beyond/2020/05/01/2cg34
127. Richard J. Joseph, *The Origins of American Income Tax* (Syracuse University Press, 2004), 6.
128. Christensen, Rasmus Corlin. 'Elite professionals in transnational tax governance.' Global Networks (2020).

Disclosure statement

No potential conflict of interest was reported by the author(s).

Guiding principles on human rights impacts assessments of economic policy reforms

Juan Pablo Bohoslavsky

ABSTRACT
In his report to the UN General Assembly on 28 February 2019, the United Nations Independent Expert on Debt and Human Rights presented *Guiding Principles on Human Rights Impact Assessments of Economic Reforms* (UN Doc. A/HRC/40/57). These set out the human rights principles and standards that apply to States, international financial institutions and creditors when designing, formulating or proposing economic reforms. Based on the existing human rights obligations and responsibilities of States and other actors, the *Guiding Principles* underline the importance of systematically assessing the impact of economic reforms on the enjoyment of all human rights before decisions are taken to implement such reforms, as well as during and after their implementation. Economic policymaking must be anchored in and guided by substantive and procedural human rights standards, and human rights impact assessments are a crucial process that enables States and other actors to ensure that economic reforms advance, rather than hinder, the enjoyment of human rights by all.

Introduction

In its March 2017 session, the Human Rights Council recognized that 'structural adjustment reform programmes and policy conditionalities limit public expenditure, impose fixed expenditure ceilings and give inadequate attention to the provision of social services, and that only a few countries manage to achieve sustainable higher growth under these programmes'.[1] The Council proceeded to request the Independent Expert on the effects of foreign debt and other related international financial obligations of States on the full enjoyment of all human rights, particularly economic, social and cultural rights (Independent Expert on Debt and Human Rights) to develop guiding principles for human rights impact assessments for economic reform policies.[2]

The drafting process for the *Guiding Principles* involved the active participation of States, international financial institutions, international organizations, scholars and experts, unions, civil society organizations and national human rights institutions. A number of public and expert consultations took place in different regions in which draft versions of the *Guiding Principles* were discussed.[3] Written contributions were also received.[4] During the development of the *Guiding Principles*, thematic reports were prepared and submitted to the Human Rights Council and the General Assembly on a range of different topics, the findings and recommendations of which ultimately constituted some of the building blocks of the *Guiding Principles*. In particular, these thematic reports include a mapping report aiming at consolidating existing human rights and other relevant impact assessment tools.[5]

The *Guiding Principles* were ultimately considered, discussed and voted by the United Nations Human Rights Council on 21 March 2019.[6] Having taken note '*with appreciation*' of the *Guiding Principles on Human Rights Impact Assessments of Economic Reforms*, the resolution went on to state that

> '[The Council] Encourages Governments, relevant United Nations bodies, specialized agencies, funds and programmes and other intergovernmental organizations to consider taking into account the guiding principles in the formulation and implementation of their economic reform policies and measures, and encourages national human rights institutions, non-governmental organizations and the private sector to give due consideration to the guiding principles in their work.'[7]

The report that follows, in its entirety, was first published by the United Nations Human Rights Office of the High Commissioner and is reproduced here with permission.[8]

Contents

Preamble

1. In its resolutions 34/03 and 37/11, the Human Rights Council requested the Independent Expert on the effects of foreign debt and other related international financial obligations of States on the full enjoyment of all human rights, particularly economic, social and cultural rights, Juan Pablo Bohoslavsky, to develop guiding principles for

assessing the human rights impact of economic reform policies, in consultation with States and all other relevant stakeholders, for submission to the Council at its fortieth session. The present guiding principles distil over two years of research and collective and participatory work with a dedicated focus on the human rights impacts of economic reforms on the human rights of millions of people around the globe and lessons learned over decades.[9]

2. Obligations under human rights law should guide all efforts to design and implement economic policies. The economy should serve the people, not vice versa.

3. While economic reform policies that could negatively affect human rights are more commonly found in the context of economic and financial crisis responses, these reforms have also been observed in less challenging economic times. This is why it is crucial to know to what extent human rights are effectively protected and respected both in times of economic crisis and in other circumstances.

4. Not all economic reform policy responding to economic crises is intrinsically against human rights, and economic reforms that are carefully formulated based on human rights can contribute to the betterment of human rights. In fact, responding to economic crises often requires actions by the Government that are dictated by the urgency to protect resources and assets that will, in the long term, serve to protect and fulfil human rights. Above all, Governments must ensure that measures put in place serve to pursue economic recovery for the benefit of the whole population, instead of only a few.

5. The realization of human rights is often affected by resource scarcity; hence, economic reform policies that affect availability of resources can negatively and deeply affect all human rights. As human rights are indivisible and interdependent, international human rights law needs to provide a consistent and comprehensive response to those economic reform policies.

6. Contractual obligations do not occur in a vacuum. Both the relationships between creditor and borrowing States and the relationship between States and their populations fall under the framework defined by international human rights law.[10] A human rights impact assessment is a structured process for identifying, understanding, assessing and addressing the potential or actual adverse effects of economic reform policies and serves to ensure that such policies are consistent with international human rights law. As they entail broad participation, transparency and accountability, human rights impact assessments also help democratize resource mobilization and spending policies.

7. More specifically, a human rights impact assessment, on the one hand, can support Governments, international financial institutions and private creditors by providing a clear and specific framework and process for assessing whether certain economic reform policies are consistent with international human rights law. On

[9] For more information and details of all these meetings and activities, see www.ohchr.org/EN/Issues/Development/IEDebt/Pages/DebtAndimpactassessments.aspx. The Independent Expert wishes to express his appreciation for all contributions to this process.

[10] See A/70/275.

the other hand, it is an essential review and accountability procedure for the design, monitoring and implementation of economic reform policies. It contributes to evidence-based and transparent policymaking as it provides an analytical basis for evaluating potential human rights impacts when choosing among policy options. Using human rights impact assessments helps identify the institutional changes required to prevent adverse human rights impacts of economic reforms in the short/long term. This is why States should strengthen their capacity to conduct such assessments.

8. The present guiding principles aim to identify and systematize existing human rights obligations, and also provide commentary on their implications. They thus offer guidance to States and other stakeholders to ensure respect and fulfilment of those obligations. The guiding principles are based on all core international human rights instruments, in particular, the International Covenant on Economic, Social and Cultural Rights, the International Covenant on Civil and Political Rights, the Convention on the Elimination of All Forms of Discrimination against Women and the Convention on the Rights of Persons with Disabilities, and their authoritative interpretation by the treaty body monitoring mechanisms, as well as, where relevant, the contribution of special procedure mandate holders. They complement and build upon relevant development-related commitments, in particular the 2030 Agenda for Sustainable Development and the Declaration on the Right to Development. Nothing in the principles should be read as limiting or undermining the existing human rights obligations of States or other actors.

9. The guiding principles also build upon relevant commitments, in particular those referring to business and human rights,[11] foreign debt and human rights,[12] human rights impact assessments of trade and investment agreements[13] and extreme poverty and human rights.[14] All these principles should be considered and applied in coordination and conjunction with one another.

I. Scope and purpose

Principle 1 – Scope and purpose of the guiding principles

The present principles provide guidance for economic policymaking, in compliance with international human rights obligations to respect, protect and fulfil all human rights. They apply whenever economic reform policies may foreseeably result in impairment of human rights. These principles are likely to be most relevant in the context of acute economic and financial crises (reactive function) but will also be relevant in less challenging economic times in the course of the design and implementation of short-, medium- and long-term economic reform policies considered or/and implemented (preventive function).

[11] A/HRC/17/31.
[12] A/HRC/20/23 and Corr.1.
[13] A/HRC/19/59/Add.5.
[14] A/HRC/21/39.

Commentary

1.1 Some economic policies, such as fiscal consolidation, structural adjustment/reforms, privatization,[15] deregulation of financial and labour markets and lowering environmental protection standards, can have adverse consequences on the enjoyment of human rights.

1.2 The guiding principles should be applied to different economic situations in which economic reform policies are considered and/or adopted. Such situations notably include: (a) acute economic and financial crises (involving sudden or gradual economic downturn and collapse of the values of public or private financial assets), where the risk of adverse human rights impacts is heightened and in which an urgent response is required; (b) medium-term economic reforms, where fiscal consolidation may stretch into multi-year processes that go beyond the immediate responses to and implications of economic and financial crises; and (c) longer-term processes, such as the systematic review of public budgets and their distributional assessments, cumulative and long-term effects of fiscal consolidation measures on human rights, or the effects of labour market reforms.

II. Obligations of States

Principle 2 – Obligations of States with respect to economic policies and human rights

States are obliged to manage their fiscal affairs and to adopt economic policies to ensure that they respect, protect and fulfil all human rights. Economic choices made by States, whether acting alone or as members of international financial institutions, must comply with their international human rights obligations at all times, including during times of economic crisis.

Commentary

2.1 States are responsible for carefully examining different policy options at any and all times and for determining the most appropriate measures in the light of their circumstances and their international and domestic human rights obligations.

2.2 Taking timely, effective and preventive measures is a critical part of ensuring all human rights during economic and financial crises.

2.3 In times of economic and financial crisis, States' efforts are often directed at trying to stabilize the economy. This comes with the risk of disregarding their human rights obligations with regard to those who suffer most from the economic crisis. Governmental efforts at stabilization can also exacerbate human rights violations. This approach is counterproductive because it is precisely during these periods that the population – in particular those who are disenfranchised, living in poverty or at high risk of falling into poverty – is in greatest

[15] See A/73/396.

need of State compliance with its obligations to respect, protect and fulfil human rights.[16]

2.4 These obligations apply to all branches of the State (executive, judicial and legislative) and all levels of government (national, subnational and local) within their allocated sphere of responsibilities.

2.5 Commitments to fiscal discipline policies, whether stated in domestic constitutions or in regional or international agreements, must not lead to sacrificing international human rights obligations. States should undertake full assessments of the potential impacts of fiscal discipline policies in different national and subnational contexts before committing to such policies.

Principle 3 – Burden of proof and obligation to conduct human rights impact assessments

States and other creditors, including international financial institutions, should demonstrate that their proposed economic reform measures will realize, and not undermine, States' human rights obligations. This implies a duty to carry out human rights impact assessments to evaluate and address any foreseeable effects of their economic policies on human rights. Consulting on, and making public in adequate formats the results of, human rights impact assessments are important components of complying with this obligation.

Commentary

3.1 States and other creditors, including international financial institutions such as development banks, must carry out a human rights impact assessment before recommending or implementing economic reform policies that could foreseeably undermine the enjoyment of human rights. States have to establish, through the steps outlined in the guiding principles regarding timely collection, sharing and discussion of relevant information, that their chosen response will not lead to human rights violations or abuses, or impermissible retrogression in human rights.

3.2 While human rights impact assessments should take account of the evidence and experience of civil society and experts, it is ultimately the State's responsibility to prove that its policies do not violate human rights. This requirement of proof means that States should approach the process of generating, publishing and subsequently updating impact assessments with openness to the available evidence and expertise.

Principle 4 – Obligations of local and subnational governments

Economic and financial crises should not be used to justify a reduction of the policy and fiscal space necessary at local and subnational government levels to

[16] Committee on Economic, Social and Cultural Rights, general comment No. 2 (1990) on international technical assistance measures, para. 9.

ensure the protection of human rights. In turn, although all levels of government have human rights obligations, the central Government can in no circumstances circumvent its responsibilities for the human rights impacts of its policies by delegating economic reform-related powers or functions to local governments.

Commentary

4.1 Effective implementation of human rights cannot be achieved without the proactive involvement of local and subnational governments. International human rights law is binding on all levels of government, and is of particular relevance when taking into account the growing global phenomenon of decentralization in recent decades. Economic reforms at the central level should also take into account responsibilities assigned or delegated to local and subnational governments within the domestic spheres.

4.2 Decentralization is not always favourable to the implementation of human rights law, and it can be especially burdensome if it is not combined with sufficient resources or policy space (both internal and by facilitating community participation) for the implementation of human rights. Recognition of multilevel governance in areas such as revenue collection, tax policy, labour reforms and solidarity across regions is crucial. The national Government remains responsible for ensuring that appropriate cross-government coordination mechanisms and processes exist and that subnational governments are given the necessary resources to fulfil their human rights obligations.

4.3 When carrying out economic reforms independently, local and subnational governments have the same obligations as States with regard to carrying out human rights impact assessments.

III. Applicable human rights standards

Principle 5 – Human rights standards and pertinent law

In taking economic action or choosing the path of inaction, States and creditors must be guided by existing international human rights law relating to civil, cultural, economic, political and social rights.

Commentary

5.1 This includes core international human rights treaties, as well as their authoritative interpretation in general comments, statements, open letters, decisions, concluding observations and recommendations issued by treaty monitoring bodies. It also includes other interpretative tools, guiding principles and recommendations developed by global and regional human rights mechanisms.

5.2 In keeping with the principle *pro homine*, the most protective human rights standards (whether domestic or international) should guide States and creditors in their economic reform policies.

Principle 6 – Indivisibility and interdependence of all human rights

Economic reform policies can negatively affect all human rights (civil, cultural, economic, political and social). Therefore, States, and creditors when applicable, should ensure that all measures are taken to respect, protect and fulfil all human rights, especially in times of economic downturn.

Commentary

6.1 While concerns about the human rights impact of economic policy measures are often focused on economic, social and cultural rights, it is crucial that States also ensure that economic policies do not have a negative impact on civil and political rights. For instance, budget cuts to public services, such as law enforcement, legal aid, education, health services or social care, may result in a failure to guarantee the civil rights to a fair trial, family life, non-discrimination, freedom from torture and cruel, inhuman and degrading treatment, or even the right to life. The right of political participation may also be undermined where economic reform policies are adopted without the meaningful participation of the affected population. In practice, the multidimensional nature of economic reform policies can jeopardize a wide range of human rights. Even where a policy appears primarily to have a particular impact on one right, it may set off a chain reaction in terms of others, owing to the indivisibility and interdependence of human rights.

6.2 States may not claim a lack of resources as an excuse for failing to guarantee human rights. For example, in the case of persons deprived of liberty, States parties have the obligation to respect the bodily integrity of such persons, and they may not invoke a lack of financial resources to absolve themselves of this obligation.[17]

6.3 It is of crucial importance to underline that certain economic measures – for example, restrictive loan conditionalities or constraints imposed by trade agreements privileging corporate interests – are clearly and directly linked to States' abilities to address phenomena that are manifest violations of multiple human rights, such as pollution, prevalence of life-threatening diseases, widespread hunger and malnutrition, extreme poverty and homelessness, among others.

Principle 7 – Equality and combating multiple and intersectional discrimination

Economic reform policies and measures must not be discriminatory, and they must endeavour to ensure equality and non-discrimination for all. For this purpose, the directly and indirectly discriminatory impact of economic reform policies on the most disenfranchised or marginalized individuals has to be assessed, and alternative measures evaluated.

As part of the requirement to prevent economic reforms from having discriminatory impacts, human rights impact assessments should seek to identify

[17] Human Rights Committee, general comment No. 36 (2018) on the right to life, para. 25.

and address the potential and cumulative impacts of measures on specific individuals and groups and protect them from such impacts. In doing so, it should be borne in mind that women are particularly exposed to multiple and intersectional discrimination. Direct, indirect, multiple and intersectional discrimination – particularly for disenfranchised or marginalized groups within society – needs to be carefully assessed and prevented.

Commentary

7.1 It is most often the combination and accumulation of individual economic decisions, such as the combination of fiscal consolidation, reforms of the labour market, taxation and public expenditure, that cause the most damage if the impacts of the decisions fall on the same population groups, simultaneously or over time. A human rights impact assessment can help identify how people confronting cumulative and/or intersecting inequalities may be affected and how to protect them from the discriminatory impact.

7.2 Identifying the particular individuals and groups that are most marginalized and discriminated against in a particular country and in specific circumstances requires a profound and sophisticated understanding of the various population groups and of the context in which a particular measure is to be taken. Groups that are frequently discriminated against include women; lesbian, gay, bisexual, transsexual and intersex persons; persons with disabilities; children; older persons; indigenous peoples; migrants; refugees; internally displaced persons; people living in poverty; the unemployed and those with precarious jobs; single parents; and ethnic, national, linguistic, religious or other minorities.

7.3 The meaningful participation of all relevant stakeholders and affected individuals and groups, including those groups at risk of vulnerability and exclusion in economic reform policy formulation, implementation and review, should be ensured across all stages of the assessments, including impact assessments. Where needed, appropriate adjustments should be made to facilitate the participation of such groups. Importantly, the participation of relevant stakeholders should also be ensured during the monitoring and evaluation phases to determine whether findings have sufficiently informed implementation or revision of policy measures.

Principle 8 – Non-discrimination based on gender and substantive gender equality

Economic reforms should prevent any kind of direct and indirect form of discrimination based on gender, in law or practice, and should promote substantive and transformative gender equality. Human rights impact assessments should always include a comprehensive gender analysis.

Commentary

8.1 The current dominant economic system is, for the most part, based on and perpetuates gender inequality and discrimination in the labour market, worsening the potential adverse human rights impacts on women. In particular, unpaid care work (i.e. care for children, older people and others) is overwhelmingly undertaken by women and often invisible in current economic analysis. Further, women are generally overrepresented in public sector positions and in precarious, informal and low-paid jobs.

8.2 Therefore, economic reforms which encourage, among other things, labour market flexibilization, reductions in the coverage of social protection benefits and services, cuts to public sector jobs and the privatization of services tend to have a negative impact on women's enjoyment of human rights.[18] Economic reform should aim to prevent gender discrimination and transform existing inequalities, instead of creating such situations.

8.3 Policies that might improve overall social indicators might not do so for women, or for particular groups of women. Human rights impact assessments, incorporating a clear gender focus and women's central participation in the assessment process, can support the realization of women's human rights in practice through contextualized analysis aimed at identifying and preventing direct and indirect discrimination; addressing structural socioeconomic and sociocultural barriers; redressing current and historical disadvantage; countering stigma, prejudice, stereotyping and violence; transforming social and institutional structures; and facilitating women's political participation and social inclusion.

8.4 During times of economic crisis, public investment in childcare and elder care can create virtuous cycles by which the investment not only addresses the care deficit through the delivery of crucial care services, but also kick-starts a multiplier effect in generating jobs and/or other effects.

Principle 9 – Progressive realization and maximum available resources

In relation to economic, social and cultural rights in particular, States are obliged to progressively realize such rights by all appropriate means, which requires States to:

(a) **Design and implement fiscal, tax, debt, trade, aid, monetary and environmental policies in conjunction with other measures, so that they are deliberately directed towards the realization of human rights;**

(b) **Demonstrate that every effort has been made to mobilize all available resources, even in times of economic crisis. In particular, States must generate, adequately allocate and make use of the maximum of their available resources to move as expeditiously and effectively as possible towards the achievement of the full realization of economic, social and cultural rights.**[19]

[18] See A/73/179.

[19] Committee on Economic, Social and Cultural Rights, general comment No. 3 (1990) on the nature of States parties' obligations, paras. 9–12; and general comment No. 24 (2017) on State obligations under the International Covenant on Economic, Social and Cultural Rights in the context of business activities, para. 23.

Commentary

9.1 In assessing potential economic policies in the light of these obligations, States should consider the following guiding factors: the extent to which the measures are deliberate, concrete and targeted towards the fulfilment of economic, social and cultural rights; whether the State party is exercising its discretion in a non-discriminatory and non-arbitrary manner; whether the State party's decision (not) to allocate available resources is in accordance with international human rights standards; where several policy options are available, whether the State party adopts the option that least restricts the enjoyment of rights; the time frame of the State's steps; whether the measures take into account the precarious situation of disadvantaged and marginalized individuals or groups; and whether the measures prioritize grave situations or situations of risk.[20]

9.2 States must not only use existing resources to fulfil this obligation but also generate potential resources in a sustainable way when the former are not sufficient to ensure the realization of rights. This requires, for example, seeking international assistance and cooperation, mobilizing domestic resources in ways compatible with environmental sustainability and with the rights of people affected by extractive industries, as well as regulating the financial sector.

9.3 States' obligation to mobilize resources includes: tackling tax evasion and avoidance; ensuring a progressive tax system, including by widening the tax base with regard to multinational corporations and the richest; avoiding international tax competition; improving the efficiency of tax collection; and reprioritizing expenditures to ensure, among other things, adequate funding of public services.

9.4 Available resources must also be measured in the light of international cooperation requested by States in cases where States cannot guarantee the enjoyment of human rights with their own resources, with such requests for international cooperation to be made as soon as possible.

9.5 Mobilizing resources to ensure the progressive realization of rights is also critical to address the minimum core content of economic, social and cultural rights as a minimum floor for protection. States cannot attribute their failure to meet their minimum core obligations to a lack of available resources, unless they demonstrate that every effort has been made to use all resources that are at its disposal.[21] Ensuring achievement of the minimum core content can serve to address the most egregious situations, such as extreme poverty, homelessness or acute malnutrition. However, minimum core content should not be construed to mean a ceiling in the efforts that are required of States.

Principle 10 – Prohibition of retrogression

Any proposed economic reform that may result in impermissible retrogression in terms of the realization of economic, social and cultural rights is

[20] E/C.12/2007/1, para. 8.
[21] Committee on Economic, Social and Cultural Rights, general comment No. 3, para. 10.

considered a prima facie violation of such rights. Measures that would result in backward steps in terms of the achievement of these rights is permissible only if States can prove that such retrogressive measures are:[22]

(a) **Temporary, in nature and effect, and limited to the duration of the crisis;**

(b) **Legitimate, with the ultimate aim of protecting the totality of human rights;**

(c) **Reasonable, in that the means chosen are the most suitable and capable of achieving the legitimate aim;**

(d) **Necessary, in that the adoption of any other policy alternatives or the failure to act would be more detrimental to the enjoyment of economic, social and cultural rights, especially if there are less harmful alternative financing mechanisms;**

(e) **Proportionate, in that the measures chosen do not unduly restrict human rights and their costs do not outweigh their benefits;**

(f) **Non-discriminatory, and have the ability to prevent or mitigate the inequalities that can emerge in times of crisis and they ensure that the rights of disadvantaged and marginalized individuals and groups are not disproportionately affected;**

(g) **Protective of the minimum core content of economic, social and cultural rights at all times;**

(h) **Based on transparency and the genuine participation of affected groups in examining the proposed measures and alternatives;**

(i) **Subject to meaningful review and accountability procedures, including human rights impact assessments.**

IV. Articulation of policies

Principle 11 - Policy coherence

States should ensure that governmental departments, agencies and other State-based institutions that take part in and/or shape economic reform policies take into account States' human rights obligations when fulfilling their respective mandates, and that policy coherence is guaranteed for short-, medium- and long-term economic reforms, in order to protect all human rights. In particular:

(a) **Adequate financial resources should be allocated for the effective implementation of social policy, fully taking into account the economic situation of the population. Social policy should be designed to address and reverse the effects of economic downturns, while ensuring respect for human rights;**

[22] See, for reference, "Public debt, austerity measures and the International Covenant on Economic, Social and Cultural Rights: statement by the Committee on Economic, Social and Cultural Rights" (E/C.12/2016/1); Committee on Economic, Social and Cultural Rights, general comment No. 19 (2007) on the right to social security, para. 42; and "Letter dated 16 May 2012 addressed by the Chairperson of the Committee on Economic, Social and Cultural Rights to States parties to the International Covenant on Economic, Social and Cultural Rights".

(b) **Fiscal policy should be used as a countercyclical tool to prevent and/or manage crises, as well as to equalize opportunities and maximize the realization of human rights;**

(c) **Monetary policies should be coordinated and consistent with other policies with the aim of respecting, protecting and fulfilling human rights;**

(d) **Financial sector regulation is required to identify, prevent, manage and fairly allocate the human rights risks created by financial instability and illicit financial flows;**

(e) **Debt policies should be consistent with broad goals related to sustainable economic development and the realization of human rights;**

(f) **Proposed economic reform measures should be informed by and align with individual and collective State measures to facilitate national and global environmental protection, recognizing the interdependence between human rights and a healthy environment.**[23]

Commentary

11.1 Social policy includes a wide range of policies, from social security (retirement/pensions and insurance, including unemployment) to labour,[24] education and health. Other areas are often affected – either directly or indirectly – by privatization of services traditionally provided for by the State, such as water and sanitation services, social housing, prisons and detention centres, and migration management. Some social policies are directed to specific population groups, such as persons with disabilities, refugees and asylum seekers or persons living in poverty. All have a clear gender component that has to be included to avoid increasing the gender divide in access to resources (education, health services, housing, labour market, etc.).

11.2 Fiscal policy can play a major role in achieving equality, tackling discrimination and strengthening governance and accountability, as well as combating poverty and funding development. Fiscal policy also has a clear and well-documented effect on economic growth: while pro-cyclical contractionary fiscal policy reduces economic growth, expansionary fiscal policy during downturns increases growth. Positive and negative changes in government expenditure are likely to have a higher than proportional impact on growth. In turn, changes in economic growth will affect the tax revenue of Governments. Domestic resource mobilization can be a tool to ensure the realization of human rights and promote inclusive growth. Increasing government revenue more directly depends on robust redistributive and progressive taxation regimes. The respective impact of revenue and expenditure variations should be evaluated in terms of the associated outcomes for economic growth, human rights and long-term debt sustainability.

[23] A/HRC/37/59, paras. 11 ff.
[24] See A/HRC/34/57.

11.3 Decisions on fiscal policy should not result in expenditure cuts that curtail the guarantee of rights, mainly in sectors such as education, health and social insurance – particularly important for women, children and persons with disabilities – or in deepening social or economic inequality and poverty through indirect and regressive taxes, such as value added tax.

11.4 Direct and progressive taxes should be prioritized. Tax policy should promote the redistribution of wealth to overcome the disadvantaged situation of the population in situations of social vulnerability (the poor, minorities and women, among others) and other priority care groups, notably older adults, children and persons with disabilities.

11.5 Tax reform measures include, for example, taxing higher-income categories and wealth more strongly; taxing certain financial transactions; shoring up the tax base; and enhancing tax collection, the efficiency of the tax administration and the fight against tax evasion and avoidance. International, binational or regional regulation is crucial for efficiency in combating evasion, avoidance, tax fraud and illicit financial flows. All States should support global norms and agreements to prevent international tax avoidance and evasion. In this regard, it is necessary that Automatic Exchange of Financial Account Information agreements be effective in order to acknowledge the final beneficiary of a transaction and establish responsibilities in cases of loss of useful resources needed to guarantee rights. Full participation and access to such information to all countries should be ensured.[25]

11.6 Decision-making processes around tax and fiscal policies need to be open to genuine public debate informed by processes of inclusive, broad, transparent and deliberative social dialogue, which should include a wide range of economic theory and evidence, expressed in language accessible to the public. These provisions also apply to tax exemptions (including tax exclusions, deductions, credits, concessions, preferential rates or deferral of tax liabilities), which reduce the public revenues that can be accrued from taxes.

11.7 Central banks are State institutions and, as such, they are obliged to comply with international human rights law and standards. Inflation and employment targets, among other targets, need to be in line with the State's human rights obligations in order to avoid any impermissible retrogressive measures.

11.8 Authorities that coordinate massive responses that stabilize the financial sector as well as those which opt for doing little to address a sovereign debt crisis need to demonstrate if and to what extent their strategies would help protect and respect human rights.

11.9 Accumulation of foreign reserves and restrictions on short-term capital inflows and outflows can often be considered effective monetary policies. However, massive accumulation of foreign reserves beyond those recommended

[25] See A/HRC/31/61.

in the rules of international financial institutions, leading to large unutilized amounts of reserves accumulated in central banks, should be balanced against the immediate needs of the State, especially from a social investment and human rights perspective. On the other hand, limiting speculative financial movements may open up space to pursue policies to facilitate the realization of human rights.

11.10 States should have a transparent and democratically discussed bailout and interest rate formation regime established by law. States should use a mix of tools to ensure appropriate global and domestic financial market regulation with the aim of curbing excessive credit growth. This mix should include measures of prudential regulation, debt sustainability analysis and capital controls.[26]

11.11 States should consider how proposed economic reforms may impact directly on or otherwise reduce a State's ability to address national ecological conditions and significant global ecological thresholds which affect the realization of human rights.

Principle 12 – Debt sustainability, debt relief and restructuring

Independent debt sustainability analysis should incorporate human rights impact assessments. Findings of human rights impact assessments should be used to inform debt strategies, debt relief programmes and restructuring negotiations, potentially triggering the latter where actual or potential adverse impacts are identified. Debt audits can contribute valuable information in conducting such assessments.

Commentary

12.1 Structural adjustment programmes are often only oriented towards short-term fiscal targets to regain debt sustainability. Debt sustainability analysis is still based on a narrow understanding of sustainability, focusing primarily on the ability of a country to pay back its public debt without having to resort to exceptional financing or major policy adjustments.

12.2 The result is that sometimes a stock of public debt may be considered "sustainable" even if its service entails the State's failure to comply with its human rights obligations because the resources necessary for servicing its debt deprive it of the financial means to realize human rights. Debt service payments should not compromise the promotion and fulfilment of human rights over time.

12.3 A more comprehensive definition of debt sustainability incorporates economic, social and environmental sustainability, meaning that debt sustainability is only achieved when debt service does not result in violations of human

[26] See A/HRC/31/60.

rights and human dignity and does not prevent the attainment of international development goals.

12.4 Debt cannot be called "sustainable" if the social and human rights dimensions of sustainability are ignored. Projections of repayment capacities of borrowing States need to ensure that the obligations of States to promote the Sustainable Development Goals and progressively realize economic, social and cultural rights can be effectively fulfilled.

12.5 Identification of actual or potential adverse impacts can guide decision-making on revision of repayment terms, on the volume of debt relief necessary to ensure that the obligations to respect, protect and fulfil all human rights can be met by States, and on the size and the distribution of losses incurred by different creditors' groups.

12.6 Systematic, independent human rights impact assessments carried out within regular debt management work and sustainability assessments can also support early identification of where constraints on fiscal space due to debt servicing are leading to an undermining of States' human rights obligations, notably towards women and other groups in situations of vulnerability. Findings can thereby contribute to timely debt restructuring, and mitigate the gravity and prevent adverse human rights impacts of economic crises.

12.7 In particular, in the context of – but not limited to – privatizations, it should be noted that States have an obligation to ensure that the fiscal risk of all debt is properly accounted for and on balance sheet and that private creditors similarly have an obligation to ensure that they do not undermine this obligation of any public-sector counterparty. The process and criteria by which States calculate the fiscal impact of certain privatization projects should be in accordance with industry-recognized best practices.

12.8 Creditors and debtors should also engage in debt relief and restructuring negotiations with the aim of supporting the freeing up of fiscal space to safeguard the capacity of States to meet their human rights obligations.

12.9 Ensuring that the findings of impact assessments systematically play a role in debt restructuring reflects the shared responsibility of creditors and debtors for sovereign debt burdens.

12.10 The environmental assessment implies an analysis of the commitment of the country's natural resources, mainly its strategic resources such as minerals and water. The social impact, the environmental remediation and the contribution to climate change must be established in the case of public debt payments based on the extraction of natural resources.

12.11 Lenders have an independent duty to ensure, to the best of their ability, that government officials are authorized under applicable domestic law to enter into the agreements and that the arrangement is otherwise consistent with such law.

V. Other obligations of States, international financial institutions and private actors

Principle 13 – International assistance and cooperation

States have an obligation to provide international assistance and cooperation in order to facilitate the full realization of all rights. As part of their obligations with regard to international cooperation and assistance, States have an obligation to respect and protect the enjoyment of human rights of people outside their borders. This involves avoiding conduct that would foreseeably impair the enjoyment of human rights by persons living beyond their borders, contributing to the creation of an international environment that enables the fulfilment of human rights,[27] as well as conducting assessments of the extraterritorial impacts of laws, policies and practices.[28]

Principle 14 – External influence and policy space

States, international or regional financial institutions and other non-State and State actors should not exert undue external influence on other States so that they are able to take steps to design and implement economic programmes by using their policy space[29] in accordance with their human rights obligations, including when trying to cope with economic or financial crises. The systematic use of transparent and participatory human rights impact assessments in the design of economic reform programmes attached to international loans can serve to support debtor States in implementing a programme of crisis response free of undue external pressure and demonstrating national ownership that allows them to meet their human rights and environmental obligations.

Commentary

14.1 Undue external influence means direct or indirect intervention in the economic affairs of a State through the use of economic and/or political measures seeking to influence States to adopt certain economic policies or to secure from them advantages of any kind that undermine the ability of States to respect, protect and fulfil their human rights obligations. Economic measures can include both conditionalities attached to financial assistance programmes and implicit conditionalities informally urged by international or regional institutions.

14.2 States in difficulty following a debt crisis or other adverse economic event may temporarily lose access to some sources of funds. In these situations, the remaining lenders have a responsibility not to use their enhanced bargaining power to exercise influence on the borrower that could lead to human rights

[27] Committee on Economic, Social and Cultural Rights, general comment No. 24 (2017), para. 37; and Maastricht Principles on Extraterritorial Obligations of States in the Area of Economic, Social and Cultural Rights (2011).

[28] Guiding principles on extreme poverty and human rights (A/HRC/21/39), para. 92.

[29] See Sustainable Development Goal 17.15; Addis Ababa Action Agenda of the Third International Conference on Financing for Development, annex, sect. I, para. 9; and General Assembly resolution 25/2625.

violations. Instead, lenders actually have an enhanced responsibility with regard to the human rights impacts of their loans and the conditions attached to them.

14.3 States should also be able to design and implement economic policies, including responses to financial and economic crises, in accordance with their human rights obligations. In doing so, they should be free from undue influence from corporations or those working to further their interests that seek to privilege corporate economic interests over, or otherwise disrupt, the realization of human rights or the environmental well-being necessary for such realization. States must take action to identify and prevent such conflicts of interest by developing a regulatory framework that ensures, among other things, that relevant interactions are transparent and accountable. Such a regulatory framework could include regulation regarding the financing of political parties and the prevention of corruption.

14.4 Host States should enact foreign investment laws in such a way that includes an obligation on investors to undertake human rights impact assessments through neutral entities in a transparent and inclusive manner. Host States and investors should undertake to use such assessments as a means of enhancing the sustainability and development impact of investments in such a way that is beneficial to all stakeholders, including investors.

Principle 15 – Obligations of public creditors and donors

International financial institutions, bilateral lenders and public donors should ensure that the terms of their transactions and their proposals for reform policies and conditionalities for financial support do not undermine the borrower/recipient State's ability to respect, protect and fulfil its human rights obligations.[30]

States, whether acting alone or within international financial institutions, as well as international financial institutions themselves, should not compel borrowing/receiving States to compromise satisfying their international human rights obligations or contribute to such compromise, either directly or indirectly. As a consequence, international financial institutions, bilateral lenders and other public donors, when granting a loan or giving policy advice in the context of economic reform measures, have an obligation to assess the human rights impact of those measures.

Commentary

15.1 Human rights impact assessments should be a mandatory element in the design of all economic reform and adjustment programmes and avoid human rights violations. This applies also to programmes developed with international financial institutions, bilateral lenders and public donors in the context of debt management and financial assistance activities. All proposed measures and loan conditionalities should be subject to a human rights

[30] E/C.12/2016/1, para. 8.

impact assessment. These should be prepared prior to the conclusion of the agreements and in time to influence the outcomes of the negotiations, and include an analysis of the impact of policies on commonly marginalized groups. In urgent situations at least, flexible instruments should be considered to allow for sufficient space to develop well-tailored adjustment measures that respect human rights. Release clauses with regard to specific conditions should be put in place where actual or potential adverse human rights impacts are identified.

15.2 The obligations mentioned in the previous paragraph include, for example, participating in debt relief programmes and restructuring negotiations in good faith through a formal process of deliberative policy engagement and social dialogue.[31] They also include actively seeking debt agreements that are financially sustainable and respect human rights. Creditors should refrain from predatory or obstructive behaviour that could compel States to act in contravention of their human rights obligations in order to repay debts or directly impact States' capacity to meet these obligations.

15.3 States cannot escape responsibility for actions or the exercise of functions that they have delegated to international institutions or private parties (re blended finance and privatization): delegation cannot be used as an excuse to fail to comply with human rights obligations, in abnegation of the extraterritorial character of these obligations.

15.4 Bilateral lenders and other public donors, including Government-guaranteed financial institutions or private institutions extending loans with government guarantees, have extraterritorial human rights obligations governing their decisions in the context of economic reform measures of the concerned States.

Principle 16 – Obligations of private creditors

Private creditors, when negotiating transactions with States or other public entities, including taking decisions in the context of economic reforms, should not undermine the State's ability to respect, protect and fulfil its human rights obligations. Among other things, these creditors should assess the human rights impacts of their own actions as well as those of the activities financed by them, unless they have ascertained that debtor States or international and regional financial institutions have carried out effective assessments, including with regard to gender equality and the environmental impact.

Commentary

16.1 In order to identify, prevent, mitigate and account for adverse human rights impacts of certain actions or inactions, private creditors should carry

[31] General Assembly resolution 69/319.

out human rights impact assessments. This requirement should be further elaborated in national action plans on business and human rights.[32]

16.2 In connection with principle 13 and commentary15.3, host and home States' obligations to protect human rights, including their extraterritorial obligations, require the establishment of adequate safeguards against negative human rights impacts resulting from the conduct of private companies.

16.3 Private creditors' obligations include the obligation to act in good faith, as established for public creditors.[33] In addition, private parties bringing vague investment treaty-based claims against States in situations of debt distress could violate this good-faith principle, particularly when such claims are brought with the hope or intent of extracting more favourable settlements than for the rest of the creditors and/or investors.[34]

VI. Human rights impact assessments

Principle 17 – Basis and purposes of a human rights impact assessment

States and creditors should carry out human rights impact assessments of economic reform policies considered and taken in response to acute economic and financial crises that are likely to cause adverse human rights impacts. States should also carry out regular and periodic human rights impact assessments of short-, medium- and long-term economic reform processes in less challenging economic times. A human rights impact assessment of economic reform policies should:

(a) **Prompt investigation of and analyse the extent to which the proposed measures, in combination with other economic measures and policies being or to be implemented, could contribute to fulfilling the State's human rights obligations or potentially undermine them;**

(b) **Serve to demonstrate how proposed measures, jointly with other economic measures and policies being or to be implemented, could impact the human rights of the whole population, particularly the individuals and groups most disenfranchised or at risk;**

(c) **Identify any prima facie retrogressive measure as well as alternative economic policy options that could be the least restrictive of human rights and avoid any impermissible retrogression;**

---

[32] See Guiding Principles on Business and Human Rights (A/HRC/17/31); and Committee on Economic, Social and Cultural Rights, general comment No. 24, para. 5. "Private creditors" include private bondholders, private banks, other private financial institutions, and manufacturers, exporters and other suppliers of goods that have a financial claim.

[33] United Nations Conference on Trade and Development, *Principles on Promoting Responsible Sovereign Lending and Borrowing*, 10 January 2012, principle No. 7.

[34] See A/72/153 and Corr.1.

(d) **Establish a (non-exhaustive) list of preventive and mitigating measures to ensure conformity of the economic reform policies considered with the State's human rights obligations.**

Commentary

17.1 An ex ante human rights impact assessment is a structured process to review alternative policy options and analyse the impacts of proposed measures on human rights.[35] The process contributes to evidence-based policymaking by making human rights impacts more visible on the basis of historical experience, and provides a firmer basis for forecasting potential impacts and assessing the effects of proposed prevention, mitigation and compensation measures.

17.2 Human rights impact assessments can provide empirical evidence to properly assess the proportionality and legitimacy of economic measures from a human rights perspective and ensure that women's rights will be taken into account. Hence, all States should prepare human rights impact assessments in order to determine whether the economic reforms under consideration are consistent with their human rights obligations. States' decisions on economic policies should be consistent with the outcome of human rights impact assessments. These assessments should be widely published in accessible forms and discussed with affected people, and include options discussed and agreed upon.

17.3 Considering ways to prevent or tackle an economic crisis includes, for example, countercyclical measures, full or partial debt relief and medium- or long-term suspensions of the creditors' payments, and tax policy reviews.

17.4 The analysis should include various policy options, including budget cuts, new tax measures, monetary policies and other adjustment measures such as labour market deregulation, that are likely to affect the population, in particular those members of the population who would be expected to suffer or have suffered a unique or cumulative impact of the measures and the groups in the most vulnerable situations. It should use a variety of quantitative and qualitative tools and methods, including participatory ones, and carefully compare the human rights impact of different scenarios including budget cuts, tax increases and measures against tax evasion and avoidance, and a review of tax expenditures.

17.5 An analysis that looks at the potential (and cumulative) distribution of impacts is necessary to ensure that the most vulnerable are not disproportionally affected by the crisis due to specific contextual and/or global conditions and that, on the contrary, they are protected from impacts, to the maximum of the available resources from the State and international community.

17.6 Taking measures during times of economic crisis requires a State to balance competing priorities and make appropriate trade-offs under conditions of potentially severe financial, political and time pressure. A human rights

[35] See Center for Economic and Social Rights, *Assessing Austerity: Monitoring the Human Rights Impacts of Fiscal Consolidation*, briefing, February 2018.

impact assessment can help States to justify hard choices if they are aligned with the normative guidance of human rights and aim to avoid discriminatory measures and minimize disproportionate impacts across the population.

17.7 The process should also include the design of economic policy responses that prevent, mitigate or provide redress (including but not limited to compensation) for impacts that cannot be avoided, taking a comprehensive view of all measures taken to respond to a crisis. Responses to a crisis may involve a range of measures that cumulatively and collectively affect the whole population. Policy responses should indeed protect all human rights of all people, and in particular those of the most vulnerable.

17.8 Human rights impact assessments of economic reforms shall incorporate complementary tools designed for and implemented in related areas. A human rights impact assessment, if carried out properly, can incorporate regulatory, environmental and social impact assessments and should contain a human rights-based budget analysis. For example, when a human rights impact assessment pursuant to the present guiding principles is conducted, the fiscal and economic sustainability of trade and/or investment agreements must be incorporated. In particular, since compliance with the obligations imposed under trade and/or investment agreements typically is ensured by the threat of economic sanctions or reparations authorized or awarded by an agreement-specific dispute settlement mechanism or international arbitral tribunal, attention must be given to the impact that such enforcement obligations, including the potential cumulative impact of such obligations, may have on public budgets.[36]

Principle 18 – Ex ante and ex post assessments

Human rights impact assessments should form a regular part of decision-making processes with respect to economic reform policies or loan conditionality, and should be carried out at regular intervals. They should be carried out both ex ante – to assess the foreseeable impacts of proposed policy changes – and ex post – that is, looking back to assess the actual impacts of policy change and implementation, in order to address such impacts.

Commentary

18.1 Human rights impact assessments should be a regular element of economic reform policies. They should be incorporated in the policy continuum, from design to monitoring to implementation. They should be started as early as possible in the policymaking process so that they can influence the choice of alternative policy options, and prior to the conclusion of agreements on programmes with creditors in time to influence the outcomes of negotiations. They should serve to look back and evaluate the short-term measures already taken and to propose adjustments as well as to provide evidence for medium- to longer-term planning going forward.

[36] A/HRC/19/59/Add.5, appendix, para. 1.3.

18.2 In the context of an acute financial or economic crisis in which the Government is forced to make decisions under extreme time pressures, it may not be possible for the State to carry out a thorough human rights impact assessment before deciding on its response to the crisis. In these situations, the Government is obliged to complete and publish a human rights impact assessment to the extent possible under the circumstances before taking any policy decisions or actions. The Government should also (a) publicly explain why it is unable to do a full ex ante impact assessment; (b) undertake a fully compliant ex post human rights impact assessment as soon as conditions allow; and (c) take steps to remedy all adverse human rights impacts identified in either impact assessment as promptly as possible.

18.3 For mid- to longer-term reforms, a human rights impact assessment can help States and international financial institutions to create capacities for adaptation to necessary changes in the economy, so as to better address the next economic and financial crisis and to ensure a robust sense of social inclusion. This is particularly worthwhile for women in situations where they are usually excluded from decision-making. Thorough and well-documented scrutiny will also contribute to evidence-based decision-making by the same or other States in future crises.

18.4 Throughout the policy cycles, economic reform programmes should be evaluated in accordance with whether they have ensured a fair and equitable distribution of social adjustment burdens, and not only whether they have reduced budget deficits and restored debt sustainability or economic growth. Such evaluations should assess the extent to which reform programmes have protected human rights, in particular those of the groups in situations of vulnerability or at risk of greater impacts, and identify gaps to be addressed.

18.5 Human rights impact assessments should not be limited to considering potential or actual adverse human rights impacts, but should also be used to identify steps to advance the enjoyment of human rights and opportunities for duty bearers to further the realization of human rights within the implementation of economic reforms.

18.6 Capacity-building in conducting human rights assessments is of crucial importance as it would make the exercise less time-consuming, more predictable, less costly, and help assessments to become increasingly accurate and comprehensive. Governments should build the systems to ensure that necessary data and information are produced and published and closely work with members of civil society during "good times" so that they are equipped to participate promptly in human rights impact assessments when necessary, whether on a regular or extraordinary basis.

Principle 19 – Participation

The right to participate should be embedded in the process of conducting human rights impact assessments. It should also be central in the consideration

of policy options, in the outcome document(s) (publication and reporting of information and the assessment), in the implementation of policy responses and in the monitoring of the impact of such responses.

Commentary

19.1 In formulating measures requiring human rights impact assessments, States and international financial institutions must allow for and seek the broadest possible national dialogue, with the effective, timely and meaningful participation of all individuals and groups, including marginalized groups and those particularly at risk of vulnerability from such policies. As women, children and persons with disabilities are generally underrepresented in both the political and economic spheres, special efforts must be made to ensure their capacity to co-decide the measures by using innovative methods of participation. Civil society organizations and actors in the broadest sense should also have adequate and timely channels for participation.

19.2 Different levels of government should also be adequately informed and consulted, and corresponding channels of communication and information should be followed, including within the legislative branches and administrative mechanisms in place for interaction among different levels of local and subnational governments.

19.3 Genuine participation can only be possible if Governments provide timely, comprehensive and accessible information on all aspects of public finance, including budgets and macroeconomic performance. Governments should also provide adequate justifications of policy choices to the population in general, and specifically to those most likely to be affected by the reform.

19.4 Several human rights should be protected in order to ensure effective and meaningful participation, including freedom of expression and access to information, freedom of the press, the right to peaceful assembly and freedom of association.

19.5 Economic reform policy measures should be adopted by the competent bodies following the procedures established by domestic law. They should be scrutinized and discussed by parliament to allow for effective political participation and necessary checks and balances.

19.6 Where labour market reforms are being contemplated, particular efforts should be made to consult, as early as possible, with local and national trade unions and employers' associations using, where they exist, national mechanisms for social dialogue. As any labour reform must include efforts to overcome horizontal and vertical gender segregation, women's representatives should also be part of this social dialogue.

19.7 Public debate and oversight over policies should start at the earliest possible moment and apply not only to policies and initiatives carried out by the State, but also to agreements with supranational institutions and/or lenders.

Conditionality packages attached to financial assistance programmes should be subjected to ample discussion, ensuring the participation of the population, and oversight and discussion by parliament.

Principle 20 – Access to information and transparency

In order to guarantee the right to freely impart, seek and receive information in a transparent manner, a human rights impact assessment of economic reforms requires a diverse range of both quantitative and qualitative data. States should endeavour to ensure that such information is available, accessible and delivered in a timely and transparent manner, and that its analysis assists in understanding the implications and impacts of the economic reform policies.

Commentary

20.1 Global and regional human rights standards guarantee not only the right to freely impart information but also the right to freely seek and receive it as part of the freedom of expression.

20.2 Obstacles to access to information can undermine the enjoyment of both civil and political rights, in addition to economic, social and cultural rights. Core requirements for democratic governance, such as transparency, the accountability of public authorities or the promotion of participatory decision-making processes, are unattainable in practice without adequate access to information.

20.3 The validity and credibility of the data collected need to be assessed in the light of clearly articulated and transparent standards that reflect the principles of non-discrimination, equality, inclusion and participation. In order to ensure compliance with the human rights requirement of non-discrimination and that due attention is paid to the situation of groups at risk of marginalization or vulnerability, it is essential that the indicators used provide information disaggregated by gender, disability, age group, region, ethnicity, income segment and any other grounds considered relevant, based on a contextual, country-level identification of groups at risk of marginalization.[37]

20.4 There are a number of methods for quantitative analysis. Well-developed approaches to modelling distributional impacts using income quintiles and deciles can be used. In order to ensure compliance with the human rights requirement of non-discrimination and that due attention is paid to the situation of groups at risk of marginalization or vulnerability, it is essential that those indicators provide information disaggregated in line with what is indicated in the previous paragraph. These human rights impact assessment standards need to be adaptable to potentially different levels of data availability and overall capacity to carry out a human rights impact assessment so that the tool can be used in a wider range of circumstances.

[37] For guidance, see, e.g., Organization of American States, *Progress Indicators for Measuring Rights Under the Protocol of San Salvador*, 2015; and Office of the United Nations High Commissioner for Human Rights, *Human Rights Indicators: A Guide to Measurement and Implementation*, 2012.

20.5 The 2030 Agenda for Sustainable Development includes a large number of indicators. Reliable and disaggregated data are needed to strengthen modelling, or at least to inform a more detailed analysis. While the indicators of the Sustainable Development Goals may not necessarily be rights based and the resulting data may not provide a comprehensive overview of all aspects of human rights, such data-collection processes could serve as a source of useful complementary information to those working in a human rights impact assessment context. However, the validity of data reported through the Sustainable Development Goals process should be carefully examined before using the data as a basis for decisions and economic policies.

20.6 In terms of qualitative data, targeted studies, surveys, testimonies and consideration of other types of analysis are paramount, including, when available, on administrative complaints, case law and jurisprudence on individual and collective cases, as they also offer a glimpse of the type of violations, trends and limitations encountered when accessing assistance, reparation and justice. Even in contexts where disaggregated data are readily available, they should always be triangulated with qualitative data on discriminatory situations.

20.7 Qualitative analyses need to ensure that contingencies in the use of quantitative models are recognized and, if possible, avoided. Such contingencies might stem from reliance on historical data, the choice of variables, etc.

20.8 International cooperation can be particularly relevant in this regard for countries with limited resources for data collection.

20.9 Transparency and wide dissemination of information are also critical when carrying out the impact assessment, including by publishing the findings in their entirety and reporting on the assessment, its conclusions and recommendations.

Principle 21 – Access to justice, accountability and remedies

States must ensure that access to justice and the right to an effective remedy are guaranteed, through judicial, quasi-judicial, administrative and political mechanisms, with regard to actions and omissions in the design and/or implementation of economic reform policies that may undermine human rights. States should ensure that the population is fully informed about the procedures, mechanisms and remedies available to them and that these mechanisms are physically and financially accessible to all.

Commentary

21.1 The right to an effective remedy includes reparations and guarantees of non-repetition. An independent, well-financed and proactive judicial branch is essential to both preventing economic reforms from harming human rights and to providing effective remedies should harm occur. A human rights impact assessment can serve to ensure that accountability procedures exist and mechanisms are in place by requiring clearly articulated and justified policy choices that have been developed through inclusive participation of the potentially affected population.

21.2 Engaging in an inclusive and accountable decision-making process strengthens the legitimacy and ownership of the choices made. Furthermore, it is likely to reduce social conflict, which can undermine democratic institutions and the rule of law. A functioning system of national, regional and international human rights accountability mechanisms, including independent and empowered national human rights institutions, is critical to this aim. States should take all measures to implement the recommendations of national, regional and international human rights bodies.

21.3 Measures covered by the present guiding principles should be agreed at all governmental levels, paying special attention to the ways in which burdens are distributed over and financial resources allocated to local authorities, which are often the main providers of social services to the population. These measures should also be open to oversight, including judicial scrutiny of applicable law, and public officials involved in the design and adoption of such measures should be accountable for any policy decisions that endanger the enjoyment of human rights.

21.4 Since corruption can play a role in the design, implementation and monitoring of economic reform policies, clear measures and mechanisms to prevent and combat corruption must be put in place with a view to ensuring accountability.

Principle 22 – Who should conduct the assessment(s)

Human rights impact assessments of economic reform policies should be independent, robust, credible and gender responsive. In this regard, each country should decide which institution(s) is/are best suited to be in charge of carrying out this exercise, based on applicable criteria.

Commentary

22.1 The present guiding principles are flexible enough to be adjusted to the particular needs of government departments, advisory bodies, parliamentary committees, national human rights institutions, courts, international financial institutions, private creditors, international human rights mechanisms, academic institutions or civil society organizations.

22.2 The appropriateness of the institution or team conducting the impact assessment should be measured against pre-established criteria, which should include, as a minimum, the following aspects: its independence from the executive branch and any creditor/creditor-aligned institution; appropriate expertise; adequate funding;[38] diversity of members of the team or body in charge of

[38] See A/HRC/19/59/Add.5.

carrying out the assessment and, notably, gender parity; engagement of affected communities; and credibility and legitimacy in the eyes of different stakeholder groups such as government agencies, international actors and civil society.

22.3 Independence from any creditor or creditor-aligned institution responsible for designing adjustment programmes is necessary in States' own assessments, given that findings can be used to inform borrowing policies and debt management, as well as triggering debt-restructuring activities. This does not preclude the participation of these actors in an assessment, or in undertaking assessments in the context of their own decision-making.

22.4 States should develop a domestic, professional and independent policy analysis capacity within the public sector to avoid dependence on private providers. Clear, rigorous and transparent criteria for appointment, regulation and accountability mechanisms should be created in advance, with independent oversight within the State, for private parties to be appointed to carry out human rights impact assessments. These private parties/corporations should be considered to be as responsible as any other entity performing a public service function. The State's delegation of a private corporation or third party does not, in any way, free the State from any of its obligations under international human rights law nor the private actor from applying all legal substantive and procedural standards enumerated in the present principles.

22.5 States should take steps to support the ability of affected communities and civil society generally to provide parallel information to assessment processes and, as far as possible, to conduct human rights impact assessments directly.

Notes

1. Human Rights Council, 'Mandate of the Independent Expert on the Effects of Foreign Debt and Other Related International Financial Obligations of States on the Full Enjoyment of All Human Rights, Particularly Economic, Social and Cultural Rights', Resolution adopted by the Human Rights Council on 23 Mach 2017, UN Doc. A/HRC/RES/34/3 (April 6, 2017).
2. Ibid., para 13.
3. For details on all consultations and expert meetings, see https://www.ohchr.org/EN/Issues/Development/IEDebt/Pages/DebtAndimpactassessments.aspx (accessed August 3 2020).
4. All submissions are available at https://www.ohchr.org/EN/Issues/Development/IEDebt/Pages/DebtAndimpactassessments.aspx (accessed August 3 2020).
5. UN Doc. A/HRC/37/54, 20 December 2017. This report was noted with appreciation by the UN Human Rights Council on 22 March 2018, which requested the Independent Expert 'to continue to develop guiding principles for assessing the human rights impact of economic reform policies, in consultation with States and all other relevant stakeholders, and to submit the guiding principles to the Human Rights Council at its fortieth session'. (Human Rights Council, 'The Effects of Foreign Debt and Other Related International Financial Obligations of States on the Full Enjoyment of All Human Rights, Particularly Economic, Social and Cultural Rights', Resolution adopted by the Human Rights Council on 22 March 2018, UN Doc. A/HRC/RES/37/11 (April 9, 2018), para 2).
6. Human Rights Council, 'The Effects of Foreign Debt and Other Related International Financial Obligations of States on the Full Enjoyment of All Human Rights, Particularly Economic,

Social and Cultural Rights', Resolution adopted by the Human Rights Council on 21 March 2019, UN Doc. A/HRC/RES/40/8 (April 5, 2019). For a discussion of state voting patterns in relation to Resolution 40/8, please see the Introduction to this Special Issue.

7. Ibid, para 3. The Human Rights Council proceeded to request the Office of the United Nations High Commissioner for Human Rights to disseminate the Guiding Principles. (Ibid., para 4).
8. United Nations Human Rights Office of the High Commissioner, *Guiding Principles on Human Rights Impact Assessments of Economic Reforms,* Human Rights Council, 40th sess., 2019, A/HRC/40/57, https://www.undocs.org/A/HRC/40/57 (accessed August 27, 2020).

Disclosure statement

From June 2014 to April 2020 the author was the United Nations Independent Expert on debt and human rights. The views and conclusions reflected in this article are solely those of the author and are in no way intended to reflect the views of any of the institutions with which the author is affiliated.

ORCID

Juan Pablo Bohoslavsky http://orcid.org/0000-0002-7059-281X

Index